THE HIGHLANDS OF INDIA STRATEGICALY CONSIDERED

THE HIGHLANDS OF INDIA STRATEGICALY CONSIDERED

WITH SPECIAL REFERENCE TO THEIR COLONIZATION, AS RESERVE CIRCLES, MILITARY, INDUSTRIAL, AND SANITARY,

D. J. F. NEWALL

GYAN

Published by

Gyan Publishing House
5, Ansari Road
Daryaganj, New Delhi-110002
Phone: 011-47034999, 9811692060
E-mail: books@gyanbooks.com

Distribution Network
gyanbooks.com
India, USA, Canada, UK, Australia

ISBN: 978-93-7447-607-9 (PB)

First Published, 1882

2nd Impression 2026

Printed at: Gyan Press, Delhi.

THE HIGHLANDS OF INDIA STRATEGICALY CONSIDERED
Author: D. J. F. NEWALL

THE

HIGHLANDS OF INDIA.

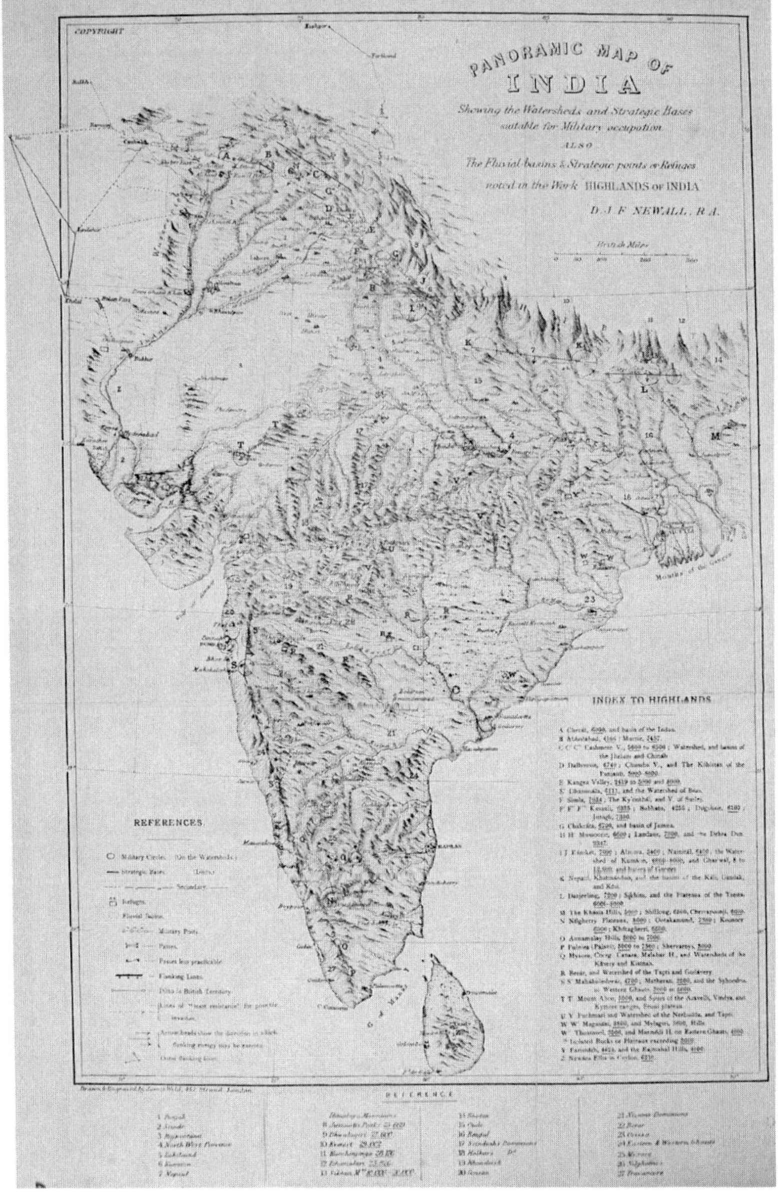
COPYRIGHT
PANORAMIC MAP OF
INDIA
Showing the Watersheds and Strategic Bases
suitable for Military occupation
ALSO
The Fluvial basins & Strategic points or Refuges
noted in the Work HIGHLANDS OF INDIA
D. J. F. NEWALL, R.A.
British Miles
INDEX TO HIGHLANDS
G Chakrâta, 6798, and basin of Jamna.
R Berar, and Watershed of the Tapti and Godavery.
REFERENCES.
Mouths of the Ganges
REFERENCE

THE HIGHLANDS OF INDIA

STRATEGICALY CONSIDERED,

WITH SPECIAL REFERENCE TO THEIR COLONIZATION

AS RESERVE CIRCLES,

MILITARY, INDUSTRIAL, AND SANITARY,

WITH A MAP, DIAGRAMS, AND ILLUSTRATIONS, ETC.

BY

Major-General D. J. F. NEWALL, R.A.
(Bengal retired),
Fellow of the Royal Geographical Society,
Member of the Royal United Service Institution, &c., &c., &c.

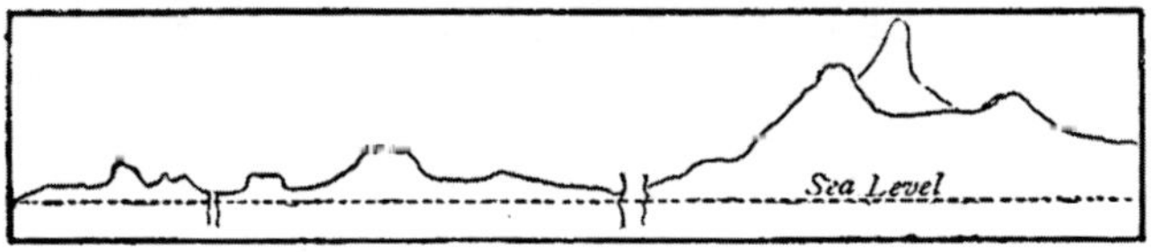

SECTION ACROSS INDIA.

LONDON:
HARRISON AND SONS, 59 PALL MALL,
BOOKSELLERS TO THE QUEEN AND H.R.H. THE PRINCE OF WALES.
ISLE OF WIGHT:
A. BRANNON AND SON, 31 HOLYROOD STREET, NEWPORT.
1882.

PREFACE.

THE following sketch of Indian Hill Stations has no pretension to the character of an exhaustive description of the Indian Highlands; it is scarcely even a guide to "fresh fields and pastures new," as our journey takes us mostly over trodden ground.

The existing Sanitaria and Hill Stations are simply regarded under their strategic aspects, and their adaptability to form sites for military or other colonies as "reserve circles," is investigated.

Short descriptive sketches of the surrounding country are attempted, and historical notes on a few of the tribes inhabiting, or closely adjacent to, these sites are added, as bearing on their military aspects; but such notices are necessarily limited, as to enter fully into a description of the various ethnological groups and races of India would be simply to write its history from early ages, which is manifestly beyond the scope of this fragmentary sketch. Neither have these papers any pretension to the character of a "guide," though incidentally hints for routes may here and there be gathered from the context, and a few geological and topographical notes are interspersed, or given in the form of foot notes.

It may be hoped, however, that in a modest way, it may tend to revive interest in a question closely associated with the *future of India;* namely, the assigning of localities for the homes of British colonists—or Eurasian and native settlers—as healthy "refuges" for the dominant race, and so, if possible, lead to a reconsideration of that most important question *a future for British India.*

Although the author has been afforded opportunities of visiting most of the places mentioned, he would nevertheless fain apologise for the many shortcomings to be found in these papers, not having ever enjoyed the advantage of the slightest official encouragement or assistance in his investigations, now extending over many years of a military life in the East.* The facts noted are simply the result of personal observation and study. He has, however, been afforded access to Government libraries containing official reports and records, and owes much to that source of information; and latterly in revising the original MSS. (written chiefly in 1874-5) especially in Sections IX., XII., and XIV., he has consulted other sources of information to supplement his own rather slender materials; and finally he has added Section XVI., as embracing matter of special interest at the present time. In this he owes much—as ac-

* I would except the generous encouragement accorded to me in youth by the late lamented Sir Henry Lawrence, at whose instance, indeed, I published the sketch of the *History of Cashmere* in the Journal of the Asiatic Society of Bengal in 1854, from which I have largely borrowed in drawing up Section I. of the following papers.

knowledged at the proper place—to various valuable papers published in the proceedings of the Royal Geographical Society—of which he is himself a fellow.

A few of these papers were printed for private circulation in India some years ago, but portions of the original manuscript were lost. As a series they were originally written (about the years 1874-5) for the Journal of the United Service Institution of India, but were found "not to suit the requirements of a purely military journal," hence they are offered to the general public instead.

The author having delivered lectures on the subject of "Military Colonization" at the United Service Institution of India; and, more recently, at the Royal United Service Institution, London; it appears scarcely necessary to further allude to a question already introduced for discussion, *viz.*, the importation into our Army System of "Military Circles"—*sub vexillo*—as a *Reserve for India.*

The lectures above alluded to form the preamble of this work; and are to be found in the journals of the Institutions mentioned.*

I am aware, however, that the idea of "Military Colonies" is so distasteful to the political ideas of the day, that I have preferred to call them *Industrial* or *Sanitary Reserve Circles:* the substitution of a word will often satisfy this public sensitiveness.

---

* Nos. 10 and 12 of the Journal of the United Service Institution of India, 1873. Also No. CXIII. Royal United Service Institution, London, 1881, forming the preamble of this work.

The illustrations are mostly from original sketches, except where otherwise acknowledged. The two isometric views (Nos. 6 and 7) are reduced—slightly altered—from Drew's "Cashmere." A few outlines in Sections IX. and XIV. are taken from Government Survey Reports. Illustrations in Section XV. (Nos. 60, 61, 62, 63) are from sketches by my brother (Captain J. T. Newall, late Asst. G. G. Agent Rajpootana States). Those comprised in the Appendix to Section XVI.—Nos. 76 to 81—are taken from the Journal of the Royal Geographical Society, and are by Major-General Sir Michael Biddulph, K.C.B., etc., to whose courtesy—and that of the Council of the Society—I am indebted for permission to reproduce them from blocks kindly lent for the purpose.

DAVID J. F. NEWALL, COLONEL R.A.,
Major-General (Bengal retired.)

Beldornie Tower,
Ryde, Isle of Wight,
1st May, 1882.

CONTENTS.

ILLUSTRATIONS.

APPENDIX.

NOTICE BY THE AUTHOR.

I am indebted to the Chairman and Council of the Royal United Service Institution for permission to reproduce this Lecture—which has appeared in the Journal—to whom also, as representatives of the Members R.U.S. Institution, I have the honour—by permission—to dedicate the following work on the "Highlands of India," of which it forms the preamble.

David J. F. Newall, R.A.

Major-Genl. (Bengal retired.)

Beldornie Tower, Ryde, I.W.
1st May, 1882.

Friday, May 27, 1881.

LIEUTENANT-GENERAL SIR C. P. BEAUCHAMP WALKER, K.C B., Chairman of the Council, in the Chair.

MILITARY COLONIZATION AS A RESERVE FOR INDIA.

By Major General D. J. F. NEWALL, R.A. (retired), F.R.G.S.

> " Res dura, et novitas regni me talia cogunt
> " Moliri, et late *fines* custode tueri."

THE subject which I am privileged to bring under your notice to-day is no new idea: I cannot claim originality in its conception; nor can I truly assert that most of the arguments to be adduced have not already been discussed and sifted by far abler hands.

The colonization of the Himalayan and other mountain ranges of India; the establishment thereon of more sanitaria; and even the planting of "*Military colonies*" has for years past been counselled by several men of mark; and their arguments in favour of such a step have been various and strong: "Reduce"—say these advocates—"the "strategic points in the plains to a minimum, and locate the bulk of "your British troops in the mountain ranges." Sanitary statistics indubitably point to this as an act of wisdom; and I hazard the suggestion that it may possibly be found equally wise in a political and strategic sense. I have myself formerly advocated such a view of the question, and in drawing up the present paper must be pardoned if I here and there borrow my own words on this subject.[1]

2. On reference to a "Lecture delivered at the Branch United "Service Institute for India, at Darjeeling, on the 30th October, 1872," I find I have instanced the Colonial systems of *Spain* and of *Portugal* —also of the Romans in Britain—as historic studies approaching the

[1] *Vide* Nos. 10 and 12 of the "Journal of the United Service Institute of India, "1873," on the "Strategic Value of Cashmere," and "On the Colonization of the "Mountain Ranges of India."

condition of British India as parallels; but although they have some points in common, the attempt to infer the future of India from the analogy of history is not valid, and has been deprecated. We stand alone in the experience of nations as regards British India, and no parallel exists in the history of the world from which to draw an inference as to its future. We must, therefore, evolve for ourselves and from our own prophetic forethought the idea of a "future India."

It is the object, therefore, of this paper to attempt a closer investigation of the probable bearings of this important question; and, first, it may be convenient perhaps shortly to review the opinions of a few able men who have made this question their special study.

Up to 1813, the opinion obtained that "a large influx of Europeans "into our Indian territories must prove dangerous to the peace and "security of those invaluable possessions."—*Letter of Court of Directors, H.E.I.C., to Lord Liverpool, dated* 27 *May*, 1813.

After this, however, a decided change in the views of the Indian Government seems to have taken place, for in 1829 we find Sir Chas. Metcalfe recording his opinion "that it is a matter of regret that "Englishmen in India are excluded from the possession of land and "other ordinary rights of peaceable subjects," and he expressed his belief that these restrictions impeded the prosperity of our Indian Empire.

Again, in 1830, Lord W. Bentinck says, "I feel most anxious that "the state of the law should be so amended as to oppose no obstacle "to the settlement of British subjects in the interior."

In 1832, when the parliamentary discussion on the renewal of the H. E. I. Company's Charter took place, we find our tenure of India compared to a "gigantic tree, its trunk and branches of vast strength, "but *resting merely by the pressure of its superincumbent weight, instead* "*of having shot its roots into the earth*!" Hence clearly recognizing the fact of our having no real grasp on the soil. Again, our Indian Empire is compared to a "Titan with arms of iron, head of brass, legs "of oak, feet of *clay*. The giant's feet of clay his weakest part, and "the first great storm may lay him low!"

What does this point at, but a want of a grasp on the soil in other words, of *colonization*?

The hackneyed simile of the "inverted pyramid" has often been applied to our tenure of India.

Metcalfe wished to colonize India.

Malcolm says "India is as quiet as gunpowder," and proceeds to urge its colonization.

Lawrence (Sir H.), as long ago as 1844, in his Essay on "The Military "Defence of our Indian Empire," advocated partial colonization, especially for *military* settlers. To quote more modern opinion, I may add that *Campbell* (Sir G.), in his work "*India as it may be*," enters upon this subject and advocates colonization. He says, "I would "have Government to encourage hill colonization to the utmost, and "especially to hold out inducements to its servants to settle in the "country." . . . .

Such, then, are a few opinions favourable to the general scheme of colonization of India; but I would go a step further, and advocate *Military* Colonization.[1]

I am aware, however, that the very idea of a *Military Colony* is so distasteful to the political ideas of the present day that I prefer the term "*Sanitary*," or, better still, *Industrial* "Circles" as the appropriate designation of the Military settlements I purpose to bring forward for discussion.

3. Now I hope I may be considered "*in order*," and as not wishing to offend the susceptibilities of any, when I remark that the "European "Colonist," the "*interloper*," as he was called, has always been regarded as an objectionable being in the eyes of an Indian Government. We know that it takes a full generation to kill a prejudice. Men, otherwise sound and far-seeing, are apt to cling to the prejudices of their early manhood; and, as advisers, are inclined to apply the traditional drag on progress, perhaps too freely at times. The traditions of the old East India Company still survive, and their sins of omission in this respect, and obstructiveness to European settlement and enterprise, have taken too deep a root to be easily eradicated. It has always appeared to me that a great opportunity was lost, as a mitigation of the dilemma of the Indian Staff Corps, "with its vast burden on the "revenue," to which the State was committed, in not encouraging surplus Officers and time-expired soldiers, discharged at the time of pressure, to volunteer for a "*Reserve*" *for India*, granting them perhaps land *in fief;* it being understood that *fief*, or fee simple, is "*that which is held of some superior, on condition of rendering him* "*service, in which superior the ultimate property of the land resides.*" It is suggested for consideration whether military "circles" might not perhaps be thus inaugurated, as one means towards the formation of a "Reserve Force for India."

4. A Russian gentleman once remarked to a friend of mine: "You need not expect to continue to hold India unless you follow our "example, and colonize;" and, indeed, the want of a "Reserve" seems manifest. I would speak with the respect and diffidence becoming an old soldier; but the absence of a "policy" on that point inspires distrust.

At any rate I would advocate anticipating the march of events, and getting as much of the mountain soil of India as possible into our own hands, and occupied by our own colonists, bound to us in military fief, before private enterprise shall have stepped in and absorbed the mountain tracts, and so in the end creating those very political complications apparently apprehended (if we may judge by the old exclusive policy) as involved in the land settlement of colonies whose citizens are not *sub vexillo;* and foreshadowing an *imperium in imperio*, antagonistic to the interests of the State.

As regards the objection that British colonists would supplant the natives, it may be remarked that colonists would bring their wealth

[1] Since delivering this lecture I have heard it stated that "there are records that "Clive, Warren Hastings, Wellington, Munro, Bentinck, Metcalfe, Ellenborough, "Dalhousie, Malcolm, Canning, and the Lawrences, amongst others, have favoured "the occupation of the hills." (HYDE CLARKE, V.P.S.S., &c.)—D. F. N.

and capital, and so renovate the land, which has hitherto been rack-rented to maintain an alien race; and the vitals of the revenue sapped to support the expensive machinery of an exotic government. We should thus be restoring to India a portion of the wealth extracted therefrom. "For at this day we find a country drained of its wealth "by men who are discouraged (if not actually prohibited by law) "from applying any portion of their gains to fructify the soil whence "they are extracted." Some day, as a means of fomenting rebellion, an enemy might point to the fact of our revenue being spent out of India, and the country thereby drained of its life-blood.

5. The Report of the Parliamentary Committee of 1858, on "the "best means of promoting European colonization and settlements in "India, especially in the hill districts and healthier climates of that "country," as well as for "the extension of our commerce with Cen-"tral Asia," embraces Dr. Martin's Sanitary Report, Dr. Hooker's "Report on Sikkim," and Captain Ochterlony's "Report on the Neil-"gherries and Malabar Hills."

It appears, however, a good deal hampered by local and partial developments, and refrains from definite recommendation of a policy for the State on those points. One of the results, however, seems to have been the collecting by Government officials of returns of "waste "lands" available for settlement.[1] They are chiefly taken from the

[1] TABLE OF WASTE LAND (1861).

District.	Total acres.	Remarks.
Punjaub, upper parts (3,000 elev.) favourable for European settlement	7,626,785	
Trans. Indus Highlands, Kohát Házára (16,479), may now be estimated	4,000,000	
Mooltan (district) suitable for indigo, &c.; hot and arid	1,510,388	
Himalayan States, Simla (Keyonthal), 5,676, 15,000; (districts 6,000 elev.) ..	20,676	
Kangra, waste land	16,136	Leased out and embarrassed with village grants.
Hooshiarpore, waste land	15,000	
Dehra Doon	204,526	
Darjeeling	250,000	
Kumaon and Gurhwhál	500,000	Approximate.
Assam, Kamroop (179,500), Cachar ..	5,000,000	Culturable, besides thousands of square miles of forests.
Damon-i-Koh (Raj Mahal)	675,840	
Madras, culturable lands (mamool) ..	13,554,333	
Bombay, Northern	1,635,666	
" Southern	2,000,000	Conjectural.
Scinde frontier	2,028	
Tenasserim provinces	628,034	
Pegu	13,146	
Mt. Aboo. Land leased to village communities	Nil.	
Mysore, table land	2,644,306	
East Berar, and the Sathpoora range ..	200,000	

special reports of 1861, and will serve to show the vast areas of waste or culturable land in India, at the disposal of the State for purposes of settlement. Some of the sites, however, are scarcely in climates adapted for *European* colonies, though others included in the larger figures are so, such as the Southern Mountains, and Khassia Hills.

6. "The Report on the Sanitary Establishment of European "Troops in India (1861)," and the "Memorandum on the Colonization "of India by European Soldiers (Punjaub Reports)," does in some sort deal with this question of Military Colonization; and a writer in the "Calcutta Review" founds thereon a definite scheme of colonization. He even lays down the precise force that would result from the scheme, and it may be roughly stated at an accession of strength to Government of a Reserve of 10,000 infantry, 700 cavalry, and 72 guns.[1]

I have only recently met with this scheme, and it has been gratifying to me to find my own views corroborated—I may say, forestalled—in this, as in some other instances, from perfectly independent sources.

7. The mention of Military Colonies leads to that of Hill Convalescent Depôts or Stations. There is an obvious connection between them. Except in the matter of *cultivation* of land; the real attribute of a *colony* (from *colere*—to cultivate), and other industrial avocations; a hill sanitarium might be made closely to approximate in its character to an *industrial circle*, such as I advocate. The garrison of the depôts as at present constituted is constantly changing, as the convalescents recover health they return to their corps; but were such garrison composed of veteran or time-expired soldiers, enrolled *sub vexillo*, as volunteers for such colony—with grants of land to Officers and men—*mutato nomine*, you have the elements of a *Military Industrial Settlement.*[2] In the sequel this especial development will be more fully

[1] The following is a summary of the Colonies (or *Regiments*, as the Reviewer calls them, vol. xxxvi, p. 220, *et seq.*, of 1861), suggested:

Punjaub, Kohisthán	3 regiments reserve.	
Kangra	1 ,,	,,
N.E. States of Punjaub	1 ,,	,,
Total	5 regiments for Punjaub containing 3,500 men of all arms.	
Simla	1 regiment.	
Dehra	1 ,,	
Darjeeling	1 ,,	
Rajmahal hills	1 ,,	
Madras Presidency	2 ,,	
Bombay ,, ...	2 ,,	
Total	12 or 13 Colonies containing 10,000 infantry, 700 cavalry, and 72 guns.	

[2] The author's former lecture on this subject, dated 30th October, 1872, was delivered whilst at Darjeeling in command of the Hill Depôt there; and perhaps his views may have been coloured by that fact.

He had sketched a plan of an industrial farm in connection with that command,

touched on. Meantime, I hazard the question: "*Could a Hill Sanitarium be expanded into such a Colony, and industrial pursuits developed in connection therewith, so as eventually to fulfil the conditions adverted to, of a self-supporting Colony or Reserve Circle?*"

Apart from their value as absorbing surplus industrial energy, and perhaps (when opened to volunteering) much of the floating vagrancy of the State, such colonies would naturally be amongst the means of securing a strategic grasp on the soil of India; affording as they naturally would do the nucleus of a *Militia* or *Reserve Force* to supplement the regular army; and, in conjunction with "entrenched camps" at the strategic points, would form rallying-points or refuges for the non-combatant portion of our nation in case of popular revolution, and would immensely strengthen the hands of Government.

Military Asylums are (or could be made) similar in general features, and might, perhaps, be considered as Military Colonies *in statu pupillari;* and might even be affiliated with such colonies, and the whole included within the protection of entrenchments, such as have been alluded to.

8. I observe that in a former lecture from which I have quoted (dated 30th October, 1872), I have enlarged on this special subject of "*Entrenched Camps*," or Refuges, remarks with which I need not trouble the present audience.

I would simply repeat that such works were strongly advocated by such authorities as the late Sir Charles Napier, Sir Henry Lawrence, and others; and I do not see why such purely military works should not in a great measure be thrown up by British soldiers, especially in the hills, where, in fact, strong working parties of various regiments do annually hut themselves, make roads, and generally enact the part of pioneers in ground selected for their summer encampments. To see the robust, rosy appearance of such men, instead of the washed-out faces one sees in the plains of India, is very cheering. I would ask, also, What more honourable employment for the British soldier than thus to construct works of grandeur and utility, such as the Roman soldiery have bequeathed to posterity as imperishable works on their native soil, as also, indeed, on the soil of this our Britain, whose occupation by Romans for several centuries bears a considerable historic parallel in some respects to our present occupation of India?[1] Should we eventually relinquish our great Indian dependency, British soldiers might thus point to something greater than the traditional pyramids of empty beer-bottles formerly attributed to us as a reproach.

If, moreover, the colonization of our splendid ranges of mountains be inaugurated; Military Colonies (or *Reserve Industrial Circles*) fostered;

and was on the point of submitting his plans to authority, when his term of command expired. As it was, he can attest that several of the Non-commissioned Staff and others realized considerable sums of money by raising stock, curing bacon, &c.

The draft of this sketch is at hand, and the questions raised in it might be reproduced perhaps for discussion with advantage, would time and space admit, as a suggestion for the industrial development of a Hill Depôt.

[1] Cæsar landed in Britain, B.C. 55, and the last Roman soldier left the country A.D. 426. The occupation of Britain, therefore, by the Romans lasted more than 450 years.

English settlers of capital and enterprise encouraged, and the other obvious means of obtaining a grasp on the soil of India carried out; we may find the India of the future fulfilling the condition of a self-protecting colony; a consummation, perhaps, hereafter devoutly to be wished by England, in case of war; when instead of a degenerate population such as some of the South American Colonies of Spain present to us at the present day, we may hope to find citizens of pure Anglo-Saxon type, as the National garrison of India: able and ready in alliance with gallant native *auxiliaries* to face a world in arms.

9. *Politics* are I believe prohibited in this assembly, I might otherwise perhaps venture on speculation as to the *Future of India*, a deeply interesting subject. I might ask, Is our national flag *India* for the *English?* or *India* for the *Indians?* I would rather hope we may be able to say, *India* for the *Empire at large* and *Humanity*. By degrees, no doubt, the two races may be welded into a common interest, and a *grand National Army* for the general defence of the Empire, as attempted to be shown, created, both Regular and *Reserve*.

As regards the planting of colonies, I would not exclude our *Native* soldiery. Colonies of *Sikhs*, *Dogras*, *Gôorkhas*, and other warlike races might be planted in certain sub-alpine points with advantage[1], the experiment has been tried in the case of Goorkhas with considerable success. *Russia*,[2] *Austria*, *Persia*, *French Algeria*, are examples of nations who have planted *military villages* as one means of holding a frontier against savage neighbours, as I have pointed out in a paper on the "*Defence of our N.W. Frontier*" (in No. 10 of the Journal U.S. Institute for India), where I instanced the Gunze or Ganz regiments of the Austrian frontier as a case in point; originally organized as a *cordon sanitaire* against that fell enemy the plague, at that time threatening an advance into Europe, they were retained after their special object had been fulfilled.

But, indeed, history is replete with such instances. We know what a success the *Roman Military Colonies* were: veritable *propugnacula imperii:* These colonies were cities or lands which Roman citizens or soldiers were sent to inhabit.[3] One-third of the land was ordinarily

[1] Perhaps in "India Alba," our newly acquired trans-Indus territory, which I have treated of in Section 16 of a work on the "Highlands of India," presently to be mentioned, I am treading on delicate ground; but the alacrity with which Russia has found an opportunity for a *congratulatory* mission to Abdúl Rahmán of Cabul is remarkable.

[2] Let us not forget that Russia is a *colonizing* as well as *conquering* Power. I would pause to say how interesting are some of the accounts one reads of Russian regiments or batteries—chiefly Cossacks—settling down on conquered lands in Siberia and elsewhere. Cut adrift from their supplies, they hut, clothe, and supply themselves with food by hunting, fishing, &c., besides agriculture and other pursuits of the Colonist. What a field for individuality! Such an expansion of Military life is indeed attractive! Could it ever be ours? Carrying with them their loyalty and cultivation—military and mental—into the wilderness, these able officers of Russia are true patriots, and they carry their country's flag into new regions of the earth; fulfilling, also, the idea of a (Roman) colony *sub vexillo*.

[3] The Tartar quarters of Chinese towns were evidently originally camps or citadels of the conquering race, antecedent to the times when the races became fused into a Chinese nationality.

set aside for the garrisons, which (in the times of the Empire) often consisted of an entire legion bodily settling on its garrison lands; but in ordinary cases a colony was led forth *sub vexillo* (which may be rendered "colours flying") by officials, triumvirs, ordinarily three in number, and the land was then and there ploughed and allotted to the volunteer colonists. These were essentially *military colonies* fostered by the State, and proved the salvation of the Empire for a time. On the other hand, the Greek colonies (as also, indeed, the North American Colonies of England, afterwards the United States of America) are standing examples of what colonies should *not* be—namely, settlements of disaffected citizens, who afterwards became bitterly hostile, and even subversive of the parent State. Is no moral to be drawn from such examples?

This, I think, forms an additional argument for *military colonization* and *volunteer corps*,[1] and with this in view it would seem advisable to get some more of the waste lands of India settled by tenants of the State bound in fief to defend the land; the defination of fief, or fee simple, being, as already stated, "that which is held of some superior "on condition of rendering him service," in which superior the ultimate property of the land resides.

10. I am bound to say, however, that arguments on the other side are not wanting: amongst them the necessity of a *seaboard* has been urged, and the *contact of ocean* insisted on as the necessary nurse of social infants, such as the proposed colonies have been termed: and predictions have not been wanting that colonies if planted in the Himalayas would soon be merged in the darkness of the semi-barbarous tribes around them, and so be lost in Cimmerian mists.

To these opinions I must demur, believing as I do that in these days railways could bring the "arts of war and peace" and civilization to their very doors if desired; and practically bring the seaboard as near to Himalaya as Ostium to Rome or the Piræus to ancient Athens.

11. It has also been urged that the culture of Indian land by Europeans *would not pay*. To this I would remark that the culture system of *Java* as introduced into that colony by the Dutch, in 1830, would seem to point to a development of the "Crown lands" of India (where they exist) well worthy of study: my treatment of this subject as a militaire must necessarily be crude and curt: suffice it here to say, that the revenue of Java was within the thirty years succeeding its introduction *quintupled*, and the happiest relations established between the European and the Native, and especially natives of rank were employed as helps to the scheme. To enter on details would, however, occupy too much space, and after all only bears indirectly on the question before us. Suffice to say, that by protecting the interests of all concerned, and cultivating with valuable products over and

[1] The Carthaginian colonies on the Mediterranean seaboard, which afforded such vast levies to Hannibal and his army during his wars against Rome, need not be cited as instances in history of military colonies aiding the mother country.

Rome had colonies on her military frontiers, both on the Rhine and Danube; in Gaul and in Dacia; also in Britain. London itself was a Roman military colony.

above the rice lands required for the food of the villagers, by contracts with capitalists, and, lastly, giving both the cultivator as well as the superintending officials, European and Native, a percentage on the outturn, the Dutch Government seems happily to have solved the problem of remunerative culture of its colonial possessions, and the European is protected from fraud and the Native from violence and force. "How different from the cultural state of India abandoned by "us to the law of supply and demand, and the unprotected and "uncontrolled principles of political economy! and the advanced "doctrine of unrestricted enterprise. In such a race the European, "following his instincts, resorts to force, and the Native, equally follow-"ing nature, to fraud, and such scandals as we have heard of in "'indigo' planting, &c., have been the inevitable result. Govern-"ment, in fact, shrinks both from taking the law into its own hands, "and so guarding all parties, the cultivator, the village community "(or landlord as the case may be), the contractor, and, lastly, itself as "suzerain entitled to *fief* in labour or land, as also from encouraging "the increased European supervision necessary to the development "of any culture system such as that of *Java*. Yet the Dutch have "introduced such with the happiest result. By supplying European "energy with the deserved Government advances on private capital, "the cheap labour of India could not fail to render the cultivation of "cotton, sugar, flax, indigo, tea, coffee, tobacco, highly remunerative to "all concerned." On this point the study of the Dutch land culture system could not fail to be instructive to all men in authority on the Indian establishment. The details are to be found in Money's "Java, or "how to manage a Colony" (1861). I have quoted and enlarged on this particular development of the waste land of India, because I should think it might be happily imported into the working of the military colonies, or industrial circles, advocated in the present paper.

A means also of increasing the revenue of India is thus indicated: but the question now occurs, "By whom is such a system to be "worked?" Not, certainly, by individual hardy soldier colonists, "(except under strict martial law), whose best field resides in the "struggle with the powers of nature such as are found in the rude "climes of America, Canada, and the Australian colonies. The hills "of India, however, present a somewhat analogous climate to the "private settler with capital, and the energy and strength of the Anglo-"Saxon might, perhaps, be thereby utilized in the struggle with the "forest and the field: but to *direct* labour gentlemen of education and "habits of discipline and good sense, such as army officers and "volunteers from overstocked professions in England, are required "rather than men of coarse Anglo-Saxon self-assertion, with contempt "for 'niggers,'" &c.

"With this reservation the Alpine fir-clad slopes of the Himalayas, "and the ever verdant plateaux of Central and Southern India—"vales bathed in perpetual spring," cry aloud for population.

Some further arguments in favour of colonization are suggested by a perusal of "The Report on Colonization, Commerce, Physical "Geography, &c., of the Himalaya Mountains and Nepaul," by B. H.

Hodgson, Esq., M.R.A.S., B.C.S., some time Resident of Nepaul. He urges several points, as follows:

(1.) A variety of climate in gradation of height from the plains to the snows; with choice of elevation. A cultivator could have his dwelling at 4,000 or 6,000, and his farms either higher or lower, yet close to his abode.

(2.) Himalayas eminently healthful.

(3.) Rainfall at Darjeeling 130″ (since less).
" at Khatmando in Nepaul, 60″.
" at Simla, 70″.

During 40 years, cholera only twice appeared in Nepaul. At Darjeeling, scarcely ever. Temperature at Darjeeling 60° to 65° from June to September, and in winter the same temperature reduced in regular ratio of 3° for every 1,000′ of elevation.

Sheep farming is a feasible project; samples of wool sent to Europe commanded 7*d*. to 9*d*. per lb.[1] He enters on further particulars too long to be quoted, ending his remarks by saying:—

"Colonization is the greatest, soundest, and simplest of all political "measures for the stabilitation of the British power in India. . . . "With the actual backing upon occasion of political stress and "difficulty of some 60,000 to 100,000 loyal hearts of Anglo-Saxon "mould, our empire in British India might safely defy the world in "arms against it."

12. As regards the planting of military villages, it is understood that some such scheme was formerly initiated in some of the larger British Colonies—Australia, New Zealand, &c.—and grants of land were made to retired Officers, both of British and Indian forces, but I never heard that veteran non-commissioned officers or private soldiers were in any way associated with them; and the scheme never got beyond the crude inception, and never in the least degree foreshadowed the coherent idea of national colonies tending to the formation of a *Reserve force.* In view, however, of certain obvious contingencies, many Officers of foresight and experience have thought that India especially may ultimately have to revert in some sort to a local army, modified, perhaps, but still the nucleus of a *Reserve*, in case of war in Europe, otherwise it might well happen that India would prove a source of weakness rather than of strength to England. In such a contingency, what better resource to fall back on than a *Military Reserve* in the Himalayas and other mountain ranges?

13. Closely associated with the question of *Military Colonies* is that of the nature of the force requisite to garrison the India of the future.

Now troops for the defence of a State may be classed as:—

(1.) Native (British).
(2.) Mercenaries.
(3.) Auxiliaries.

[1] The whole of the table-land of Thibet is no doubt a grand wool field; and its development might form one of the collateral projects of Himalayan "Industrial "Circles."

(1.) As regards the first class—British troops. The general purport of this paper is how to supplement the present British mobile garrison by a *Reserve* or *Militia*, in other words a local territorial army; it finds its advocacy in the preamble.

(2.) As regards the *Mercenary* system. Under its old aspect it has broken down by the mutiny of 1857, and that great standing danger to our British Empire in the East, so apprehended by men like Malcolm and Metcalfe, has been in a great measure swept away; and in regard to its partial resuscitation by our present large Native Army, we may inquire: "*In what light must we* "*regard our Native troops?*" Surely scarcely as "mere mercenaries!" Are not their interests yet sufficiently identified with our own to justify our calling them a "*National Army?*" I think so, and I would therefore, as, indeed, has been already suggested, associate them with ourselves in the experiment of *Industrial Reserve Circles*, which it is the object of this paper to discuss.

(3.) The third class of troops. *Auxiliaries* have scarcely yet been tried. The idea of small contingents or brigades to be furnished by certain Native Princes to co-operate with the regular forces of the State has scarcely ever been tried, though, indeed, of late a few thousand Sepoys of the Sikh Princes of the Cis-Sutlej States did take the field as a support during the late Afghan War, a happy precedent, as I think. To quote my own former words:—"I know not whether the day may have "yet arrived when our great feudatories such as Cashmere, Patiala, "Scindia, and others, should be entrusted with the independent main- "tenance of recognized *Corps d'Armées*, as portions of the grand "Imperial Army of India. They exist as a fact; might it not, therefore, "be well to call them out occasionally as auxiliaries for exercise with "the Regular Army? By this means, possibly a portion of the British "troops might be released from service as local custodians, and "advantageously massed in healthy localities, such as hill districts, "elsewhere. This leads me to reassert the postulate already put for "consideration, viz.: The hills for European; the plains for the "Asiatic soldiery! And the strategic points occupied and prepared "as refuges or entrenched camps, as a rule, in the close vicinity of "the industrial circles which would partly constitute their garrisons."

14. I might here dwell on our just claim to the services of our Native feudatories, whose integrity we guarantee from foreign and domestic enemies: self-preservation demands that we should in these days bring under more effective control, not only the contingents, but the entire armies of those States, and a most popular measure it would be, I think; and a force thereby raised, animated with a chivalrous rivalry, and jealous of each other to an extent just sufficient to ensure their fidelity to the British Government, the palladium of their honour and distinction. I put this for consideration, for I believe a territorial auxiliary Native army might be organized, on some such principle, and the whole welded into a grand National army of India really formidable to our foes and sufficient to guarantee the safety of India against all comers.

Contingents of the armies of our allies, *not being our feudatories*, form a different branch of this subject, which simply points to a *Reserve* or interior defence: I hesitate to give an opinion on such matters, which are beyond the scope of this paper: I may say, however, that battles have been gained ere now with the aid of auxiliaries[1]—*Plassy*, for instance—but they must be our servants, not *masters*, as history so frequently gives us instances of in the case of allies called in to aid. "It "is in *himself* and his own courage alone that a prince should seek "refuge against the reverses of fortune." So said one who knew the world of men and nations!

15. *Reserve regiments* or circles have been mentioned, and elements of one such were sketched in the former part of this lecture whereby an accession of strength to the State was estimated at 10,000 infantry, 1,000 cavalry, and 70 guns, all European troops, as a result of one scheme of the kind.

An experimental idea was also suggested in a sequel to the lecture from which I have quoted as given at Darjeeling, 30th October, 1872, for the formation of three small colonies to contain 100 men each, the expense of which, so far from being a burden to the State, was set down as an approximate saving in ten years of 130,000*l.*

Could I obtain the consent of my able collaborateur on that occasion (Captain F. Henderson, H.M. 107th Regiment), I could almost wish to reproduce *in extenso* his able lecture, entering as it did into the actuarial aspect of this question. To that gentleman, as also to Dr. Ambrose, who kindly supplemented my original address with sanitary statistics bearing on the same question, I was indeed most grateful: and I feel that as regards my present lecture, all was then said in a happier form than that I have now been enabled to reproduce. The three lectures—(1) on the Political and Strategic; (2) on the Sanitary; (3) on the Actuarial Aspects of Military Colonization—are to be found in No. 12 of the Journal of the United Service Institute for India, and form a trilogy (so to term it) which with the subsequent discussions on the subject (when we had the advantage of several able opinions) put forth all I could collect on this, to my idea, important question.

16. Little excuse seems needed for entering on the sanitary aspect of the case, when we observe that Dr. (Sir J. R.) Martin reported to the Court of Directors, H.E.I.C., that in the forty years embraced from 1815 to 1855, a total mortality occurred amongst the British troops of 100,000 men, "the greater portion of whose lives might have been saved "had better localities been selected for military occupation in that "country." Now each British soldier has been calculated to represent 100*l.* The State, therefore, in that item, lost 10,000,000*l.* sterling.

Such issues, moreover, are borne out by statistics mentioned in the able lecture I have alluded to by Dr. Ambrose, H.M. 58th,—the Medical Officer of the Depôt at Darjeeling,—and a most able Officer. Amongst his figures I find the death-rate of British soldiers'

[1] The Romans employed auxiliary troops, paid and often led by native kings. These troops drew *rations* and sometimes *clothing* from the Roman State.

The auxiliary State brigades suggested in the text find their prototype in these.

children in India for 1854 was 68·83 per 1,000; from 1864 to 1869 it rose to 94·41 per 1,000 in Bengal; and for the year 1869 was reserved "the unenviable notoriety of being the period in which 145·22 out of "every 1,000 European soldiers' children fell victims to the climate: "speaking roundly, the children of our European soldiers, the very "large majority living in the plains, have in each year been all but "decimated."

As a *per contra* to this, the increased health and consequent lessening of the death-rate to 39·9 in the hills is given. Other statistics on this head exhibit a death-rate lessened by six-sevenths in the hills.

Dr. Bryden's report to Government on the employment of British soldiers at road-making in the Himalayas, chiefly in the Punjaub Hills, during the term 1863–69, contains further proof, if proof were needed, of the salubrity of these mountains: it appeared that of the 2,500 men so employed, the death-rate was only *one half of what it is in the Army in England.* "But," asks Dr. Ambrose, "why go on multiplying "instances in proof of the wonderful salubrity of our hill climates? ". . . . The Royal Sanitary Commission to which I have alluded, "after hearing and weighing evidence given by such men as Lord "Lawrence, Sir Henry Durand, and Sir Ranald Martin, made the "following recommendation regarding the geographical distribution "of an European army in India:—

"1st. To reduce to a minimum the strategic points on the alluvial "plains; and to hold in force as few unhealthy stations as possible.

"2nd. To locate a third part of the force required to hold these "points on the nearest convenient hill stations or elevated plain . . ". . and to give the other two-thirds their turn."

This recommendation has been in part carried out, but scarcely in the thorough manner stated; but instead *palatial* barracks have been erected in the plains, and the rate of mortality and invaliding amongst our British troops, notwithstanding all our sanitary reforms, is scarcely diminished. I think I could suggest one or two concurrent causes of this, but in this place such cannot be entered on, beyond saying that heat and *overfeeding*, and lassitude engendered by want of wholesome industrial work, are some of those causes.

17. Now, as regards the first steps to be taken towards the formation of an industrial reserve circle or colony, such as have been alluded to, should such be ever inaugurated.

Assuming that such colonies should be *sub vexillo* (under martial law) with a regular military commandant and staff, it remains to suggest what sort of man we should endeavour to secure for our military colonist. At the discussion of this question on the occasion to which I have referred, it was generally agreed that able-bodied men between 20 and 40, if possible married men, would be at the expiration of their first term of service the most suitable: Artisans, husbandmen, and stockmen, each man possessing some craft highly desirable, if not imperatively necessary.[1] Non-commissioned officers and men of

[1] Of 100 men, 60 to be labourers, 40 mechanics; and it was further suggested

good character to have the option of volunteering, and this volunteering should be accompanied by an offer of a free grant of land, varying in extent from 3 to 25 acres according to locality and the special industrial avocations of the projected colony, and I fear it must be supplemented by a grant in aid of money. I see 1,000 rupees (say 100*l.*) was fixed upon as the least sum to start the colonist on his legs. The details of the start would be too voluminous to be entered on in this lecture. The internal organization, interior economy, and the Government legislation and supervision would alone absorb more space than can be allotted in this paper, which is necessarily of an *introductory* character.

The undertaking would necessarily be at first of an experimental nature, and would doubtless require much patient thinking out and elaboration to reduce it within anything like practical limits: the following tabulated average, however, as drawn up by Captain Henderson, may be given as a rough estimate of the undertaking suggested:—

ROUGH ESTIMATE OF THE COST OF 300 SOLDIERS FOR A PERIOD OF 10 YEARS.

	R.	£
Approximate cost of 1 soldier, per annum	1,000	100
" " 300 " " ..	300,000	30,000
Approximate cost of 300 soldiers for a period of 10 years	3,000,000	300,000

ROUGH ESTIMATE OF THE COST OF 300 COLONISTS FOR A PERIOD OF 10 YEARS.

	R.	£
Cost of conveying 300 men to the hills, at Rs. 50 per head	15,000	1,500
Grant in aid of Rs. 1,000 to 300 men ..	300,000	30,000
Staff allowance for 3 Colonies at Rs. 1,000 per mensem each for 10 years	360,000	36,000
Contingent allowances for 3 Colonies, at Rs. 1,000 each per mensem for 10 years	360,000	36,000
Compassionate fund for 3 Colonies, at Rs. 1,000 each per mensem for 10 years	360,000	36,000
Arms, ammunition, accoutrements, clothing, &c., for 300 men for 10 years ..	150,000	15,000
Building Government offices and staff residences at 3 stations	150,000	15,000
Total ..	1,695,000	169,500

According to which estimate a saving of 1,305,000 rupees (130,000*l.*)

that the permission to marry to young soldiers on the completion of their first term of service might form a very strong inducement to volunteer as a military colonist.

in ten years would accrue on the profit side, leaving a respectable margin for unforeseen expenditure.

Captain Henderson concludes his instructive lecture by quoting the words of Sir Henry Lawrence, who has already been alluded to in the preamble of this paper, as an advocate of military colonization, and for my part I cannot but consider that it must commend itself to all well-wishers of the European soldier and his family. It is interesting also to observe how nearly Sir H. Lawrence, forbearing to go into details, hits off as it were by intuition about what the actuarial calculation corroborates.

It would be quite impossible in this *introductory* lecture to enter upon further details. The remaining space allowed must now be devoted to a cursory sketch of some localities adapted for the placing of such colonies as have been suggested.

18. The sentimental aspect of military colonies as affording pleasant homes for Englishmen in the East, and its moral advantages to the soldier, need not here be mentioned. Such, perhaps Utopian, ideas were introduced into my lecture on this subject in India; and (if I mistake not) were sneered at as visionary. Utilitarians as we English sometimes are inclined to be, we are, perhaps, too apt to regard our soldiers simply from a financial point of view, and to think of them as mere machines for war—food for powder in short—but after all they are *men*, and their value moral as well as material. It is believed that the philosophic soldiers of Germany owe much of their success to the full recognition of the Napoleonic maxim, that the "moral is to the "material as 3 to 1;" and no doubt the probable improvement both in the physical and moral health of the soldier from military colonization scarcely admits of question. Setting aside humane views, is it not our *interest* to fortify the soul and spirit of the soldier, amidst the grand aspects of nature and the breezes of a temperate zone? I may, perhaps, be pardoned if I here quote my own former words, which I see annotated as "*Arcadia rediviva, the sentimental aspect of military* "*colonies*."

"Gazing on the charming landscape, perchance in fair Cashmere, or "green Kangra, on the grassy slopes and downs of the Neilgherries, "or even at this tea-growing 'bright spot' Darjeeling, the idea has "sometimes occurred to me that haply in this fair land may arise the "homes of a happy Anglo-Saxon population; perchance in times to "come of cheerful English homesteads amidst the orchards and sheep-"walks of the north; or the tea and coffee gardens of the south in "which the Indian veteran might cultivate his plot of land, and rear "a healthy family, his robust sons growing up the future defenders "of the State. . . . . Then, should the clouds of war arise and "danger to the State, I have pictured a robust and valiant citizen army. "—*The Reserve Force of India*—ready to descend full of health and "confidence on the foe! These ideas are perhaps Utopian, but after all, "why should some such future for the mountains of Hindostan "not be?"

I must not forget, however, that I am addressing a calm-judging audience on a practical question. I must refrain from such sentimental themes; I need not to indulge in rhetorical platitudes but proceed to the strategic aspects of the question.

19. The occupation of a ridge of mountains forming the water-parting, whence issuë the rivers which fertilize the adjacent lowlands, must at once strike the eye of the military critic as the true line of domination of the plain country embraced within those rivers.

There is one Hill country (were it ours) above all others, calculated both from its topographical features, as well as its geographical position, to afford flanking strategic value for "Military Colonies" such as I would advocate, viz., Cashmere.

This position I have sought to establish in a former paper entitled "The Strategic Value of Cashmere," in connection with the defence of our N. W. Frontier, and I suggested that the flanking value of that country as commanding the five Doäbs embraced within the five Punjaub rivers was inestimable, and should form a prominent feature in any Imperial scheme of defence for the Punjaub and N.W. Frontiers of India. If that position be conceded, it follows as a corollary, though perhaps with less emphasis than in the more marked case of the Punjaub, that the mountains flanking the entire Gangetic valley, viz., the Himalayan watershed, whence issue the rivers that flow into it, must, in like manner, be the true crown of domination of the deltas embraced by those affluents, and therefore probably the true points for occupation by a dominant race, so numerically inferior *in partibus infidelium*.

Instance, that troops massed in Hill Stations between the River Sutlej and Jumna (*i.e.*, Simla and its circle) are free to march and deploy on the whole Cis-Sutlej States and N. W. Provinces, without the obstacle of an intervening river, as was instanced during the mutiny of 1857, when the troops there in garrison marched to the siege of Delhi.

Again, troops in the ranges of *Garhwhâl and Kumäon* should command the Doäb, through the Dehra Dun, as far even as Allahabad.

The group of Hill Stations represented by *Almora*, *Nainee Tal*, and *Raniket* should command Rohilkund, Oude, &c., as far as the Ganges.

Troops at Darjeeling should command S. E. Tirhoot and Bengal as far as the River Brahmapootra, and so on. The principle admits of modification owing to local causes, but in its general aspect may, I think, be regarded as valid.

Here, then, are some of the localities on which reserve circles should be placed; but no doubt there are many points in other parts of India equally available; such as the Neilgherry plateau with the Annamallay and Palney mountains in the south. The Sahyoodria, or Western Ghauts, in the west, and perhaps a few isolated blocks or summits throughout India, such as Mount Aboo, the Omerkantuk plateau, would do for smaller refuges throughout the land; once let the principle of *Reserve Circles* be conceded, and many suitable localities will be found. The Khassia hills might be named; Pachmari and a few elevated regions in Central India, in the vicinity of Seöni and Rajmehal; and, should we retain our lately acquired territory across the Indus, perhaps sites for *native* reserve circles or Colonies may be found in the Highlands of *India Alba*.

20. I have here the MSS. of a work which I have called "The "Highlands of India," wherein I have attempted to describe somewhat in detail these and other localities which seem suitable for military occupation, most of which points during my lengthened service in the East I have had opportunities of visiting personally.

The index on the face of the map (now before the audience) comprises the majority of these highlands, and I have assumed 4,000 feet in elevation as the demarcation of the temperate zone, above which malaria, that dire foe of Europeans in India, ceases to be formidable, though still sometimes active even between 5,000 and 6,000 feet.

The work in question will embrace perhaps 250 pages or more, and is, of course, too voluminous to be entered on except in this cursory manner here; but should time allow, I may perhaps have the honour of reading a few extracts bearing on some of the localities I have named, and so on the general subject of this lecture.

I will now ask my audience to look at the map of India before them.

I point to *Cashmere* and the Kohistán of the Punjaub, which subtends the arm of the Himalayas called the Pir Pinjal, behind which lies the valley of Cashmere.

Were Cashmere ours, I would at once say: "Here is your main "defensive *Refuge* and *flanking* strategic circle for the whole "frontier of Northern India—the very bastion and fortalice of the "land,"—and my reason for this opinion is that the country of Cashmere flanks the entire path over which any invader from Afghánistán could pass; as also covers the side doors towards which a certain rival Power is always creeping; on this head I cannot, I believe, do better than refer to the lecture I have alluded to on the "Strategic Value of Cashmere" (No. 10, "Journal of the United "Service Institute for India"), from which I find I have quoted in the work on the "Highlands of India," now before me.

It has ever been my wish to associate my military diagnosis of this question—the *Defence of India*—with the military occupation of Cashmere as within the scope of a grand Imperial system of defence for British India; and I hold it should be *subsidised*, as it seems our treaty obligations bind us too tightly to free our hands in this matter. Doubtless our ally, H. H. The Maharajah of Cashmere, the son of an astute and (for an Asiatic Prince) a steadfast and reliable friend to the British Government, which set him on his throne, has hereditary claims on us—and sufficient *savoir vivre* to support our views in all ways. His interests and ours, indeed, are (or *should be*) identical. I will not dilate on this theme, which is, moreover, fully treated of in the paper quoted.

Failing this there are sub-Alpine spurs and ranges in the Kohistán, subtending the Highlands of Cashmere, where localities may be found for stations—fit for colonies—as guards to the Indus and N.W. Doäbs of the Punjaub, such as Murrie, and Abbottabad, &c.

Passing S.E. along the Himalayan subsidiary watershed, we find the station of Dalhousie, dominating the Bári Doäb, and (though less effectively) the Rechna and Jullindar Doäbs. I should consider this an excellent locality for one of the Reserve Circles, Colonies, or Regiments we have been considering. I should incline to prefer it to *Kangra*, named by the reviewer already mentioned. At Kangra, I think a Volunteer Corps should have its head-quarters and consist of mounted infantry, διμακαι, or dragoons, as the old mounted foot-soldiers were called, *mounted rifles* of the present day. This lovely district is, as is well known, one of the chief centres of the tea-planting interest, and already a considerable European population reside there.

Going south, down the Himalayan watershed, we arrive at Simla—that imperial mountain already mentioned—where I have in my work placed what I designate the *Keyonthál* Refuge, from the name of one of the small Hill States comprising its precincts.

Chákráta, a station in the fluvial basin of the Jumna.

Mussoorie with *Landaur*, dominating the Dehra Dun, which some authorities have at times sought to recommend as a capital for Hindostán, and a future seat of government. No doubt this sub-Alpine region dominates the Doäb and Oude as far even as Allahabad, and in that sense might be called the capital of *Hindostán* (which is a term only properly applied to that region of India alone). Sir George Campbell, in his work, "India as it may be," has, indeed, insisted on the peculiar eligibility of Mussoorie with Dehra Dun in this point of view, and without going quite so far as that able author, it may be safely conceded that there is much force in the suggestion.

The Kumäon Hills,—Almora, Raniket, Nainee Tal,—have been mentioned as dominating Rohilkund and N. Tirhoot. They are fully described in my work. But I must pass on southwards.

Here we find a fine hill country, "Nepaul," one of the best, indeed, in the whole range, unfortunately rendered unavailable to us from the fact of being out of our territory and independent; were it otherwise, probably the Valley of Khatmandoo would afford a fine site for settlement. It is also fully described in the work.

We now pass on to Darjeeling, and the region of British Sikkim, where no doubt splendid sites may be found for industrial development or colonies such as I have advocated. With this district, having been in command two years, I am well acquainted, and can affirm that no better locality can be found throughout India for one of the small experimental colonies, the elements of which I have sketched.

Passing across the Brahmapootra, we find the *Khassia* Hills, fully described in this work, chiefly from the works of Hooker and others. This is almost the only hill district in India not personally visited by me.

In the south of India, that noble plateau the Neilgherries seems in every way suitable for a large reserve circle or colony, and having had ample opportunities of observing it, I have entered rather minutely on its resources.

I would associate the Annamally and Pulnay Hills with this group.

Other blocks of mountain such as the Shervaroys and some small ranges rising above 4,000 feet, near the mouth of the Godavery, together with Coorg, Canara, the Wynaad, and the Mysore table-land, are treated of, but can only be just mentioned here.

Crossing the Toomboodra into the Dekhan we find ourselves in Mâhârâstrâ, the land of Sivaji, the Mahratta, the "Mountain Rat," as his proclivity for hill forts caused him to be called by his enemies the Moghuls. The Syhoodria Mountains or Western Ghauts are found to be the great buttress or mountain littoral of Western India, and contain a few sites for *sanitary* circles such as Mâhâbulêshwar, Mahteran, and the sites; for camps echelloned along the summits of the Ghauts from Khandâla to Deolâlie. There are several summits, also, such as Mander Deo, Amber-Khind, Singhur, and others, rising to eminences above the zone of malaria, and presenting favourable *pieds de terre* for convalescent depôts and sanitaria; but most of the positions are cut off by torrent and flood in the excessive rainfall of the monsoon, and are of too restricted an area to enter into our consideration as sites for colonies, or even very large military circles.

I have entered very fully, however, on the *Hill Forts of the Dekhan* in my work, some of which are fine impregnable sites for refuges for a dominant race, numerically weak amidst rebellious populations.

Thence I have passed on into Central India, and from the plateau of Omer Kantak as centre, being the watershed or waterparting of the land (7,000), whence issue the great rivers Sône and Mahamuddy, which find their exit into the Bay of Bengal (the former through the Gangetic Valley), as also of the Nerbudda and Tapti, which, flowing westward, fall into the Indian Ocean north of Bombay, I have thence traced the courses of the various ranges such as the Vindhya, Keymore, Rajmahal, Mahadeo, and Pachmári, &c., which ramify north-east, south, and west, and buttress in the table-land of Central India, forming steep escarpments in the courses of the rivers named. They afford but few sites for colonization of Europeans.

Thence I pass across the Nerbudda into *Upermal*, the *Highlands* of Malwah or Rajpootána, till arriving at the *Aravelli* Mountains (the "*strong refuge*") I find the station of *Mt. Aboo* capable of holding a *small* reserve colony, valuable for its *strategic* position.

Various *pieds de terre* forming temporary refuges from the heat of the plains subtending them are sketched: such as a few of the *Droogs* of Southern India, Mt. Parasnauth, in Raj Mahal; the Mágásani and Mylagiri hills near Balasore, in Cuttack; and a few rock fortresses and elevated plateaux are cursorily alluded to, but they do not enter into our consideration as fit localities for *Colonies*.

I had ended my sketch of the Highlands of India with section 15 —Mt. Aboo and the Aravelli spurs,—when the Afghán question arising, I made bold to add section 16, on the Highlands of *India Alba*, including the Kurrum basin (of which I have some personal knowledge). The Suleiman Ranges, on which are found the small sanitariums of Sheikh Boodeen; Fort Munro; and Dunna Towers (South), as also Peshin and the basin of the Lora, which, with the *highlands* dominating them, I have termed *India Alba*, the ancient

Arachosia of geographers. In this I have been much indebted to the valuable papers of Sir M. Biddulph, who lectured in this theatre, of Sir R. Temple, who lectured at the Royal Geographical Society, of Mr. Clements Markham, C.B., the able Secretary R.G.S., whose valuable papers on Afghanistán are almost text books on the subject: and of Captain Holdich, also a lecturer in this Institution, a most able military surveyor, whose paper has also appeared in the Journal of the Institution.

We are now retreating from our objective, Kandahar, and the subject *Highlands of India Alba*, may, perhaps, possess but diminished interest: nevertheless, if we uphold the provisions of the Treaty of Gundamuk, much highland territory will fall within our frontier, and will have to be taken into consideration.

In former papers I have long been inclined to advocate frontier military villages, as a buffer or zone of defence against savage neighbours who, in their raids, would necessarily first fall foul of our warlike villagers and receive at their hands a "Borderer's "Welcome!" And here I think I see an opening at various commanding points, to plant colonies of our loyal native subjects, who, in fact, form part of the scheme for the formation of a *reserve force for India* which it has been my object to suggest: but which from various causes I fear I have but feebly put before you, trusting more to the discussion which I hope may ensue, and elicit valuable opinions, rather than to my own crude and imperfect paper on the subject, which,—deprecating any dogmatic assertion of personal opinion—I offer simply as introductory and tentative.

HARRISON AND SONS, PRINTERS IN ORDINARY TO HER MAJESTY, ST. MARTIN'S LANE.

THE HIGHLANDS OF INDIA.

INTRODUCTORY.

IN this work it has not been the object to enter on any extended geodesy of the Indian Highlands.

(1.) Following the steps of our imaginary perambulation of the Mountain Ranges of India, we first examine the great *Himalayan* chain which extends 1600—or even 1800—miles along the N.E. frontiers of India from the Indus to the Brâhmâpootrâ, with an average width of 100 or even 150 miles. The general features of this gigantic range are too well known to need general description. The temperate zone embracing altitudes between 4,000 and 10,000 feet above sea level is chiefly noticed, and details of points selected for description will be found in Sections I. to VIII. of this work.

(2.) The Mountains of the South of the Indian peninsula are next investigated; such are the *Nilgherrie, Annamallay,* and *Pálnay* Mountains, together with their spurs or offsetts, such as the *Shervaroy* hills, the *Southern Ghauts, Coorg, Canara,* the *Mysore* table land, &c., with a few isolated blocks of mountain on the Eastern Ghauts, and near the mouths of the River Godávery, described in Sections X to XII.

(3.) The *Syhoodria Mountains* or *Western Ghauts* extend 800 miles down the Malabar coast, whose southern extremity is sometimes held to terminate with the gap of Ponany near Coimbatore—blend in with the great mass of the Nilgherries in Lat. 11°30′ north, and form the western littoral of India. This range from north of Bombay to the gap named attains elevations of from 4,000 to 7,000 feet above sea level: prolonged across that gap, may be considered to extend as far as Cape Comorin, embracing the Annamalay, Palnay, and Travancore Mountains, the geological formation being identical. The great elevated block of mountain called the *Nilgherries* is of arbitrary classification. Strictly viewed, the Nilgherries are simply an elevated plateau of the Syhoodria Mountains or Western Ghauts, forming the bluff terminating at the gap of Ponany mentioned above. The details are described in Sections X. to XII. of this work.

The *Syhoodria* Mountains or *Western Ghauts* are in fact the great western buttress of the elevated Indian plateau called *The Dekhan* or *Mâhârâshtrâ,* in the north, and *Bálághaut* south of the River Toomboodra. This table land dips to the north-east, and is highest in the south, being 3,000 feet near Bangalore, and the Mysore country averaging an elevation of 2,500 feet, whereas at the north it scarcely rises to 1,000 feet, or 1,200 feet near Nagpore and the country subtending the Seöni plateau. On the north-east however it rises into several ridges or elevated plateaux, such as Omerkántuk, &c.

(4.) *Omerkántuk,* 7,000 feet, may be considered the central water-parting of India, on which are found the sources of the *Nerbudda* and *Tapti,* as also of the *Sône* and *Máhánuddy,* the former draining westwards into the Indian ocean, and the other eastwards into the Ganges and Bay of Bengal. This may therefore be termed the *Great Divide,* and is in fact the most elevated watershed of Central India. The table land of Central India, however, at its edges rises into various ridges of hills, to which local names have been applied. The *Vindhya* range (properly so called only to north of the Nerbudda) is sometimes considered as extending right down the east and south of this plateau, even into the Southern Ghauts. *Geologically* this may be a true classification, but for purposes of topographical description, untrue. Radiating from this central watershed plateau of Omerkántuk are found the axes of several ranges with steep escarpments. The true Vindhyas trend north and westwards, parallel to the Nerbudda of whose valley they form the northern boundary. They do not rise beyond 2000 feet in elevation, and terminate near the west coast. The *Sátpoora* Mountains—in which is situated Páchmári—also run parallel to the same river, and constitute its *southern* boundary. They scarcely average 2500 feet above sea level. These two ranges buttress in the north of the Indian table land. On the east, towards the Ganges, the *Kymore* hills north of the Sône, and the *Rajmahal* hills south of that river may be considered the eastern slopes or offsetts of the same watershed plateau. They will be described more fully in the body of this work—Sections XIII. XIV.

(5.) The *Khássia* hills &c. of South-east Bengal are independent of this classification, and are described in Section IX.

(6.) The *Arravelli* range on the North is also a separate range, and forms a great defensive barrier of North India, extending 300 or 400 miles along the northern desert, with a width of from twenty to sixty miles. It blends in with the Vindhyas on the west. It is treated of in Sections XIV. and XV.

(7.) The *Droogs* (or Doorgas), those singular islands of the southern table lands are mostly built on spurs or elevated rocks of steep ascent, sometimes reaching 3,000 feet or more. They are succinctly described in Section XII.

(8.) A separate Section (13) has been also given to the *Hill Forts of the Dekhan*, as interesting *pieds-de-*

B 2

terre of the "Highlands of India;" but many of the points described do not rise to 4,000 feet, which has been assumed to be the "zone of malaria;" above which the true "Highlands" suited for European settlement and occupation commence. Below this zone lies nearly the whole of central India, which may be considered as bounded *north* by the Vindhya mountains, which, descending in steps or terraces to the Harrowtie and Chittore ranges, extend north as far as the Aravellis, comprehending a region called the *Upermal* or "Highlands" of Rajpootana; *South* by the so-called Eastern Ghauts; *East* by the table lands of Omerkántuk trending south-east into the Rajmahal hills; *West* by the great Syhoodria or Sáhyádri range of Western Ghauts which forms the littoral of Western India.

(9.) The original design of this work had scarcely contemplated crossing the River Indus; but Section XVI. has been added, and will be found to contain a brief notice of the great *Suliemán* ranges—east and west—as well as of the *Pushtoo* hills, and the mountain systems bounding the basins of the Rivers Kurrum and Lora, portions of "Highland" territory recently incorporated within the limits of British India, to which region I have—following ancient geographers—applied the term *India Alba*, the ancient Arachosia.

This short preamble may perhaps suffice to indicate the heads of the general subject embraced in the following work.

The Index on the face of the Map will show the consecutive order in which the details of the subject are treated, and the approximate elevations of most of the regions forming sections of the "Highlands of India" are also there given. I have added a foot note* showing the elevations of some of the principal

---

*MOUNTAINS.

The following are the altitudes of some mountains,—

Deodunga (Mount Everest) ... 29,002 feet

mountains; and the length of the chief rivers of India, whose basins are described in the work.

Peak K 2 (in Baltistan) W.	...	28,865 feet
Kanchinjanga ...	...	28,156 ,,
Dhaulagiri	...	26,826 ,,
Chumalari	...	23,944 ,,
Manda Devi } Gurwhál and Kumäon		25,700 ,,
Budri Nauth } Gurwhál and Kumäon		23,221 ,,
Nanga Purbut (Cashmere)	...	26,629 ,,
Sulieman (Takt) ...	...	11,300 ,,
Mount Aboo (Aravelli)	...	3,850 ,,
Vindhya, not exceeding	...	2,300 ,,
Satpoora ditto ...	...	2,500 ,,
Sahyadri (Western Ghauts)		4,000 to 7,000 ,, in S.
Nilgherries (Dodabetta peak)	...	8,760 ,,
Annamallays highest peak	...	8,835 ,,
Eastern Ghauts, not exceeding	...	3,000 ,,

RIVERS.

The length of a few Indian Rivers is as follows,—

Indus	Miles to the sea	1,700
Ganges ...	,,	1,500
Jumna (to junction with Ganges, 780)		1,500
Sutlej (to the Indus 900)	,,	1,400
Jhelum (ditto 750)	,,	1,250
Gunduck (to the Ganges 450)	,,	980
Godavery	,,	850
Krishna	,,	700
Nerbudda	,,	700
Mahanuddy	,,	550
Tapti	,,	460
Cavery	,,	400

---

* The numerals after names of places throughout this work show their altitudes in feet above sea level.

THE HIGHLANDS OF INDIA.

SECTION I.

CASHMERE.

HAVING glanced at the political and strategic aspects of the proposed "reserve circles for India;" having also attempted to show that the watersheds are the true positions for military occupation, it remains to indicate a few of the sites best adapted for their location; and to this end a brief description of some of the present hill stations appears not inappropriate. (1st), because many of them are capable of expansion beyond their existing limits. (2nd), because they are mostly situated on the watersheds which it is urged, form the subsidiary strategic bases,* and (3rd), from the fact that the circumjacent lands and territorial possessions are mostly our own, and already partially settled, so that society need not be disturbed, nor vested interests depreciated by the selection of such points for expansion into "reserve circles." Some of these localities have already been briefly indicated in the papers contributed by me to the United Service Institute for India. **Reasons for considering the present hill stations available as sites for military "reserve circles."**

(2). Foremost amongst them stands preëminent "Cashmere." "Who has not heard of the Vale of Cashmere?" It is a hackneyed quotation; nor are we **Cashmere Valley.**

* "Tactical bases" might perhaps be a more correct form of expression, for though strategic points doubtless exist, there can be no doubt that the *ocean* and seaboard is our true strategic base for the whole of India.

here called upon to consider its roses and romantic aspects (albeit that no really wise man will reject the "beautiful" as an element of mundane politics), but rather its sanitary and strategic capabilities, especially as containing sites adapted for a "military colony" or "reserve circle." It may, however, be objected *in limine* that to speculate and lay down laws for the disposal of a neighbour's estate may savour of the questionable and premature; but it is forced on our attention if we really contemplate the probable march of the political history of India.

Its political future forced on our attention.

Its flanking strategic value dwelt on as guarding the N.W. approaches to India.

(3). Having in a separate paper* expressed strong opinions on the value of its flanking position as bearing on the defence of our north-west frontiers, I believe I cannot do better than refer the reader to that paper (*vide* extract given below), and to the Map which accompanied.† A mere glance at the Map and Index to Military Events noted in the margin, which shows the routes of invading armies, cannot fail to convey an idea of the value of this State as a flanking defence to the Indus and the greater portion of the Punjab Döabs, and consequently as guarding the approaches from the north-west passes, and frontiers from Affghanistan into the Punjab, and so into India. I cannot but consider it as essential to the future safety of our Indian possessions, and the sooner the political necessity of its absorption within our defensive system is recognised, the better. In saying this I would refrain from suggesting any aggresive views subversive of political good faith. I would simply put for consideration how such an end could be accomplished without a breach of treaty obligation or of international good faith; but that Cashmere, sooner or later, *must* be incorporated within our army system of defence, I entertain no sort of doubt whatever.

---

* No. 12 Journal U.S.I. for India, 1873.

† No. 10 Journal U.S.I. for India, 1873.

"The importance of Cashmere in this point of view, "as the pivot of our advanced frontier, cannot be over "estimated, flanking as it does the approaches to and "from Northern India, and especially guarding by flank "pressure 'the Khyber,' that old conquering route of so "many invaders, both of ancient and modern times. "As an illustration, let us take the earliest invasion on "record, that of Alexander the Great, about B.C. 325. "Starting from Balkh, that conqueror, passing through "(Is)Kandahar and Kabul, appears, after emerging "from the north-west passes, to have turned north into "the Swât Valley, where, having formed alliances with "the frontier chiefs and overrun the country on the "right banks of the Indus, he apparently crossed that "river at or near Torbela,* thence advancing through "Hazára to Dhumtore, and the modern Rawul Pindi, as "far as the river Jhelum, found himself there opposed "by the warlike Porus, who may probably be styled King "of Lahora. He was there detained several weeks seek-"ing a passage. Now was the time for Cashmere to have "asserted herself, and had the chief of the 'Caspatyri' "at this crisis, vigorously issuing from the passes, fallen "on the flank of Alexander's army in aid of the gallant "Porus defending his native land, in that case 'Mace-"donia's madman,' being a hero and a great military "genius, *might* perhaps have found a remedy and fought "his way to victory; but by all the laws of warfare he "ought to have been cut off, and his army reduced by "famine or the sword; but a fatuous prince—I think "Mihira-Koola or Meerkul (surnamed Hustinuj, des-"troyer of elephants†)—then ruled Cashmere, and the "opportunity passed of emphasizing for all time the "value of the flanking position of the Cashmere State; "for be it noted that this manœuvre might have been

Extract from Lecture on "The Strategic value of Cashmere," 6th February, 1872.

---

* *Attock*, lower down the river, is usually considered his point of transit; probably his army crossed in two divisions.

† Or Ravána of the first Gonardya dynasty, according to a corrected list.

"repeated at each river of the Punjab, and with especial "force at Goozerat and Wazeerabad.

"Nor has Cashmere, during subsequent and more "modern invasions of India by the same route ever "played other than a quiescent part; and the importance "of her flanking position has never therefore been made "sufficiently prominent; nor have her resources on such "occasions been skilfully availed of by the potentates "engaged in the defence. Had they been so, it is diffi-"cult to conjecture how such invaders as Timour Lang "(Tamerlane), Baber, Mahmoud, Nadir Shah, etc., could "ever have passed the rivers of the Punjab in safety, "for of course the defending army could operate on "their communications, and take them in reverse at "each river; but the Lahore State and Cashmere were "too often rivals instead of strong allies, and so both "fell under foreign invasion.

"Thus much as to the importance of Cashmere as "guarding the flank of what may be called the "Khyber "line of least resistance" into India. Now to turn to its "other (or north-east flank, traversed by the route from "Kashgar and Yarkund over the Kara Koorum, *viâ* Leh "and the Tang Lung pass into Roopshū, and so into the "Lahoul and Kūlū Valleys just now being opened out "for trade. Not much is to be said for this route. Let "it be noted, however, that where traders and their "animals can pass, wild troops can also pass. It need "not be noted that the Cashmere State absolutely com-"mands and holds that route.

Routes from Central Asia.

"Lastly, as regards the routes from Central Asia "leading direct into Cashmere itself. The course of the "following historical sketch will tell of at least two "invasions of that country from Kashgar and Yarkund "apparently by the routes of Leh and Iskardo of armies "several thousands strong;* and in early times we read "of armies advancing from Badūkshán *viâ* Yassin and

* *Vide* the History about 1539 and 1557.

"Gilgit into the Cashmere Valley;* and we may appre-"hend that in the event *(quod Dii avertent!)* of future "war with Russia, pressure in the form of *threatened* "invasion would be resorted to by a subtle enemy, and "in all events an opening to political intrigue exists in "that quarter not to be disregarded. Nor, to speak "plainly, are these routes so inaccessible to the threat-"ened assaults of barbarous hordes (of Kirghiz and "others) from the plateaux of Central Asia, at present "under the protectorate of Russia if not already "incorporated within that empire, as it has been the "fashion of the advocates of 'masterly inactivity' to "proclaim.

"Let me not be thought to exaggerate this into a "grave source of danger; above all, let me not raise that "demi-extinct ghost Russophobia! Of course the object "of any hostile demonstration in that quarter would be "to endeavour, by disturbing the minds of our frontier "subjects, to keep amused in the north-west as large a "portion of the garrison of India as might be. A state "of things may, indeed, easily be conjectured when "Russia or other nations would employ every means to "threaten and attempt to intimidate all our colonies in "general, and so lock up therein as large a portion of "our small British army as possible; and north-west "India seems by no means exempt from pressure of "this nature.

"Enough has been said, I suppose, on the value of "the position of Cashmere as a 'frontier state.'

"We may assume the good faith and loyalty of our "ally and feudatory, the present chief of Cashmere. "His interests and ours are (or should be) identical. "As regards the attitude of our great northern neigh-"bour, the policy of 'masterly inactivity,' as it has been

---

* Probably over the Bárághil Pass which is a very easy pass, not exceeding 12,000 feet elevation, and by no means so inaccessible a route as has been supposed.

"called, has hitherto kept us from exerting such legiti- "mate influence in our frontier states, and the Northern "Khanates, as might have arrested the advance of Russia "a step further back. Several of these states have more "than once demanded officers to drill and organise their "armies.* Such states, if supported, become the pickets "or outposts of our main line of defence, and regarded "as such would afford time to our main defence to get "under arms and prepare for the shock of war; exactly "such breathing time as that ponderous, slow moving "animal, John Bull, requires to get on his mettle.

"Cashmere may perhaps be regarded as a bastion or "grand advanced salient, and its resources should, I "hold, be absolutely subordinated to the general defence "of India. We may assume, I trust, the good faith and "loyalty of its chief who holds this most important post. "I know not whether the time may have arrived when "our great feudatories such as Cashmere, Pattiala, "Scindia, and others throughout India, should be quite "entrusted with the independent maintenance of *corps-* "*d'armee* to be considered as portions of the grand "Imperial Army of the State. Why not? It would "seem that a balance of power subordinate to imperial "interests might be established by some such measure; "the sword of Britannia being held in readiness, like "that of Brennus, as Arbiter of the East. Thus also "releasing so many brave British troops at present "locked up throughout the land, and frittered away as "local custodians whom it would seem might be more "advantageously massed in more healthy localities "elsewhere."

Corollaries derived from the foregoing remarks

(4). The History of Cashmere then—an abridge-

*As regards Cabul, it is believed that the Affghans—a high spirited, independent race—are best left to fight their own battles till their national existence be threatened; they will then probably call in foreign aid. That would probably be the time to depart from the policy of "masterly inactivity." The power that then firmly assists will be dominant in Cabul politics. [This was written in 1872.]

ment of which it is proposed to present—would seem to point these lessons of polity,

1st—That the resources of Cashmere and the Punjab should mutually support each other.

2nd—That strategically Cashmere flanks and commands the approaches to India through the Punjab Döabs, and is therefore in the highest degree valuable to the defence of India.

3rd—That Cashmere (and North-west India) is not absolutely closed against invasion, or at least hostile pressure, by the routes from Central Asia, *via* Kashgar, or Gilgit.

4th—That Cashmere must be regarded as lying within the general frontiers of India, and be included within the scope of any general imperial scheme of defence for British India.

The following are briefly a few of the chief climatic and physical characteristics of this fine country.

Geological and topographical description of the Valley.

(5.) The alluvial plain or Valley of Cashmere at about 6000 feet* elevation above sea level, may be defined as the basin of the Upper Jhelum or Behut; it lies embedded in mountains between 33° and 35° N. Lat. and 74 E. Long., and extends from S.E. to N.W. The river is fed by innumerable streams and rivulets from the mountains along the margin of the snow-line. The valley is situated in the middle of a temperate zone which is most fitted for European settlement and industrial developments. It is a lacustrine deposit, formed by the subsidence of a vast salt lake, which at a remote period covered its surface. The supposed depth of this original lake (Suttee-Sír) being, from

---

* The following elevations of four separate points in Cashmere Valley give an average of 5,858 feet above sea level for the general *terre-plein* of the valley,—

Shupeyon	6500 feet	average 5,858 feet
Shahabad	5600 ,,	
Srinnuggar	5235 ,,	
Suheyum (burning ground),	6100 ,,	

The Source of the River Jhelum at Virnag—10,000 feet.

geological appearances amounting to proof positive, fixed at about 900 feet; a partial drainage appears to have been caused by some natural convulsion, followed by attrition of the sandstone rocks at the gorge of the valley through which the waters of the Jhelum now escape. This lowered the surface of the lake about 700 feet, leaving a fresh water lake (at first 200 feet deep) still covering its entire surface with the exception

The "Karewahs" appropriate sites for cantonments.

perhaps of the Karéwahs, or plateaux of elevated land, which jut into the valley at various points. These plateaux are several hundred feet above the plain, and would form very appropriate sites for summer cantonments; especially the "karéwah" or plateau of Islamabad presents one of the finest sites in India for such a settlement.*

(6). The mountain kingdom of Cashmere may, like other Himalayan profiles, be considered as divided into three zones, viz.—the Lower Zone (in the *south* forest and morass, in the *north* stony ranges) up to 3500 or 4000 feet unfit for European habitation; the Temperate or Middle Zone up to 8000 to 10,000 feet most fitted for European settlements and industrial developments, and an Upper Alpine Zone up to 20,000 feet and the snowy solitudes. Cashmere, however, is much broken up with lateral ranges and subsidiary watersheds, owing to the divergence of the main Himalayan axis into the arm called the Pir Pinjal, beyond which the Valley of Cashmere or basin of the river Jhelum or Vetasta constitutes a cleft or break in the conditions noted of a regular succession of ranges rising from 3000 to 16,000 feet in elevation. The Rutton Pir (7000) a branch or spur south of the Pir Pinjal,

*A sketch will show the way the alluvial deposits of clay, etc., are often found in high valleys of the tributaries of the Upper Indus—in Zanskar as high as 12,000 or 14,000 feet. The "Karewahs" (alluvial plateaux) of the Cashmere valley are thus formed. Above Cashmere the whole valley of the Indus contains lacustrine deposits, and the river most probably, in remote ages, ran through a chain of lakes, as the Jhelum at the present day within the Cashmere Valley.

II.

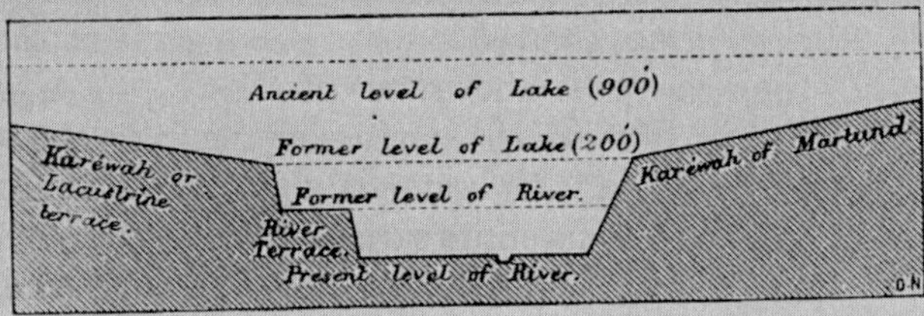

Section of a Karewah, showing also the formation of fluvial terraces in the Himalayan mountain streams. Section I.

III.

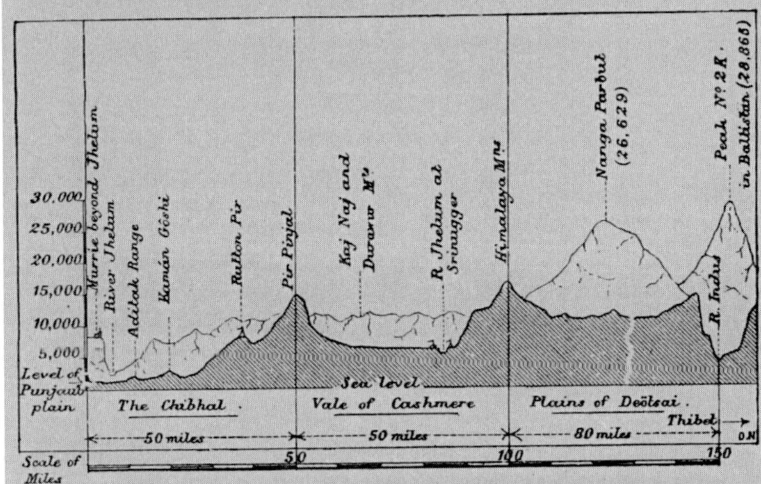

Two sandstone ridges Rutton Pir, syenite. North, gneiss—also limestone much contorted. Lower hills sparsely wooded with *pinus longifolia*. Slopes of Pir Pinjal, cedars and pines.	Diluvial—old sea beaches (karewahs), containing marine & lacustrine fossils 400, 600, & 800 feet above *terre-plein* of valley. Mountains plutonic; trap, basalt, and limestone.	Rugged country with peaks of granite and gneiss—a few horneblende rocks. On the Indus, diluvial and fluvial terraces with old beaches Himalaya Mountains trap and basalt.

SECTION AND ISOMETRIC VIEW ACROSS CASHMERE. Section I.

appears to me to contain some favourable sites for military occupation, being in fact the true strategic base guarding the basin of the Chenab from the north west.

(7.) There are twenty-four passes leading into the valley, about half of which bear on the strategic points in the Punjab, and are marked thus.*

Passes.

*Baramoola Pass, open all the year round.
*Poonch or Publi; joins No. 1 at Uri.
*Goolmerg or Ferozepore, open in April.
*Tosi Maidan, open in May { Here the Sikhs under Runjeet Sing were defeated in 1814.
*Sung-i-Sufaid, open in June.
*Pir Pinjal, open for foot 20th April, horse 20th May.
*Nundur-Sir; joins No. 6 at Allahabad Serai.
*Sedau pass, ditto, more difficult by Budul, Rihursi, and Aknoor.
*Koori, near the Kosi Nag; joins No. 8 at Budul, best in Cashmere { The Sikhs, under Runjeet Sing, took the valley by these Passes in 1819, having executed a flank march from Rajoorie.
*Water Nárah to Jummoo, always open.
*Banihál, ditto, open in May.
*Sir-i-Bul to Kishtwár, always open.
Mirbul, open in May.
Nabūgnyah, ditto.
Pakilgöan, open 20th June.
Durás, the great pass into Thibet.
Kôh-i-Hámon, for foot only.
Bunderpore to Iskardo, 1st June.
Lólâb, not for horses, always for foot.
Kurnáwer to Mozufferabad, ditto.
Kurnán, Bringas, Satasur, and Rehámau.

The defence of these passes was in ancient times entrusted to hereditary mullicks or chiefs.

(8.) The chief mountain peaks to the north, with their approximate elevations are as follows, viz.—

Mountains.

"Dudina," the "Mountain of Clouds,"	14,000 feet
"Wustur Wun," the "Forest Covered,"	12,000 „
"Pandau Chuk," the "Giant King,"	15,000 „

"Hárá Mookh," the "Head of Siva," 16,900 feet.

The highest peaks of the Pir Pinjal attain about 15,000 feet elevation. The great peak of "Nanga Purbut," to the north of Cashmere exceeds 26,000 feet.

Mountain Ranges. The main axis of the Himalayas is probably north of Cashmere, though the Pir Pinjal may be regarded as its southern arm; in fact, the range is divided into two branches by the valley, the northern range trending away north to Baltistan, and the southern or Pir Pinjal ending in a bluff at Baramoola, with offshoots west and north across the Jhelum called the Kaj-Naj Mountains (13,000). The "Rutton Pir" (8,000) range is Cis-Himalayan, and would afford, in my judgment, valuable sites for military purposes in the future, as it commands more effectually than the valley proper the plains of the Punjab. Its garrison would have no snowy passes to traverse during the winter months, and its climate is all that could be desired, as it rises 7,000 to 8,000 feet above sea level. In this range I believe a site for a military station, or stations, having the same strategic bearing on the Rechna Döab and the River Chenáb, as Murree and its watershed ridge has on the Sind Saugor Döab and River Jhelum, could be found; in other words, taking those two rivers respectively in reverse and flanking the Döabs embraced by them.

Rivers, Lakes, Springs. (9.) The water communications of Cashmere, consisting of a system of rivers and lakes, traversing the entire valley, would constitute a considerable element of strength in any well concerted defence of the valley. Canals, also, in many directions intersect the country and connect the water system, being deep enough for boats. There are three navigable rivers in the Cashmere Valley beside the Jhelum (which is the main artery of the country)—*i.e.*, the Bringee, Vesau, and Liddur. The River Vesau rises in the Kosah Nag at 12,000 feet elevation. The Sedau Pass leads thither, as also the Kuri Pass. The beautiful cascade of Arabul, near Heerpur, is found in the course of this river towards the *terre-plein* of the Valley of Cashmere. There are numerous tarns or lakes, *e.g.*, Lakes.

Mársir	...	Lake of Snakes
Társir	...	„ Trees
Khooshálsir		„ Delight
Achásir	...	„ Water-nuts
Mânusir	...	„ Spirits—Demons
Hákrsir	...	„ Weeds
Dullsir	...	„ City Lake
Wooler	...	„ Great Lake, &c.

Ebbing and Mineral Springs.

There are many ebbing springs in Cashmere,—such as Virnâg, Echibul, Basák Nâg, Sunker Nâg, Neela Nâg, &c., some of them having medicinal properties: they are mostly in the limestone rock.

The valley is drained by the Jhelum, and forms its upper basin. This river (the Hydaspes of the Greeks) has a course of 380 miles within the hills above the town of Jhelum—whence it derives its name—during which it falls 8000 feet, being 21 feet in the mile; but its fall in the valley itself is not more than three feet per mile, rendering it sluggish and deep. Its total course is about 620 miles to its confluence with the Chenâb. It receives the Kishengunga and the Nainsook—its two great intramontane tributaries—after leaving the valley. It is an outlet for the timber and other produce of the valley. It is said that Alexander the Great built the boats for the transport of his army to the sea at Jhelum, from timber floated down from Cashmere.

Topographical.

(10.) The Ruins of Ancient Cities attest its former flourishing state; they were about seven in number, and the ruins of many of them can be traced to the present time, *e.g.*—

Ancient Cities.

1. "Wentipore," built by Rajah Ven (or Awenti).
2. "Bejbiharrie," built by Hurrie Chunder.
3. "Anant Nâg," (now Islamabad).
4. "Srinugger," an ancient capital built by "Asoka" supposed site Martund.

5. "Parihaspore," built by Lalitaditya just below the present city of Srinugger, the present capital, which was built by Provarsen 450 A.D.
6. "Narapore," said to be below the River Jhelum near Sambul.
7. "Padinapore," sacred to "Lucksmee."

Dependencies. The ancient population of the valley and its dependencies is supposed to have reached three millions under the Hindoos.*

Temples. The temples constituting the remains of its ancient architecture are of the Aryan order (Ariostyle), and are to be seen at Martund, Pyach, Pandretun, Lar, Puttun, and elsewhere. They have been ably described by Cunningham and others.

Bridges. There are thirteen bridges over the Jhelum, seven being at the city. They were mostly built by the Hindoos antecedent to Mahomedan conquest. Jehangir built three, Zeinúlábúdín one, Futteh Shah one.

Houses. The houses in Cashmere are built of wood, four stories high; and flowers are often planted on the roofs. The people inhabit the third story, the lowest being devoted to cattle, and the highest to clothing and valuables.

Boats. In the time of Shah Hamedan there were 5,700 boats on the rivers and lakes of Cashmere, and in the time of Akbar upwards of 3000 boats paid tax. But the details of ancient Cashmere statistics can be found elsewhere,—notably in the "Aeen Akbari."

Attractive features of the country. (11.) It may here perhaps be expedient to dwell a little on the attractive features of this fine country as a field for colonists or settlers *sub-vexillo;* in other words of a "military reserve circle." I would remark

---

* These dependencies were, Thibet, Kishtwar, Gilghit, Hurshall, and Burshall, Pakli, Dardo, Ladak, Kalmuk, Kasial or Kal—and even Kabul and Kandahar were formerly incorporated in the Soubah of Cashmere under the Moghuls. The sides of the hills were terraced, and afforded much more cultivation than at present, of course supporting a larger population. The remains of ancient culture and fruit gardens attest this decay in population.

that many of our present hill stations—Simla itself for example—are located on foreign territory, so that it may be hoped no insuperable impediment exists to the establishment of such settlements, if not in the Cashmere Valley itself, at any rate in the Kôhistán or hill-country adjacent — perhaps Cis-Himalayan. I have written elsewhere—"A noble valley not less than "80 miles in length and 25 in breadth, at a general "elevation of 6000 feet above the sea; its climate tem-"pered in summer by the cool breezes from the snowy "peaks of its girdle of surrounding mountains, with a "rich soil the gift of a lacustrine origin, bright with the "waters of a thousand fertilizing streams and fountains, "and balmy with the odours of groves and flowers in-"digenous to the soil, forms no sterile cradle for a new "race called forth from the barren steppes of Thibet "and Tartary, and the mountains of the surrounding "watershed. From the chill plateaux of Deotsai, "Thibet, and Zanskár, from the sandy wilds of the "Punjab, the favored people of Káshyapa flocked across "the passes of Himáleh and the Pir Pinjal into the fair "valley to which they had been called." And the same attractions and more exist as in the days of the first Aryan immigrants.

Cashmere as viewed by the Aryan immigrants.

(12.) Some of the finest sites perhaps in India for villages are to be found in the spurs and lateral valleys which branch out of the main basin of Cashmere. Here, nestled amidst groves of plane-trees (chenârs),* walnuts, and other grand forest trees such as the fir, the oak, the pine, the elm, the poplar, and others, with

Equally applicable to present times.

* The Moghul emperors caused chenâr trees (platanus orientalis) and poplars to be planted near every Cashmere village, whether as a sanitary or picturesque measure is not stated. In the former point of view, I think the present ruler might try "eucalyptus globulus," the gum-tree, in addition to his present flora in the valley proper, as supposed absorbents of malaria, though perhaps the climate would be too severe in winter. I have, however, seen the tree flourishing elsewhere in the Himalayas at elevations of 5,000 or 6,000 feet, and in the Nilgherries at 7,000 feet, and higher.

brawling rivulets of pure water rushing down the mountain slopes; green with fresh sward and spangled with wild flowers, the flora of a temperate zone, are villages which may vie with those of the Alps or Switzerland in picturesqueness. Fruit trees of all kinds abound, and the natural types of most vegetable products are found in this favored land. The apple, pear, quince, plum, apricot, cherry; currant, mulberry, walnut, here flourish *in situ.* Most European trees are found, and many others, such as the chenâr, peculiar to the country, abound; and liberal nature here yields ample crops of cereals and tubers to the hand of moderate labour and industry. Grapes may be added, from which some wine is made, and this industry is one capable of development; amongst other products, saffron made from the crocus is exported, and oil is expressed from the walnut; the attar of roses is celebrated. The people eat the Singhâra (water-nut); also the root of the *(nadree)* esculent lotus, which adorns the lakes of Cashmere. The shawl and *papier maché* work is celebrated. Horses and cattle are of a small but hardy kind. Flocks of sheep numbering thousands roam the hill sides, and fatten on the fresh pasturage up to the snows. Wine, cider, beer, honey, saffron, timber, wool, and grain, are thus, amongst others, products of Cashmere. Here, if anywhere, could the dream of Arcadia be realized, and the glories of the golden age formerly attributed to the land of Káshyapa be restored, and the romantic spirit of the west imported into this favored Eastern Eden: nor do I speak alone of the valley proper, but of all the Kôhistán or mountain country of Cashmere. Nor are these elements of prosperity its only attractive feature. Close at hand is the home of the Arimaspians, the gold hunters of Herodotus; where also borax and gems are found. In the noble forests around the valley, mines of wealth exist, metalliferous ores and timber to any extent abound, and any amount of water power is

Cashmere villages

Agricultural and pastoral capabilities, products, &c.

Not confined to the Valley only, but to the entire Kohistan.

Forests.

ready to the hand of industry and enterprise, which at present runs as waste to feed the normal marshes of the valley. Not here need one fear the effeminate langour of an Indian Capua to corrupt man's heart, whilst all the manly pursuits congenial to the Anglo-Saxon race could be nurtured and are easily obtainable. The bear, the ibex, the stag, the chamois, and other game abound, and all the manly virtues could be educed in their pursuit by hardy settlers. Game.

Probably there is no part of India better, if as well, suited (were it ours) for settlers, or for a military reserve circle, than the territories of the Maharajah of Cashmere. But it must be added that the winter climate of the valley proper up to March or April is not good, being cold, and damp, and foggy, and not unlike that of the British Isles.

It would be obviously out of place to specify exact localities for military villages or settlements, as probably the Native Government would scarcely sanction any such undertaking, except perhaps in very limited localities—Goolmerg, Sónamerg, and the Sinde Valley, Naboog Valley, and the Karéwahs* may however be named, and the slopes of the Rutton Pir have already been mentioned. It is therefore only permitted us to sigh for what *might have been*—that sad point of retrospect in human affairs.

Should Cashmere, however, in the dim future which lies before us, ever be garrisoned by British or auxiliary troops, considerable care would have to be exercised in selecting healthy sites for barracks and cantonments, for it must not be overlooked that the "valley" has been more than once invaded by epidemic cholera of a very malignant type, and the other diseases incident to a malarious climate are prevalent. As a set-off against this, we have besides the "karéwahs" already Climatic effects considered.

* The Karéwahs of Cashmere are those of Martund, Nonágar, Pampur, Khanpur, &c., they are dry and would form fit soil for *cotton*: another industrial development.

mentioned, choice of elevation in numberless lateral valleys which branch out of the main basin, gradiating to any required elevation, and containing any amount

A field for the engineer.

of level ground for building purposes. The *terre-plein* of the valley itself presents a glorious field to the scientific engineer for drainage and reclaiming of the land generally from its normal marsh and swamp.

It is believed that by careful drainage and water-works, the entire character of the valley could be changed, and the development of malaria arrested. Granted the vast labour and expense requisite to effect this, still it would present a noble object for a great Government to undertake, and in the end prove amply remunerative. Cereals would take the place of the present rice cultivation; orchards, sheep-walks, and pastures would supplant the malarious swamps at present existing, and a long train of advantages too obvious to need enumeration would result. Suffice it to say here that Cashmere might become one vast granary and supply the commissariat of an army, both in grain and live stock. To enter on detailed statistical speculations on this head, would occupy a larger space than in this cursory sketch can be allotted.

Financial aspect.

14. As the country is at present under a Native Government, specially jealous of its finance, it is difficult to arrive at any just approximate valuation of this fine country. We have in the "Aeen Akbari" detailed data of its capacity in former times, and it is believed that were the population brought up to the census of Akbar (1592 A.D.), a net revenue of one million sterling would not prove an excessive estimate; and after ten years of occupation that amount might be doubled.

Area of territories comprising ancient Cashmere

15. The Kingdom of Cashmere has greatly varied in dimensions at different periods of its history. Many of the surrounding countries, such as Little Thibet, Zanskár, Gilgit, and even Cábul, were formerly incorporated within its limits. From time immemorial

IV.

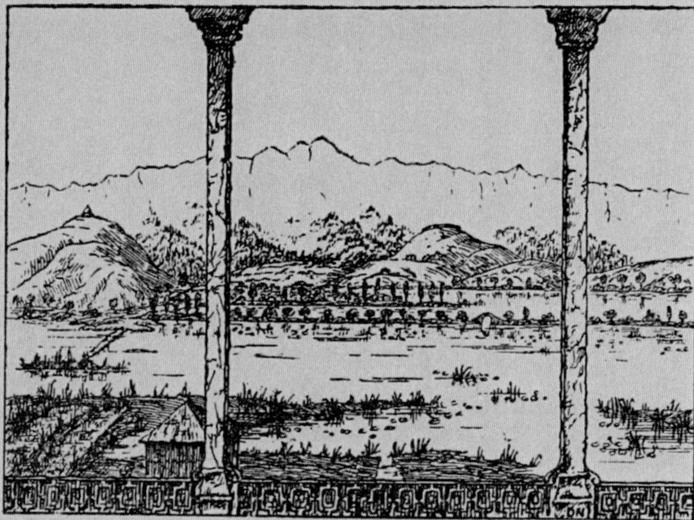

City and Lake of Cashmere, looking south-west towards the Pir Pinjal. Section I.

V.

CASHMERE VALLEY. Village of Mulwun, showing the "Karewah" of Martund with the Duchin-para in the distance. Section I.

the taxes have been taken in kind, so that the revenue depends much on the character of the ruler. In the time of Akbar—who took half the cultivator's profit—the revenue amounted to £1,000,000 sterling, but in his time Cábul and Candahár were included in the province as stated above. Its revenue under the Patháns was about £330,000; under the Sikhs (who took two-fifths) not more than £66,000 (for Cashmere Valley only); under Golâb Sing (who took seven-eighths), perhaps £600,000. Under the present ruler it is officially stated to be about £400,000, but may probably exceed that estimate.* Revenue, its fluctuations and the causes of such.

16. The Cashmere Valley is divided into two large natural sections or districts—the "Kámráj" and the "Miráj"—the former containing sixteen and the latter twenty pergunnahs, four of which were formerly allotted to Islamabad, the revenue being twelve and twenty lakhs respectively (£320,000).† The Valley divided by the river Jhelum into two sections containing 36 Pergunnahs since early times.

The "Aeen Akbari" enumerates the exact number of soldiers quartered in each pergunnah, as also the exact quota of revenue derived from each village. It may be stated generally that the ground revenue of the

* The population of the valley of Cashmere during the rule of the Sikhs was estimated by Hugel at 200,000, of which the city of Srinugger contained 40,000, and this may partly account for so low a figure of its revenue in those times (£66,000). At the period of his visit, the country had been drained of its inhabitants. At present (1874) it is probable that 80,000 may not be an excessive estimate of the number of the inhabitants of the city, and 1,000,000 of the entire country of Cashmere.

† Abul Fuzl in the statistical account of the country, *circa* 1600, as contained in the "Aeen Akbarie," states that under Kasi Ali the Cashmere Valley produced upwards of thirty lakhs of khurwahs (mule loads) of rice—3,063,050 is the exact number—each khurwah being three maunds eight seers, or about 256lbs. The value of a khurwah varied, but generally one rupee per khurwah may be assumed as an average. This, be it remembered, is the estimate of the times of Akbar; at the present day rice is ten times the price. Its present area has been officially estimated at 25,123 square miles, with a population of less than one million (750,000), and an estimated revenue of £400,000 per annum, but this is probably a low estimate.

valley alone slightly exceeded £300,000 per annum; it further gives a list of villages amounting to upwards of 4,000 in number in the valley alone—a fact which sufficiently attests the flourishing condition of the province under Akbar.

Garrison under former native Governments.

17. According to the same authority (Abul Fuzl), the military force of Cashmere under Akbar was 4,892 foot, or garrison artillery, in 37 garrisoned fortresses, and 92,400 cavalry. The Pathans had 20,000 troops, the Sikhs had 2,500, or two regiments. The Cashmeries of the present day are a timid race easily ruled. The force maintained under the late ruler, Golâb Sing, in 1851, was as many as 19,000, and it is believed that the present chief, "Runbeer Sing," could bring 20,000 men into the field.* Such being the material resources of the country, it might be asked whether we as suzerain obtain a fair compensation for the security guaranteed to the Cashmere State. That the country is open to invasion is evident. A mere glance at the map and index, showing the historical events of the past 500 years, will at once point that fact; and it is believed that without our support Cashmere could not exist long as a kingdom in face of its warlike and aggressive neighbours—its masters in times not long passed.

18. Before leaving this enticing subject, and seeing

---

* The following is a list of Golâb Sing's Army in 1851-2, in which year the author saw the chief part of them, *en route* to the siege of Chilas, which fell that year:—

COMMANDANTS,			
Davee Sing	... one regiment	...	1,000 men
Dhurm Sing	... two ,,	...	1,600 ,,
Steinbach and Lochun Sing	,, ,,	...	1,800 ,,
Beja Singh	... ,, ,,	...	1,800 ,,
Hajee Singh	... ,, ,,	...	1,600 ,,
Golaboo	... one ,,	...	1,000 ,,
Soondur Singh	... ,, ,,	...	1,000 ,,
Bussunt Singh	... ,, ,,	...	800 ,,
Goojadur (Poorbeas)	,, ,,	...	700 ,,
Kuliandur	... ,, ,,	...	1,000 ,,

that our "manifest destiny," is to civilize (if not colonize) the great Indian peninsula, I would ask, "Are there no means of bringing about a pacific solution of this question?" I would point out that the present ruling dynasty (Dogra) has no special territorial sympathy for the people and soil it governs. I hazard the question —Whether some arrangement could be effected whereby a rectification of territory, satisfactory to the reigning chief, might be brought about, and the north west frontier—conterminous with so much of Cashmere territory—brought thereby more perfectly within the "zone of defence" of a British Imperial military system. Failing this I think that a contingent under British officers should be considered of.

Could some rectification of frontier be effected by treaty?

19. I have scarcely touched on the romantic or picturesque aspects of this fair land; its sublime mountains and noble forests, its placid meres and sparkling fountains, its fruits and flowers and floating gardens; let travellers and poets tell of such! Suffice if we can here point out more emphatically than has hitherto been done its strategic and military value and resources, and rescue from neglect and abandonment to the forces of evil, moral and physical, this fair kingdom, one of the chief bulwarks, as it might well become, of our Indian Empire; whence haply in times to come may re-issue the effigies or type of a future

---

Amuriepultun	...	one regiment	... 1,000 men
Meean Huttoo	...	,, ,,	... 800 ,,
Davee Sing (2nd)	...	,, ,,	... 1,000 ,,
Adjutant	...	,, ,,	... 1,000 ,,
Tumboorchee	...	...	... 200 ,,
Topchee	...	...	... 500 ,,
Ghorcherra	...	...	... 300 ,,
Rohillas and Sikhs		...	... 1,400 ,,
Motee Singh	...	...	... 500 ,,
		Total	... 19,000 men

It is now, I believe (1874), officially returned at 26,975 of all ranks, a respectable force "numerically."

colonial India, and of a civilization restored to this its virgin matrix, for assuredly the primitive types of things are to be found in this cradle of the East.*

To complete this sketch a notice of the historical and military events bearing on the strategic position of Cashmere will now be given.

HISTORICAL NOTICE.

Historical note on Cashmere.

20.—THE sole authority for the history of Cashmere prior to the 13th century, is an ancient Sanskrit chronicle, the "Rajah Taringini," the slokes comprising which were collected by Kalhâna Pundit about 1,200 A.D., in the reign of Jye Sing of Cashmere.

Its early history is obscured by fables and myths, both Hindoo and Mahomedan, for both claim the valley as one of the cradles of their Theistic faith. All, however, agree in stating—and geology corroborates the statement—that the valley was at one time a vast (salt) lake, the pressure of which seems at some remote period to have formed an outlet for itself at the western corner of the valley, where the barrier of sandstone rock at Baramoola seems to have been rent by some cataclysm followed by attrition, whereby the waters of the valley escaping formed the present

* In Cashmere, or its girdle of mountains, is to be sought the home of the Arimaspians (hunters of gold) alluded to by Herodotus, and of the Kaspatyri of Arrian and Strabo. It was doubtless one of the chief seats of empire when India was at its best and most flourishing period of civilization amongst the nations of the East, and from this centre probably issued the learning (such as it was) of the Brahminical priesthood now spread over India, and the martial clans of the Great Surájbuns and Chándrábuns stock of Rajpoots, the very pith and backbone of the ancient warlike Aryans of India, now how depressed and semi-effete! To restore such high destinies were worthy of the British Government!

Jhelum or Vitasta.* This natural geological event, approximately fixed by chronologists at about 2,666 B.C., is attributed by native annals to the agency of a mythical personage (Káshiapa) the múni or divine progeny of Brahma, but the fables which involve the myth are too fantastic and puerile to need insertion. The most rational chronology seems to approximate this event to the epoch of the Mosaic deluge.†

Authorities differ as to the origin of the original stock of Cashmere. I should consider, however, that its mountains may have been sparsely peopled by the Naga aborigines of the ancient Khassia range, and that an early wave of Aryan conquerors of India followed. We find traces of the primitive form of religion to have been that of the "Tree and Serpent" **Ancient religion.** worship in prehistoric times. Upon this seems to have been engrafted the Brahminism of the Aryan conquerors of India, afterwards merging into Boodhism, and the original stock superseded and all but transfused by Toorks and Kulmuks of Central Asia, followed by Moghuls and other immigrants. Mahomedans, indeed, assert that the original inhabitants were a tribe from Toorkistan, who shortly after the Mosaic deluge emigrated thither. As an approximate estimate of the religion of Cashmere antecedent to the time of Akbar, we may quote "Ferishta," who states that in his time there were 45 places of worship to Mahadeo, 64 to Vishnoo, three to Brahma, 22 to Boodh, and nearly 700 figures of serpent gods in the country; and this notwithstanding the destructive activities of

* The modern Jhelum is formed by the junction (near Kanibul) of the three streams Arpet, Bringh, and Sandrahan. The higher Cashmere mountains are of trap and basalt, but the lower hills are of limestone and sandstone "often much contorted, and holding marine fossils." Beaches are also found.

† The Samaritan Pentateuch dates the deluge at 2,938 B.C., ordinary computation at 2,349 B.C., the drainage of Cashmere 2,666 B.C.; therefore is clearly referable to the Mosaic deluge.

several iconoclast Mahomedan kings; by this we clearly recognise the ophistic character of the native religion. Aryans from India, and Toorks or Tartars from Central Asia, under hereditary khans or chiefs, appear to have ruled for long periods, and several fabulous or semi-fabulous dynasties, extending over nearly 2000 years are enumerated, until we at length find Ogregund (or Gonerda I.), emerging from the obscurity of fable

Gonerda I., 1367 B.C.

a recognised sovereign of Cashmere. He may be held to have reigned about 1400 B.C., for we find that this belligerent potentate fell in the wars of the Koraus and Pandaus, perhaps in the battle of Korau Ket, 1367 B.C. The next conspicuous character on the page of ancient Cashmere history is King Lava (or Laoa), who is stated

Lava 950 B.C.

to have introduced Brahminism about 950 B.C.; he was a contemporary of Darius Hystaspes. At this early period we find Cashmere subject to invasions from Central Asia, with which country it was evidently more closely connected in ancient times than since the ruin caused by Ghengis Khan in historical times. We find three Tartar brothers reigning about 400 B.C., evincing conquest from Central Asia; indeed, the "Rajah Taringini" informs us that in the following reign of Asoka, Cashmere was overrun by Mlechchas or Scythian hordes, the fragments apparently of ancient Media or Toorkistan. The great Asoka reigned 284—246 B.C.;

Asoka, 246 B.C.

he was a contemporary of Antiochus the Great. His epoch is a well-known landmark in Indian history; he was converted to Boodhism, and his kingdom extended over the greater portion of the Indian peninsula from the Indus to the mouths of the Ganges.

After this period the sovereigns of Cashmere are known to history with tolerable accuracy, but the dimensions of the kingdom are vaguely defined. The chronicle claims Cashmere as the seat of government of nearly all the provinces north of the Nerbudda and the Gangetic valley, but it seems probable that the valley was merely the occasional summer residence of several of the dynasties who reigned in Upper India; indeed, it is expressly stated so in the "Rajah Taringini." The Kuttoch dynasty of Naggarkote (Kangra), or at least the chiefs of Jummoo (the ancient Abbisaros), appear to have been closely associated with Cashmere. The ancient kings, perhaps, moved *to* Cashmere for the summer, rather than *from* it in winter, like the Moghul emperors and governors of a subsequent age. However, whether the seat of government or not, Cashmere undoubtedly exercised far greater influence on India in ancient than in modern times.

In later times it was associated closely with the Rajpoot Kingdoms of Anhálwára and Malwa, and its kings gave laws to those principalities as subordinate fiefs, if we may believe the chronicles. Próvársén, the Conqueror, who founded the present capitol city of Srinugger (450 A.D.); Mégwáhun (Mégháváhāná 350 A.D.); Zeardutt (Yúdishtur 600 A.D.); Ballitádit (Balláditya 592 A.D.); Lalitáditya (714 A.D.), are all great names in the Cashmere chronicles, and led armies out of Cashmere for conquest of parts of India. The *Verma* dynasty ascended the throne 875 A.D., and reigned 84 years. In all, six dynasties are named as reigning at different periods, and all are called Kings of Cashmere: Lalitàditya is stated to have led an army from Cashmere and overrun the Punjâb, Kanouj, Behar, Bengal, the Dekhan, Ceylon, Malwa, Delhi, Cabul, Bokhara, Thibet, and "so home" to Cashmere. He perished in the snowy mountains near 'Skardo in an attempt to invade Kashgar, and with him may be said to have died the glory of Cashmere as a kingdom.

Provarsen 450 A.D.

Verma Dynasty. A.D. 875

Thirty-seven insignificant princes—steadily declining in power—succeeded this great monarch; till at length the native rulers, disgusted at the effete stock of ancient kings, which seems to have reached its climax of folly and luxury in the person of King Hurshun, set up several puppet kings as cloaks to

Decline of ancient Cashmere in 13th and 14th centuries.

their own designs. Feebleness and anarchy ensued as the natural result, and things were about at their worst when, in the reign of Jye Sing (about 1200 A.D.),
A.D. 1200 Kulhána Pundit began to collect the slokes of that ancient chronicle of Cashmere, called the "Rajah Taringini," almost the sole real authority for its past history. After this we approach historical times. Feebleness invites aggression; we accordingly find in the reign of King Zeshyumdeo an army of "Toorks" invading Cashmere from Cabul. The hereditary commander-in-chief of the country, the brave Malchund—the support of the throne—marched to meet them. In order to discern the enemy's force Malchund, disguising himself as a common runner, is stated to have penetrated into the enemy's camp and to have pinned with his dagger, at the pillow of the Toorkoman general,* a letter of menace. The history adds that the latter on awaking and discovering the same, was so terrified, that he precipitately fled to Cabul with his army. Malchund is stated to have led an army into Hindostan and re-populated Malwa, which hence acquired its name, its ancient one being Kamput.† In the weakness of the ruling power, Malchund alone, or his sons after him, maintained the frontier, and built a chain of forts to guard the passes, their stronghold being Kucknigéra in the Lar. "About this time," *says the Chronicle,* "Káshyp-murra began to be called Cashmere (Kashmir),"‡

---

* The reader is reminded of the Biblical story of the treatment of Saul by David, and indeed the Persian Commentator, through whose translation I read the "Rajah Taringini," apparently interfuses his history by many stories derived from Arabic sources; such are, of course, to be received with caution as authentic history.

† It is doubtful whether this refers to the modern province of "Malwa." It seems rather to refer to a portion of the Cis-Sutlej territory, whence the name of Malwa Sikhs derives.

‡ The word "Kashmir," on the authority of a Persian annotation of the "Raja Taringini," has been interpreted as a modern rendering of Káshypmurra, the land of Káshyapá. A modern author (Bellew)

This family alone sustained the declining power of Cashmere, now become a legitimate object of prey to any bold adventurer. Supported by these nobles, King Sunkramdeo, about the middle of the 13th century, made a feeble effort to sustain the fading glories of Cashmere. Then the throne fell into the **A.D. 1300** hands of a family of feeble Brahmins, who soon fell before the energy and subtlety of a new race. Its ancient religion was subverted, and its history merged in that of a new line of Mahomedan Kings. From this date (*circa* 1300 A.D.) Cashmere became the arena on which military adventurers from Central Asia, Toorkistán, the Punjab, and the countries immediately surrounding it, waged incessant war, not only against Cashmere, but with each other, and in fact the country had become so enfeebled as to present a tempting object of ambition to any such state as could raise an army for its conquest.

Mahomedan History commences, circa 1305 A.D.

The Mahomedan history may be said to commence with the year 1305, about which period three foreign adventurers—each operating from his own point of action—entered on the arena of Cashmere politics, and eventually (1341 A.D.) overturned the Hindoo dynasty represented by Queen Kotadévi. From this date thirty native Mahomedan kings reigned, and sustained themselves with great energy against foreign invaders till 1587, when the country was subdued by the Moghul Emperor Akbar. It remained a province of the Delhi Empire till 1753, when it was surrendered to Ahmed Shah Abdallie, under whom it remained as a viceroyalty of the Dooranees or Affghans till 1819, when it was conquered by Runjeet Singh, the Sikh King of the Punjab. In 1846 it lapsed by treaty to the disposal of the British, who placed Golâb Sing, the

---

suggests it to be referable to "Káshimir, the place of the Káshi inhabitants of these ranges," and allied to Káshgar, Kasi (Benares), &c. &c. The Emperor Baber in his autobiographical memoirs, attributes the name to the tribe "Kas" dwellers on the Upper Indus.

Dógra chief of Jummoo, on the throne, in whose family it has since remained.

A chronological index of the military events since 1300 A.D., tending to point the strategic importance of Cashmere, is annexed, as an epitome of its history from that date. Any further detailed historical sketch of this fair country, however interesting, would be manifestly tedious and out of place here, and the foregoing is only adduced as illustrative of the military importance of the kingdom in ancient times, as well as of the facility with which its soil, however mountainous, has been traversed in all ages by foreign invaders from all points.

Chronological Index to the Principal Military Events since A.D. 1300:—

1300—Armies of various surrounding Nations enter Cashmere and endeavour to subvert its Government.

1320—An army of 70,000 Toorks penetrate into Cashmere and lose 20,000 in battle, the remainder (50,000) perish in the snows of the Pir Pinjal.

1326—An Army of Toorks under Urdil brought to terms by Queen Kotadévi of Cashmere.

1350—Shahab-oo-deen, King of Cashmere, conquers Thibet, Kashgar, and Cabul, and subsequently (1356) invades Hindustan with a vast army by way of Kishtewar and Kangra—Defeats Firoz Shah, King of Delhi, on the Sutlej.

1423—Zein-ul-ab-ood-deen (or Boodshah) invades Kashgar and Thibet with an Army of 120,000 men.

1473—Tazie Khan, Commander-in-chief of the Cashmere Armies, invades the Punjab, to punish Tàttàr Khan, Chief of Lahore (a Gukker).

1487 to 1506—Civil War between contending factions in Cashmere of Cháks, Rehnas, and Mágrèys, supporting either the legitimate King Mahomed

VI.

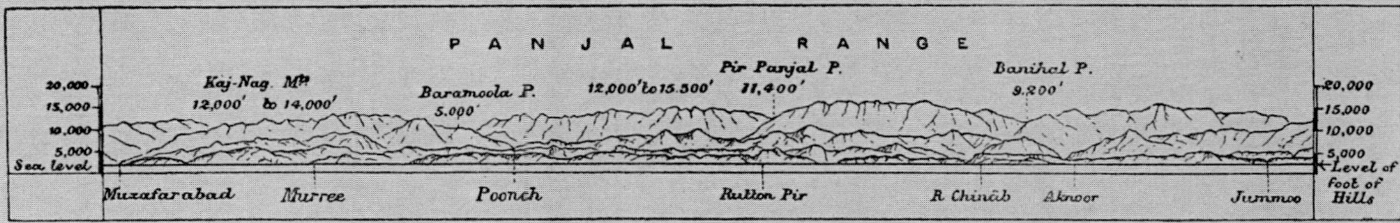

Isometric View of the Pir Pirjal and Mountains between the Pinjal and Cashmere Valley. Section I.

VII.

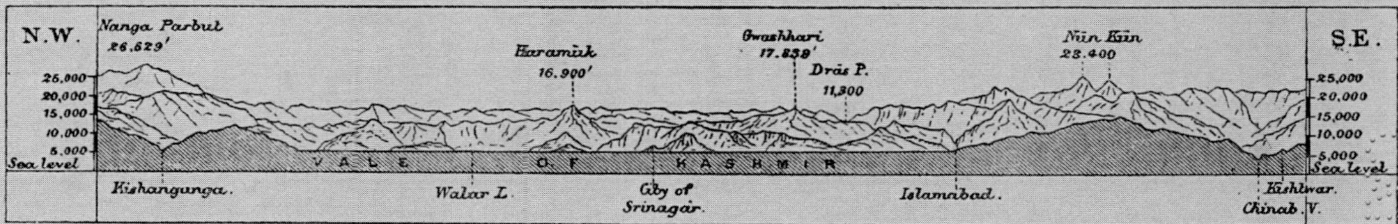

Section of the Cashmere Valley, and isometric view of the Himalaya Mountains beyond. Section I.

Shah, or his uncle, the pretender, Futteh Shah. **Military Events.**

1489—The Cháks forced to take refuge in their strongholds in the Kamráj. Taragaom destroyed 1492.

1512—Mohomed Shah and his Allies from the Punjab invade Cashmere by the Poonch road; recovers the throne at the Battle of Poshkur.

1520—The Cháks defeated in the Lar Pergunnah by the Rehnas and Mágréys with Allies from Hindustan, but rally and hold the field.

1528—Allie Beg and his Cashmere Allies invade Cashmere and defeats Kajee Chák in the Bongil Pergunnah.

1530—Mizra Kamran invades Cashmere, is defeated by Kajee Chák near Srinuggur.

1537—Kajee Chák defeated by Syud Khan of Káshgár and Mirza Hyder in the Lar Pergunnah; treats with the Kashgarries, who withdraw.

1540 to 1550—General rally of the Cháks; but discontented Chiefs of Cashmere ally themselves with Mirza Hyder, invade Cashmere, and defeat Kajee Chák, who dies of wounds at Thannah.

1551—Mirza Hyder then re-introduces armies of Kashgarries and other foreign races to keep down the native chiefs; who, however, rally, form a combination, and under Dowlut Chák, defeat the Kashgarries. Mirza Hyder slain, and the Fort of Inderkote taken.

1556—Gazie Khan (Chák) defeats the Rehnas with an allied Moghul Army from Delhi at the Battle of Kuspa.

1557—Gázie Khan Chák defeats with great slaughter an army of 12,000 Kashgarries, under a nephew of Mirza Hyder.

1558 to 1580—Armies of Môghuls, Tátárs, Toorks, Kashgarries, and Ghukkas, repulsed by the Cháks and native Cashmere Armies. The "Cháks" acknowledged as the sovereign family.

1582—Yoosoof Shah defeats Lohur Khan and Allies.

Military Events. 1584—The Emperor Akbar sends an Army against Yoosoof Shah, King of Cashmere.

1585—The Emperor's Army (under Bhugwan Dass) utterly defeated and nearly destroyed in the Mountains of Hazára, by Yakoob Shah of Cashmere.

1586—Akbar sends an Army of 30,000 horse against Yakoob Shah, who is deserted by his nobles, and flies to Kishtewar.

1586—General rally of the Cháks, who, under Yakoob Shah, encamp on the Takt-i-Súlimán and defeat "Khásim Khan," drive his Army into the city, where they remain besieged till reinforced by 20,000 men from Delhi. Yakoob Shah is then forced to surrender to Akbar (1587), and Cashmere passes under the sway of the Môghuls.

1587 to 1752—Cashmere enjoys comparative peace under the Môghul Emperors, until a force under Abdoola Khan—sent by Ahmud Shad Abdállie—seizes the valley, which thus passes from the sway of the Môghul throne under that of the Dooranees (1752).

1740—Rebellion of Abul Burkut.—The Kishtewarries called in as allies, plunder the city and valley.

1753—Rebellion and defeat of Raja Sookh Jewan, a native chief.

1769—The Dooranee Governor, Ameer Khan (Sher Jewan), revolts from Ahmud Shah Abdállie, till Timor Shah succeeds to the throne of Cabul (1773) and despatches an army to recover

1773—Cashmere. A battle fought near Baramoola ends in the defeat and capture of Ameer Khan.

1785—Timoor Shah again invades Cashmere to chastise Asád Khan, a rebel.

1793—Zemaun Shah invades Cashmere, recovers the valley, and visits the country (1795).

1800 Abdoola Khan enlists an Army of 30,000; is summoned to Cabul.

Military Events.

1801—Zemaun Shah invades India, but precipitately retreats and is dethroned by the Barrukzyie family—Abdoola Khan returns to Cashmere, revolts and defies the new Shah, Mohomed Shah.

1806—Mohomed Shah invades Cashmere under Shere Mohomed, who defeats Abdoola Khan, takes the valley, and sets up for himself.

1807—Mohomed Shah sends an Army to invade Cashmere; the whole army is made prisoners, but treated kindly and released by the Governor.

1807—Cabul convulsed by the rival claims of the Barrukzyie and Suddoozie factions.

1801 to 1810—Runjeet Sing rising to power.

1812—Futteh Khan Barrukzyie proceeds to Lahore and enters into a treaty with Runjeet Sing, who gives a force of 12,000 men, and the combined armies invade Cashmere, and gain possession of the country—but misunderstandings subsequently occurring, war is declared between the Sikhs and Affghans.

1814—Runjeet Sing invades Cashmere, is repulsed by the Governor, Azim Khan Barrukzyie.

1819—Runjeet Sing again invades Cashmere; this time successfully—The army under Misr Dewan Chand executes a skilful flank movement and takes the enemy in reverse, defeating the Pathan Governor (Jubbar Khan) and occupying Cashmere.

1839—Mutiny of the troops in Cashmere.

1840—Golâb Sing of Jummoo—with other chiefs—puts down the mutiny, invades Thibet, which he reduces, but his General (Zorawer Sing) is subsequently defeated and killed by the Chinese.

1842—Rebellions on the frontiers of Cashmere.

1845, 1846, 1847—Invasion of British India by the Sikhs; their defeat at Ferozeshahur, Moodkhee, Aliwal, and Sobräon (February, 1846) and Military occupation of Lahore—Surrender of Cashmere to Golâb Sing of Jummoo, who becomes Maharajah.

———o———

SECTION II.

THE KOHISTAN OF THE PUNJAB.

MURREE (7,457) AND ITS DEPENDENCIES. ABBOTTABAD (4166). CHERAT, ETC.

Murree (7,457) with its dependencies and the Kohistan of the Punjab afford valuable strategic sites.

1. A BRIEF notice of Murree and Abbottabad with their dependencies, and other sub-Alpine sites in the Kôhistan—5000 to 8000 feet—of the Punjab, would supplement the foregoing description of Cashmere, for although within British territory, they partake of the characteristics of the sup-Alpine tracts of that country, especially as bearing on the military approaches to India from the north-west, in which point of view their flanking position is equally, or even more, valuable than Cashmere itself. A short topographical memorandum is appended, which tends to show that in its sanitary aspects Murree is highly valuable. The land available for settlement in the immediate vicinity of this station is not extensive, but it has been found capable of some expansion in the direction of Goragullie (6,439), and Geedagullie (8000), also at Kyragullie (8000), where a battery of mountain artillery has its summer station. Here several hundred British soldiers, employed as pioneers on the hill-roads, annually hut and locate themselves for the summer on the pine clad ridges adjacent thereto, thus establishing a chain of posts between Murree and the military station of Abbottabad, at present held by native troops exclusively, and forming a point strategically of high importance as a guard to the Indus.

British pioneers in the mountains between Murree and Abbottabad.

2. The Flats of Kooldana (7,060), three miles north on the Cashmere road, also have, I believe, supplied a

site for troops additional to the convalescent depôt of Murree, which contains 400 men. In fact, ridges and blocks of hill from 6000 to 8000 feet in elevation radiate in several directions from Murree both towards the north-west and Abbottabad, as also south and south-east, forming the watershed overlooking the intramontane course of the River Jhelum. I know not, however, that suitable sites for European settlers are to be found within this last named region—a somewhat rugged tract of mountain interposed between the plains near Pharwalla (the ancient stronghold of the Gakhars destroyed by Baber in 1523) and the Jhelum. It extends as far south as Meerpûr, where that river leaves the mountains, near the probable site of Alexander's battle with Porus. I am not aware that this tract has been much explored with a view to purposes of locating troops, but I imagine the altitudes of the hills decline as they approach the apex of the peninsula block of mountain indicated.

3. The following altitudes of points in the vicinity of Murree embrace an area of expansibility within which—failing Cashmere—a reserve circle as a guard to the Indus might perhaps be established:— **Altitudes in the vicinity.**

Tope	...miles, 3;	N.E.;	elevation,	7,315	feet
Charihan	„ 3	E.	„	6,903	„
Tréte ...	„ 6	S.S.W.	„	4,212	„
Douna ...	„ 4	S.W.	„	5,684	„
Bheemkot	„ 5	N.W.	„	7,028	„
Kooldana	„ 3	N.	„	7,060	„
Chumbi	„ 7	N.	„	8,751	„
Chumari	„ 5	N.N.E.	„	6,920	„
Góragullie	„ 2½	S.S.W.	„	6,439	„

N.B.—These distances and bearings are taken from the tower on Observatory Hill, and "as the crow flies."

The forest area around Murree has been calculated at 11,000 acres, but the "whole tract cannot be less than 200 square miles, half of which is cultivated, and the other half available for pasturage and fuel." The flora **Topographical.**

of the upper ranges assimilates to that of Cashmere, and contains a greater proportion of European species than any other hill station. Mochpoora is clothed with deodar to its summit, and pines, firs, oaks, rhododendrons, walnuts, and other forest trees of a temperate zone flourish at their generic altitudes within the area specified.

The Lawrence Asylum.

4. We must not forget the Lawrence Asylum below the observatory hill, healthiest of all the children's sanitaria throughout the land—save and except Darjeeling Loretto Convent. Here nearly one hundred soldiers' children have been lodged and educated since 1861. This would of course be included within any fortified area as suggested. The happy cheerful faces of the children here sufficiently attest the salubrity of the climate.

General features.

5. Who of the dwellers of the Punjab knoweth not Murree and its fir-topped hills redolent of ozone and picnics, its wooded shades and forest walks and misty "khuds" (hillsides); its bright culture down the valley sides gleaming through the foliage of the woods; its pleasant club where many a true frontier soldier is to be met,—the rendezvous of sportsmen bound for Cashmere and the snows! At Murree also is the summer residence of the Lieutenant-Governor of the Punjab, and the head-quarters of Government and of the frontier force. In summer how pleasant a place is Murree after the blazing heat of the Punjab plains; and in winter how quiet and calm and Christmas-like the snow-fringed paths and forest walks of this valuable sanitarium of the Punjab, which forms an important strategic flanking support of the Sind Saugor

Strategic aspects.

Döab, the left point of the lower flanking line of our sketch map. I will not dwell on its advantages, as it requires no great acumen to see how important a part it might—in conjunction with Abbottabad—play in any complication wherein Attock and the line of the Indus was compromised.

VIII.

Murrie Church (7,457) Punjaub, from the Cashmere Road. Section II.

IX.

View of the Tartara Mountain from Peshawer. Section II.

6. We must pass on (24 miles) to Abbottabad, which has been mentioned as a point of much strategic value. Situated on the debouchement of the only military road from Cashmere towards the Indus, it commands that river and the Hazára country. It guards also Attock (1,200), and the plains of Châch (1,500), and even stretches a hand to the Yoosoofzäie country, by the valley of the Sirun, Torbéla, and Topi, across the Indus. We must consider it as a position of great importance. Though not much over 4000 feet elevation above sea level, it is essentially a "hill" station and very healthy; its grassy slopes and "marches," and its hill sides bare of forest, present excellent training ground for troops; and within 10 or 12 miles the pretty little dependent mountain spur of Tandiánee (8,845) forms a charming summer resort for the sick of the Abbottabad garrison.

Abbottabad a point of much strategic value as a guard to river Indus, and N.W. Passes.

Altitudes.

7. The heights and distances of some of the surrounding hills embracing a fine area may as well here be given (taken from Abbottabad church, as the crow flies,)

Abbottabad Church,	miles;		4,166	feet elevation
Sirhan Hill	2½	S.	6,243	"
Bazmar	7½	S.S.W.	5,050	"
Jundoki	4¾	S.S.W.	4,923	"
Bilihana	6	W.	6,192	"
Naimar	5	N.N.W.	4,803	"
Bhutroijee	4	N.	4,951	"
Tandianee	10	N.E.	8,845	"
Musta	8½	E.	8,435	"
Tope	6	S.E.	6,645	"

N.B.—The area includes fine sites for "military villages" as a frontier guard, such as have been at times advocated.

8. At Abbottabad a Goorkha corps has become in a manner localized, and in fact forms a native "military colony," such as might indeed be formed of various castes throughout the plains in view to balance of native power. The agitation recently got up regarding

A military colony of Goorkhas there established.

the present state of the "poor whites," and Eurasians of India, strengthens further these suggestions. They also might be formed into colonies or circles, some in the plains, and be worked up into the defensive system suggested. The garrisons of these two stations supplement the force located at the important station of Ráwal-Pindee; they form the present support of Attock and the Indus, and guard the north-west frontiers; and *as long as Cashmere is friendly* they may suffice to that end.

Cherat (6,000) in the Kuttock Hills.

9. Before leaving the north-west frontier, mention must be made of Cherát (6000), a small sanitarium for British soldiers of the Peshawar Valley, situated in the Khattock Hills (6000), some 20 miles from Peshawar city. Though bare and somewhat uninviting, it is nevertheless—as a local sanitarium—of much value. Its site, in consonance with strategic principles, commands the Kohát and Khyber Passes, and as long as the Peshawar Valley be held by British troops, this little post will maintain its value. Personally, I am only acquainted with the place in its crude inception, and scarcely aware to what point progress may have brought it. It is about 5000 feet or 6000 feet above sea level, and its ordinary summer garrison averages 800 to 1000 men. These live chiefly in tents, there being at present (1874), I hear, only three small barracks capable of holding some 30 men each. The officers live in wooden huts. Until the rains set in, the heat here is often very great, the thermometer rising to 100° in the shade, and even at night standing at 94°. The chief benefit of the place seems to be that it is out of the malarious vortex of the Peshawar Valley; and as soon as the rains set in a steady, cool breeze from the plains blows day and night, and reduces the temperature to about 72°.

The situation of Cherát is pleasing, as being on the summit of a ridge between two valleys. On one side you look down on the Peshawar Valley, and on the other on the Bunnoo Valley, and you get a bird's-eye view on both sides. Cherát is subject to very violent storms, which often blow down the tents, and are frequently accompanied by hail and heavy rain, but do not last long. There are no trees, only shrubs 15 inches in height. The hills are rocky, the roads good, but water has to be brought on mules or bullocks from a distance of three miles.* The rains last six weeks or thereabouts. The climate is especially healthy for young children, who seem to thrive there better than in more elevated stations such as Murree. I have dwelt on the description of this small sanitarium because it is possible that this position may be destined to supersede the station of Peshawar as a garrison for British troops; its strategic value is the same, and in some respects superior to Peshawar itself; its plateau should be made into an entrenched camp, and the salient and defensive points fortified by small redoubts and epaulments so as to contain a permanent garrison. The "Meer Kaláñ" Pass leading on to this range is practicable for artillery: it leaves the main road at Pubbie *via* Jalouzaie.

10. There is a small hill station or sanitarium called "Shaikh Boodeen" (4,500),† in the spurs of the Súliemán range (6000—12,000) bordering the Derajat, which may, in point of elevation and climate, bear a favorable comparison with Cherát. It is chiefly resorted to by officers of the Punjab frontier force as a pleasant relief from the lassitude of the plains during the heats of summer. It may be named amongst the sanitary refuges of the Punjab. Shaikh Boodeen in the Derajat.

11. The refuge called the "Dunna Towers," a small sanitarium or cool retreat for Shikarpore, Jacobabad, and the north-east portion of the Sinde Valley, about Dunna Towers in Sinde, &c.

---

* It has been suggested that hydraulic rams might be substituted here, and elsewhere in the hills where water is scarce, each step being of a vertical altitude of say thirty feet.

† Vide Section XVI., Para. 2.

50 miles south-west of Mehur, is beyond the limits of this section of our subject; as is also Fort Munro in the Súliemán Hills, near Deyra Ghazie Khan.

HISTORICAL.

Historical note on the Khuttock Tribes.

12. An historical sketch of two tribes, whose annals are bound up with the military history of the Western Döabs of the Punjab, will now be given, without which any sketch of the past condition of the Peshawar Valley and Sinde Saugor Döab would be incomplete.

The Khuttocks are descended from the Kartánees, and were originally from Sháwal, whence—under the leadership of their great chief Akore, they dispossessed the Orukzyes of Térie and Kohât, and spread over the Peshawar Valley and Khuttock Hills as far even as Bunnoo along the Indus. This chief founded Akóra on the Cabul river during the reign of Akbar, and allied himself to that emperor, furnishing a contingent of horse and foot in his service to keep open the road between Attock and Peshawar. He ruled 41 years, and was succeeded by his son Tohuja Khan, who is stated to have reigned 61 years. Both these chiefs were murdered, and the third in succession, Shahbaz Khan, after 31 years, also came to a violent end, being pierced through the head by an arrow! Khooshal Khan was the fourth chief, and was an ally of Shah Jehan, who employed him in many military enterprises. He was ultimately, like his fathers, killed in action against a Mahratta force near Hussan Abdál.

The Khuttocks are divided into two branches, the eastern and western clans are rather an industrious race (for Affghans), and retain their former bravery. They have on several occasions acted as our allies. It is in their hills that Cherát is situated. The Sikhs resumed all the plain country of Khuttock, and the present tribes are mountaineers, and chiefly restricted to the range which bears their name between the Bunnoo and Peshawar Valleys. Humbled as they now are, it still is not too much to say that the communications with Cabul of the entire northern Punjab, were formerly at the mercy of these tribes and that of the Gakhars, an historical notice of which latter tribe or clan will conclude this section of the subject under review.

Formerly custodians of the communications trans Indus.

HISTORICAL NOTICE OF THE GAKHARS.

13. At Murree (and Ráwalpindi) we find ourselves in the heart of the country of the Gakhars, a clan which acquired much strength, and played a considerable part in history during the 14th, 15th, and 16th centuries. Some affect to trace their descent from the soldiers of Alexander the Great, and assert that the word Gakhar is merely a modern form of Gakr, Gruk, or Greek; others again point to Central Asia and the Highlands of great and middle Thibet as their cradle; whence they are said to have issued under Sultan Kâb early in the Christian era; a few of their most distinguished chiefs—several of whom are stated to have invaded Cashmere—will be mentioned below. Their stronghold of Pharwalla (near Ráwalpindi) was destroyed by Baber about 1523 A.D., and their power considerably curtailed. A branch of this tribe occupied the salt range and country south of Jhelum, Rhotas being one of their strongholds, also Dangali in the Kohistân; they frequently invaded Cashmere, and on more than one occasion are stated to have actually usurped the government of that country for short periods. About 1008 A.D., Gukhar Shah (son of Kabul Shah) was established Sovereign of the Sinde Saugor Döab by Mahmood of Ghuznee. In 1008 was fought the great battle between Mahmood and the Hindoo confederate army under Anand Pal, Rajah of Lahore, wherein the Gakhars played a conspicuous part, and

Historical note on the Gakhars.

Pharwalla destroyed by Baber, 1523 A.D.

1008 A.D.

brought 30,000 warriors into the field, who led the van so nearly victorious at the great battle of Hazro near Attock. The victory, however, ultimately went to the Mahomedans. About 1200 A.D. the Gakhars were dominant in the Middle Punjab, and held the communications between the Indus and India, imposing black mail on all sides. They often, from that time till 1523, when their stronghold of Pharwalla was destroyed, rebelled against and defied the Moghul emperors.

Battle of Hazro.

Gakhars dominant in middle Punjab.

The Gakhars opposed Tamerlane in his invasion of 1398, but were defeated. In 1399 Jasrot Khan (Gakhar) intimidated the whole country and pillaged Lahore. In 1475 a Cashmere army is stated to have invaded Lahore to chastise Tátár Khan (a Gakhar), who had usurped that state. In 1523 Tátár Khan and Hati Khan were chiefs of the Gakhars; the latter destroyed his brother, but was himself killed by Baber, who stormed his stronghold of Perhôlah (or Pharwalla). In 1530 A.D. Sultan Sarang—the greatest of Gakhar chiefs—succeeded, and allying himself steadfastly to Humaioon, defied the usurper Sher Shah. He was, however, defeated, and ultimately beheaded by the latter; and Dangáli, the second stronghold of the Gakhars in the Sinde Saugor Döab, was plundered and destroyed. His successor Sultan Adam, however, restored Pharwalla.

Oppose Tamerlane 1398.

1475 A.D.

1530 A.D. Allies of Humaioon.

During the wars of the successors of Akbar, Prince Kamran, foster or uterine brother of Humaioon, sought an asylum amongst the Gakhars, but was delivered to Humaioon and blinded. Sultan Adam having subsequently rebelled, was defeated and captured by Akbar. That emperor divided the territory of the Gakhars between Adam and his nephew Kamal Khan, son of Sultan Sarang, the old ally of Humaioon. The power of the Gakhars seems to have declined under the vigorous sway of Akbar and the Moghul empire till about 1730, when Mukherib Khan (Gakhar) made a strong effort to restore their power, but was subsequently defeated and slain in 1761 by the Sikhs, and his country annexed up to the Jhelum. In 1765 the Sikhs, advancing, absorbed the whole of the Gakhar territories, and expelled them a second time from Pharwalla, their ancient stronghold, which they had re-occupied. From this date the clan was effectually broken, and merged in the Sikh kingdom of Runjeet Sing.

1765 A.D.

Finally absorbed in the Sikh Kingdom of Runjeet Sing.

SECTION III.

THE KOHISTAN OF THE PUNJAB.

DALHOUSIE (6,740); CHUMBA; KANGRA VALLEY; DHARMSALA (6,111); KULU; AND THE SMALL HILL PRINCIPALITIES IN THE KOHISTAN OF THE PUNJAB.

Dalhousie (with Bakloh and dependencies) an excellent site for a military reserve circle.

1. PROCEEDING southwards from Murree, we next (after a long stride) come to the Station of Dalhousie (6,740), which, with the native outlying station of Bakloh (5000), comprises a fine site for a sanitarium, and is capable of expansion in several directions as a military hill circle, for which also its strategic position is excellent, flanking as it does the Bari Döab—and though less effectively—the Rechna and Jullundur Döabs. The Mahomedans—no bad selectors of sites dominating lines of country—evidently recognised the value of this position in having built the fort of Pathánkote (1,200), now a ruin, on the high road to Lahore, to which point troops can at any season be conveyed, as no river intervenes to check their march. This formerly fine fort was built by Shah Jehan; it was an excellent native fortress, and its situation most valuable. It should not, to my thinking, have been allowed to fall into decay, and its very site alienated by Government. It was on the old high road from Cashmere to Kangra, the Nâggakôt of past times.

Pathankote a valuable site as a support to the Bari and Rechna Doabs, also perhaps Jullundar Doab.

A linking post in the watershed of the Chenab, requisite between Murree and Dalhousie Circle.

2. A glance at the map will show, however, what a long intermediate step in the link of flanking defence —nearly 200 miles, and across three difficult rivers— has thus been taken. Doubtless one or more posts on the subsidiary watersheds between the Jhelum and Rávi (in other words in the basin of the Chenâb) is a desid-

X.

View of Snowy Range from "Kujjear," near Dalhousie. Section III.

XI.

View in the Barmawar Valley, Chumba. Section III.

eratum, and I think the "Rutton Pir" might be found to contain eligible sites for flanking support. This range extends from Poonch to the Kúrie Pass. It is in Cashmere territory, but is this side the Pir Pinjal, and hence free of the snowy passes, and on the whole I name it as probably containing favorable sites for subsidiary flanking supports to the direct defence of the Punjab rivers. This want of support is partly obviated by the station of Sealkote, which, however, is itself dominated and outflanked by the Cashmere posts at Rajaori (3000), Aknoor (2,500), and Jummoo (1,500), not to mention that the old main imperial roads from Cashmere converge at Aknoor some 40 miles distant. Dalhousie is situated in Chumba territory, the capitol of which is distant some 16 miles across the Rávi.

Chumba: its strategic value much depreciated for want of proper outlet.

3. Chumba does not possess much strategic value in its present state of development, as it is (like Badrawar) much shut in by the territory of the Maharajah of Cashmere, who has pushed his hill frontier abutting on the plains as far as Bissoli on the Rávi; indeed, the basin of the Siáwa river which falls into the Rávi above Bissoli, and constitutes its last considerable intramontane tributary, is within Jummoo territory, and belongs to the Maharajah of Cashmere, whose transit rules are very strict, so that practically the only outlet of Chumba is by Dalhousie, or possibly across the Chuári (3000) Pass in the Kangra Valley, as the great range of the "Dhaola Dhar" (white mountain) effectually shuts in the upper valley from the plains of Chumba (or Barmáwar). A note* on the

* The Rávi—the Hydraotes of the Greeks—from its source in the glaciers of the Bara Bonghál in Barmáwar to its junction with the Chenâb, near Shorkote, above Mooltan, may be nearly 600 miles in length. It is the most tortuous and least navigable of the Punjab rivers after entering the plains, and its intramontane course the most rapid. Its course through Barmáwar and Chumba is about 150 miles, within which it falls 115 feet per mile. Its chief tributary—the Badhul—rises in Muni-Mahésh glacier, and near its confluence is found the ancient seat of the Chumba or Barma family, where the

upper course of the Rávi will give a general idea of Barmáwar, which is in fact the basin of the Upper Rávi. The sketch map will show the strategic points and watershed both of this and of the Kangra district.

The Barmawar Valley difficult of access.

4. As to the Chumba and Barmáwar Valleys, although it is believed that Sir Donald McLeod (whilst Deputy-Commissioner) and others proposed to establish sanitaria therein for the residents of Dharmsála and Kangra, it was found that the access to them over the passes of the Dhoola Dhár—such as Keársi, Warus, Thamsir, etc., all over 15,000—was too steep and difficult to warrant the attempt, though as local refuges and sanitary *pieds de terre* their climate were doubtless beneficial in a high degree. From the causes named the strategic value of the upper valley of the Rávi is rendered ineffective as a base, its only outlet being, as above stated, either by Dalhousie or over the Chuari Pass into the Kangra Valley, where the great Dhaola Dhár range declines in height.

The Jot.

5. The station of Dalhousie is on a ridge, whence on one side the plains as far almost as Umritsir and Sealkote on the Chenâb, may be seen in clear weather. It may be defined as a congeries of hill tops which branch out west from the great mountain Diarkhoond (9000) in a series of descending steps, *viz.*—Bukróta

country is called Barmáwar. The next great tributary of the Rávi —the Sewl—joins it below Chumba; it rises near the Säah Pass, and rushes through some very remarkable clefts and gorges. It drains a considerable basin between Chumba and Badrawar. On the watershed ridge containing the western basin of this hill-stream a support of Sealkote and the Rechna Döab might perhaps be found. As it approaches the lower hills, the valley of the Sewl opens out into a fine fertile valley with wide river terraces far above the present level of the stream; it is called the "Garden of Chumba," and supplies the capitol and Dalhousie with wheat. Jummoo territory has been so far extended east that up to the Rávi the watershed is absorbed or rendered ineffective as a flanking base. I am not aware of the hereditary claims the Maharajah may have to this watershed, but strategically it has a very injurious effect on Chumba, whose development as an auxiliary fief is paralysed thereby.

(7,600), Térah (6,840), Putrain (6,820), and Balún (5,687). This is the spur on which is situated the convalescent depôt, which contains 400 men. At Bániket (5000), about 100 British infantry soldiers—employed as pioneers—are located. Although at various levels, these points are all connected by good roads, railed off from the "khuds" (sides of cliffs). Fine malls are thus formed round the various hills at some distance from the summits, which are covered with oak foliage. Here the houses of the principal inhabitants are built. The sylvan environs of Dalhousie embrace Kujeár, a lovely spot in the Kála-Tope forest; and Diarkhoond, redolent of pines and wild flowers, with the valley of Chumba and the basin of the Rávi. These points—with Bakloh (5,490) where a Goorkha corps is located—embrace an area of expansibility within which a glorious "reserve circle" could be established. I would also, perhaps, associate artillery, and even cavalry in this circle; the matériel and horses to remain at Pathánkote or nearer, under sufficient escort. To sum up, a circle radiating to Chumba, Pathánkote, Bissoli, and Noorpoor, would embrace a block of mountain containing as a centre the sanitarium of Dalhousie, within which might be established a "circle" such as would, I think, form an excellent support for Lahore, Umritsur, and the Bari, Jullundur, and Rechna Döabs.

6. The population of this country is Hindoo, Rajpoot, Dogra, etc., with some Sikhs and Mahomedans. Its ethnological traditions are warlike. A remarkable tribe called "Guddies" inhabit the mountains and valleys of Barmáwar and the Dhaola-Dhar. They are distinguished by a curious head-dress. They seem to be the descendants of a Rajpoot tribe which in the 15th or 16th century immigrated into these mountains, and established themselves in Chumba, Barmáwar, and the skirts of the Dhaola-Dhar. The whole country, however, is full of ethnological groups of great

Ethnological remarks.

Guddies

E

interest, and there are—in the Kūlū Valley especially—tribes, even villages, quite distinct from the populations surrounding them, and speaking a totally different language of their own.* Tea planting has not been attempted in the immediate vicinity of Dalhousie; it is believed that the climate north of Kangra is too severe for that product. An outlet to produce exists in the Rávi, which is navigable by "mussocks" (skins of buffaloes which are inflated and serve to float rafts), downward from near Chumba. I myself have thus made the voyage to Sirdhona Ghat near Madhopore, the head of the Bari Döab Canal, in four or five hours, whereas it is a journey by the road of fifteen to twenty hours at least.

The Ravi a natural outlet for the produce of Chumba timber, etc.

7. Associated with this circle, but involved in a maze of hills and ravines, useful perhaps as independent linking posts, we have the hill forts of Noorpoor (3000) and Kotila, whilst Kangra (2,419), and the hill station of Bhágsu (4000) contain garrisons essentially self-reliant, which probably also might be available as supports to the Jullundur Döab. That of Dalhousie, however, could be thrown across the Beas *viâ* Patháukote even in the rainy season with perhaps greater facility than the former could be marched through the somewhat tortuous hills lying between the Kangra Valley and the Jullundur Döab. I do not, therefore, insist on these hills as a strategic base; suffice if they hold their own and protect their settlements, and serve as a sanitarium for settlers. This is, perhaps, the very best amongst the numerous hill tracts to be enumerated in this series. At present (1874) there are, I believe, about two companies of British infantry in garrison at Kangra, detached from Jullundur. In view to possible contingencies, I think

Linking Posts.

Garrison of Kangra and Bhagsu.

* Mullouna, in the Kūlū Valley on the River Parbuttee, is an example whose inhabitants are totally unlike those of Kūlū, Lahoul, or Spiti, do not even understand their language; and can give no account of their own origin.

shelter might be prepared for the same number of volunteers and others. The Kangra fortress (2,419) would then—as, indeed, it did in all ages—form a rallying point or refuge for that country-side in times of trouble, and there is ample room within the fortress for that purpose. I think also sanitary measures such as removing some of the decaying and half-ruinous walls, and sloping off the grassy ramps should be adopted. I cannot do better than at this place introduce extracts from Mr. Commissioner Barnes' able Settlement Report on the Kangra Valley and district.

Extracts from Mr. Barnes' Settlement Report of Kangra Valley.

Kangra Proper.

"Kangra proper is a long irregular tract of country "running north-west and south-east. Its extreme "length is 108 miles, and average breath 30 miles. "The entire superficial contents are 2,700 square miles. "On three sides it is bounded by native states. On the "west flows the river Rávi, which divides the district "from Jummoo territory. On the north a stupendous "range of mountains, culminating to a height of 16,000 "feet above sea level, separates Kangra from the hill "principality of Chumba. Along the southern frontier "lie the level tracts of the Bari and Jullundur Döabs, "represented by the districts of Deenanugger and "Hoshiarpore."

Fort Kangra captured by a Sikh chief.

Para. 56.—"In 1781-82 Jye Singh laid siege to Kot "Kangra. Throughout the revolution of the preceding "30 years this fortress had remained in the hands of "the Moghul Governor, and an idea of the strength and "reputation of this stronghold may be gathered from "the fact that an isolated Mahomedan with no resources "beyond the range of his guns, could maintain his po- "sition so long and so gallantly."

Surrender of Fort Kangra to British

Para. 82.—"In March, 1846, a British army occupied "Lahore, and obtained the cession of the Jullundur "Döab and the hill tract between the Sutlej and the

E 2

"Rávi. And here an incident occurred which shows "the prestige of the Kangra Fort. Notwithstanding "our successes, and in despite of the treaty dictated at "Lahore, the hill commandant refused to surrender. "The British Resident came up in haste, and Dewan "Deenanath, the Minister at Lahore, exercised in vain "both supplication and menace. At last—after a delay "of two months, when a British brigade had invested "the fort, and the plan of attack was actually decided "upon—the resolution of the Sikh governor gave way, "and he agreed to evacuate on condition of a free and "honorable passage for himself and his men."

Prestige of Fort Kangra.

Fort Kangra in 1857.

"Was garrisoned by a wing of the 4th Regiment "native infantry, who were relieved by a wing of 2nd "Hill Regiment from Dhurmsalah on the breaking out "of Mutiny."

Fort Kangra in 1870.

"During the Kooka disturbance at Loodianah, the "Fort of Kangra was looked to as a place to move to "in case of danger* by the tea planters at Pallumpore."

Fort Kangra in 1875.

"Is garrisoned by two companies of Her Majesty's "81st Regiment, and half a company of 1st Goorkhas."

8. The first extract gives the boundaries of Kangra district. The other extracts and notes give something of the history of Fort Kangra. It appears to be well suited for becoming the head-quarters of a reserve force for the district, should such be formed. Its present garrison is two companies of Her Majesty's 81st Regiment and half a company of Goorkhas. There are many native pensioners in the district, the majority of whom are Dogras, Rajpoots, and some Goorkhas, who have settled in the neighborhood of the 1st Goorkha Regiment. At Pallumpore are situated the tea plantations, and several of the planters have served in the army. Fort Kangra is eight

* This is an infallible test of the value of such posts of vantage as refuges. Such points as Mooltan Fort, Attock, Kangra, and others, should not be dismantled or allowed to fall into disrepair *till other refuges are established;* yet I have known the thing done frequently.
D.J.F.N.

XII.

View of the Kangra Valley--with Dharmsala, Bhagsu, and the Dhaola Dhar Range, from the north gateway of the Fort. Section III.

XIII.

Fort Kangra, the ancient Nagakot. Section III.

marches by a good cart road from Jullundur, and about the same distance from Simla (*viâ* Nadoun on Beas) by a hill road requiring mule carriage.

Dhármsála (6,111), a pleasant hill station of this district—15 miles from Kangra—is situated on a spur of the great Dhaola Dhar range (16,000), which towers above the Kangra Valley, and throws out several spurs into the valley between Dhármsála and Palunpore, both of which are situated on spurs. At Bhágsu (4000) is situated the military cantonment of Dhármsála, where a native corps of hill rangers is located. **Dharmsala.**

9. The Kangra (3000 to 6000) and Kūlū (5000 to 8000) Valleys present manifold attractions to the European settler, and have already been availed of to a considerable extent. At present many flourishing tea estates exist in the Kangra Valley and its skirts. The Pallumpore Fair, established for the convenience of traders from Yarkund, Kashgar, and Central Asia, is held in November annually, and presents an opportunity of studying the character and habits of these races, who appear—after all is said—an intelligent, law-abiding and honest people, as far as my slight opportunities have led me to consider them. I believe I may indicate this as one of the best districts for a "reserve colony," could land be obtained, though, as aforesaid, its strategic position is of little value for purposes of imperial defence, yet it is good as an inner guard, well sheltered from the probable storms of politics and war. Kūlū, in the basin or valley of tho Upper Beas, which rises near the Rotung Pass (13,000 elevation) is peculiarly beautiful. It is wider than most Himalayan valleys, with wide terraces of cultivation. The river runs swiftly (with a fall of about 60 feet per mile) but not violently, through a "strath" or wide glen, and forms islands at various places, fringed with alders; the higher slopes are crowned with deodar, and several kinds of pine and oak, whilst deodar, fir, elm, alder, poplar; and fruit trees round the

Kangra (upper) and Kulu valleys as Tea Districts specially adapted for European settlers.

Not valuable as a strategic base, but rather as a refuge or "inner guard," sheltered from the storms of politics and war.

villages dot the *terre-plein* of the valley. The ancient capital was Nugger, on the left bank. The modern capital Sooltanpore, 12 miles lower down, also on the left bank, is a great mart for traders of many provinces, and covers a large area of ground.

The Beas and its tributaries.

Nine large mountain streams join the Beas as tributaries in this portion of its course, the Parbuttie being the chief, and contributing nearly as large a volume of water as the Beas itself. The Bijoura divides Mundi from Kūlū, and irrigates several tea plantations. The Maráli Forest here extends down the river on both banks, and contains some fine deodars, especially around the sacred temple of Barwa. The Bubboo Pass leads into the Kangra district. From Bedath to Larji several tributaries join. The Ul River, from the snows of Bara Banghâl and the Dhaola Dhar, falls into the Beas at Mundi. The fall of the Beas here is about 40 feet per mile, and the river flows smoothly through a green and gently sloping plain country. Above this river—at Futikol (Goghurdhor)—is the watershed ridge between the Beas and Ul, and a splendid locality for a settlement could there be found. The Sookhét on the left bank is the next great tributary, and rises in the principality of the same name, from the Sikander Dhar (Alexander's furthest): after this the course of the Beas rather increases in swiftness. It receives five more tributaries from the Dhaola Dhar through the Kangra Valley, and flows moderately strong at a fall of 40 feet per mile. It then cuts the Sewâlik range, debouches at Mirthal, turns due west, skirting the base of the lower hills, where it loses its Alpine character; again turns south, and after a course of 50 miles further joins the Sutlej at Hurree-ke-Pattan, the site of the great battle of Sobräon in 1846. Total length of the Beas is equal to 350 miles.

Topographical.

Few who have wandered in this beautiful district, viewed its green recesses, surmounted its circumjacent hills, or have climbed the "Jôt"—the Kuarsi Pass

15,000—and peeped into Barmáwar (5000 to 8000), who have crossed the Bubboo Pass, and travelled into Kūlū (5000 to 7000), and the valley of the Beas, but will bear me out in saying that no more delightful district exists in India. Indeed, the writer, who has personally visited nearly "all," is inclined to give the palm to this as the "Arcadia" of the tea planter or military colonist. Its fertility, especially for tea; its great metalliferous wealth, at present all but quite undeveloped; its glorious pine forests and splendid scenery, all invite admiration. The Beas forms a fine waterway through the country, and an outlet for its timber and produce, and drains the basin of the Kūlū valley. In certain places it may be navigated downwards by the traveller on "mussuks," which have been defined as buffalo hides inflated, on which a slight frame is super-imposed as a raft, as before described. Besides nine large tributaries, every small lateral glen pours its tributary stream into the Beas, and in Kūlū the sounding cascades gleam on the hill sides as one passes along the roads. Water power to any extent, suggestive of industrial avocations such as saw-mills, etc., is thus presented. Mines of copper, salt, crystal, lead, etc., are known to exist. On the whole, if the idea of colonization be once accepted, I should anticipate a fine future for this glorious district.

Game. The district abounds in small mountain tarns or lakes swarming with fish, chiefly maháseer. Bears, leopards, chamois, hill antelope of many kinds, abound in the surrounding hills; whilst the feathered game is represented by the jawáhir, moonál, koklás, and káléj pheasants; forming the paradise of sportsmen.* **Area of Kangra district.** The area is 16,136 acres of waste land well adapted for settlers, but is hampered by grants and fiefs to villages

* *Sookhét*, a small principality of this region, trans-Sutlej, contains much game—goorul (chamois) and pheasants innumerable, besides leopards and a few bears. Sookhét is seen across the Sutlej above Belaspore, where also is a ferry.

and native holders. A brief historical sketch of Kangra (2,419) as the capital or centre of this charming district has been added.

Small Principalities of the Kohistan.

10. The small principalities of Mandi (4000), Sookhét (5000), and Nadaun (3000), have scarcely been noticed in this sketch, as they possess so little military value; they may be regarded as partaking of the general characteristics of the lower Alpine Himalayas, and their history is much associated with that of the Kuttoch dynasty of Kangra, of which they were mostly fiefs. Of course the chiefs have their genealogical fables, usually carrying their family back into the mythic ages.* We may regard them as nearly all more or less related to the Kuttoch family so long dominant at Kangra, a sketch of which kingdom will now be given, as including the majority of these principalities of the Kohistan of the Punjab—its constituents.†

Ancient fiefs of Kangra.

The Fort of Bajra, near Mandi, is 6,168 feet in elevation. This principality contains a good deal of level land, which has been availed of by the present chief—an intelligent and cultivated nobleman—for the growth of tea and other valuable products.

Kumlagurh (4477) is another wonderful stronghold or *cul de-sac* of this district, being a fortified valley, completely surrounded by mountains, well worth a visit.

The traveller has now been carried over the hills of the Sikunder Dhar, near to Alexander's altars, to Belaspore—the capital of the small state of Kahloor—

* As an example of the extravagance into which ancestral pride will conduct the genealogies of native chiefs, I may instance that the first "Khuttock" is stated to have been created by the perspiration on the forehead of the Kangra goddess; and to have started into life fully armed—like Minerva from the head of Zeus—a godlike man prepared for mighty deeds. This remarkable event occurred 11,000 years ago, in the silver age of mankind.

† In the mountainous regions adjacent to the Sutlej, and below Kanáwer, it has been computed that as many as 32 petty Rajahs rule small principalities.

Cis-Sutlej. Over the Sutlej* we arrive at Simla (7,034); that imperial mountain, which, however, being the viceregal summer residence, must be treated of in a separate section.

HISTORICAL NOTICE OF KANGRA AND THE KUTTOCH FAMILY.

11. *Kangra* (or Nágrkôt as it was anciently called), can doubtless claim a very remote antiquity of origin, and may be regarded as having been the seat of ancient kings, from times before the Christian era. The Greek historians of the period succeeding Alexander the Great (325 B.C.) allude to the Kohistan kingdom of the Northern Punjab, then under the Kuttoch dynasty. **Historical sketch of Kangra.**

The early Mahomedan invaders appear to have overthrown this kingdom, but to have treated Kangra—which nevertheless they plundered—with unusual consideration, for they restored the great idol in 1044 A.D., from which date till about 1360 the Hindoos continued to rule, in fief to the Mahomedans. In 1360 A.D., Feroze Shah Toglak again plundered Kangra, and seems to have held sway there until 1388 when he received Prince Mahomed Toglak on his flight from Delhi. **Mahomedan invasion A.D. 1044.** **A.D. 1360, Feroze Shah Toglak.**

The Emperor Akbar, who conquered Kangra—*circa* 1580—spared the Kuttock Chief Dhurm Chand, and **Akbar, 1580.**

* The Sutlej, rising in the head waters of the Mansaráva Lake in Great Thibet, flows 280 miles to its junction with the Lé or Spiti River (fall of 9,400 feet, or 83.8 per mile). Thence west-south-west for 180 miles to Belaspore, with a fall of 39 feet per mile. From Belaspore to Roopur 100 miles, where it leaves the hills. Roopur to Loodiana 120. 50 miles further on it receives the Beas at Harree-ke-Pattan, close to where the historical battle of Sobräon was fought 1846. Thence 400 miles, where it joins the Chenâb. Total length, 1,130 miles. Here it is called the "Panjnud," from its combining the waters of the *five* Punjab rivers, *i.e.*, Sutlej, Chenâb, Beas, Jhelum, and Rávi. It is the Hesudras of the Greeks, and the Hypanis of Strabo. Much history has been enacted on its banks. The "Hakra," the "lost river" which formerly ran through the Marōsthāli (region of death)—as the Indian desert is called—to the Runn of Katch, is by some stated to have been a channel of the Sutlej. Mahmood and Timoor both crossed the Sutlej at Pak Putton, the principal ferry of those days. Also Ibn Batuta the Arab traveller, who gives the above particulars.

restored him. The Emperor Jehangir "took a fancy" to Kangra, which he named Chota (or Little) Cashmere, and resided there frequently.

1752 A.D. The Dooranees under Ahmed Shah Abdalli.

The Moghuls (1752 A.D.) were dispossessed of the fort by the Affghans or Dooranees, under Ahmed Shah Abdalli, who held it till 1782, when the Affghan Governor Taifoola Khan (who was besieged by the Sikhs at the time) died, and his followers surrendered. It may tend to point the value of Kangra in old times to mention that his compatriots had been driven out of the Punjab 16 years before by the Sikhs, who, however, were unable to take the fort thus isolated and cut off from all support. They now, however, acquired this last stronghold from the Affghans, and after several changes of hands, bestowed it on Sansar Chand, the legitimate chief and descendant of the ancient Kuttoch kings. This chief, by conquest and intrigue during the next 20 years, extended his power over nearly all the states comprising the ancient kingdom. However, he (Sansar Chand) drew on himself the hostility of the Goorkhas, who at that period held the Keyonthâl and hill states up to the Sutlej. Called in as allies by the chief of Kūlū, then at war with Kangra, they overran Sansar Chand's country, and plundered the Kangra Valley, but were unable to take the fortress. Runjeet Sing came to its support, and the Goorkhas retired across the Sutlej. Runjeet Sing thus became master of the situation, took nearly the entire kingdom, leaving the Kuttoch chief only the Fort of Kangra and a few villages to support the garrison: eventually, on the death of Sansar Chand, the principality was absorbed in the Sikh kingdom, and so remained till the date of the war with the British on the Sutlej in 1846, when Kangra lapsed to the British. The Sikh Governor holding out, a force under Sir H. M. Wheeler advanced to its capture, and on a battering train arriving the fortress was surrendered, and has since remained in possession of the British, and been garrisoned by our own troops.

1786 A.D. Sansar Chand.

A.D. 1838, Runjeet Sing.

SECTION IV.

SIMLA,

WITH ITS NEIGHBOURING STATIONS. THE KEYONTHAL, AND BASINS OF THE SUTLEJ AND GIRI.

SIMLA (7,034), KASAULI (6,335), SUBATHU (4,253), DUGSHAI (6,100), JUTOGH (7,300), ETC.

The Keyonthal (as defined in this sketch) comprising Simla, Dagshai, Subathu, Jutogh and Kasauli, suggested as the second central Himalayan refuge

THE above are included in the country of Keyonthâl, otherwise Kyūnthâl (5000 to 7000), which may be defined as a block of hill territory between the Sutlej and the Giri, properly not above 15 miles square, at a general elevation of 5000 feet. It formerly comprised several small hill estates—such as Kahlour, Theōg, Ghoond, and Kóte, and "marched" with Sirmoor. It comprises an area of 5,676 acres, and its district, as roughly dotted in the sketch map, a further 15,000, making a total of 20,676 acres of land for settlers. The Keyonthâl refuge thus defined is artificial, and its limits as given are about 40 miles square. It is now, I believe, in Pattiála territory, but it is surmised that it might be easily resumed by amicablo concession from the Pattiála chief; and comprising as it does some of our most important hill stations, clustered round the summer seat of Government—Simla—would form, in my judgment, an admirable site for a large central "Refugo" or "Reserve Circle." This district was overrun and garrisoned by the Goorkhas early in the present century (1809). The stronghold of Maloun,* which under their brave commander, Umer Singh Thappa, they defended long against the "British force" under Ochterlony in 1815,

---

* Maloun, in the principality of Kahloor, is about 4,450 feet elevation. It capitulated to Sir D. Ochterlony on the 15th May, 1815.

is included in the area of the Keyonthâl. This country, together with the adjacent State of Sirmoor, was conquered by Feroze Shah Togluk, King of Delhi, about 1379, and remained tributary for some time to the Emperors of Delhi.

An excellent strategic site for a grand reserve circle.

2. The foregoing group of hill stations presents an aggregation of military posts forming, in the main, an excellent strategic site, dominating the entire Cis-Sutlej States, and the north-west provinces Trans-Jumna; as indeed was exemplified during 1857, when troops were hurried to Delhi, and deployed on the plains of the north-west during the height of the hot and rainy season; in short, no river presents any obstacle to such a military development. I would remark, however, that a central "refuge" for the impedimenta and families of this district is desirable. The so-called "Simla panic" of 1857, when this district was denuded of troops, was doubtless weak, and may be sneered at as even pusillanimous, but after all may be accepted as the index to a necessity recognised in the hour of danger and trouble. That much-vilified writer Machiavelli, has said "There is no better fortress for a prince than the affection of the people," nor, as regards the hill tribes, did that fail us in the perilous year 1857. I would counsel the salient points of this hill district being strengthened. We must consider it as a valuable strategic or tactical base, bearing the same relation to the north-west provinces and Cis-Sutlej States, as Cashmere has been described as doing towards the Döabs of the Punjab; and it is even more practically effective to that end for reasons mentioned above, *viz.* —the non-intervention of troublesome intersecting rivers or mountain ridges.

3. If the visitor to Simla will take the trouble to walk out as far as the exterior road round "Observatory Hill," and look well at the panorama, he cannot fail to recognise the ridge of the basin of Keyonthâl, here proposed as one of the great central refuges of the

XIV.

View of Simla from Mahasoo. Section IV.

XV.

General View of the "interior" Country near Simla from "Nakunda."
The "Shunkun Ridge" in the distance. Section IV.

country, which, moreover, north-west, contains that strong and interesting position of Maloun, held by the Goorkhas so obstinately, as before mentioned.

4. A few brief notes on the stations already mentioned and embraced within this area, would complete and supplement the description of the strategic features and military positions of this district. The united garrisons—including volunteers—may be estimated at 3000 or 4000 men.*

Sunawar Military Asylum should be protected as a refuge in case of trouble, and included in the "camp of Keyonthal."

5. It has to be mentioned that a Military Asylum, containing some 500 children, is included in the area of the Keyonthâl. What a "hostage to fortune," and how necessary a refuge in the hour of peril with such a gage for victory! Neglect in forming judicious refuges at points throughout the land may yet, if not rectified, prove the ruin of our cause in the perilous times to come. What better summer employ for the soldiers of this garrison than to entrench this fine "camp of Keyonthâl"—containing so much value—with redoubts, etc., at certain strategic points!

This, then, after Cashmere and Dalhousie, I would select as a second great bulwark of Northern India—a veritable *propugnaculum imperii.*

Industrial capabilities and natural features.

6. A few words as to the natural features of this fine district, and we may pass on. Who that has visited Simla can forget its pine-covered hills and cultured valleys, gleaming away far below the mountain sides into the misty "straths" and purple glens and gorges; its flush of rhododendron forest and groves of oak and ilex, its wild flowers and breezy ridges—haunts of the chikôr. The glory of novelty has long since faded from the writer's mind, and he finds it difficult to impart to his words the enthusiasm of youth as formerly felt on viewing these fair mountains

---

* There is a British regiment at each of the stations—Dugshai and Sūbáthū—a depôt of 600 men at Kasauli, and a Goorkha regiment at Simla, with a battery of mountain artillery at Jutôgh.

so as graphically to paint the scene.* The northern road conducts the traveller to still finer scenery in the "interior" as the country outside Simla is called. The forest of Nakunda is almost unique even in the Himalayas, and is filled with koklás, and káléj pheasants; and chikôr are abundant everywhere. The true water-sheds are on the Shunkun and Huttoo Ridges, where rise the Giri and the Pabur, and this may be held to form nearly the northermost limit of the Keyonthâl, as a few miles further on takes one into the valley of the Sutlej. Here one of the oldest established tea estates—the Berkley—is to be seen. I am not aware that tea, as a speculation, has been very successful in these hills, as few, if any, other gardens are to be found. Breweries flourish; saw-yards might pay. Farms for rearing live stock for the Simla market have been found a success, and various branches of arboriculture are fairly successful. There is one source of profitable labour that one day may possibly lead to vast developments beyond all present thought and calculation—I mean *gold;* it probably exists, but except slight washings in some of the mountain streams and ravines, has not been scientifically searched for. The matrix—"the father and mother of gold" as the pyrites are called—have been noted by tried projectors, metallurgists, and travellers. Here and there the gypsum crops out under the very feet of the traveller almost on the high roads. Reports have been submitted to Government on this head, but it is believed it is not desired to encourage the idea of "diggings" so near to placid, imperial Simla, where, if I may be so bold as to assert it, the traditional drag is applied to progress of this kind, as calculated to

Gold probably exists in the Keyonthal "in situ," as also in superficial interfusion?

"Diggings" stink in the nostrils of authority.

---

* As regards the social aspects of Simla, they must be left to the traveller, novelist, or social critic. Who, of the *ancién régime* could not draw on his memory for reminiscences of old Simla, Queen of Indian "watering places!" Its provincial magnates and little great men, its exotic swelldom, and dandies male and female! Let them pass.

attract the "interloper"—that dreaded and objectionable being—whose *raison-d'être* is scarcely recognised by a large class of Indian magnates. In the years to come, however, the haro cry of justice against ourselves which has lately been heard in the land, in behalf of the poor whites and Eurasians, will have to be considered of as a grave question. These classes might, perhaps, ere it be too late, be worked up into the defensive system of a landwehr or "reserve," *sub vexillo*, which it is one of the objects of these pages to suggest.

Ditto Eurasians and poor Whites.

7. Here, if anywhere, under the eye of Government, might the experiment be tried. The Lawrence Asylum here seems to demand a word of notice. The instruction of the children at the Sunáwer Asylum in agricultural and handicraft trades might perhaps be more fully developed. The writer of this paper was instrumental in collecting the first batch of children ever sent to the Sunáwer Asylum in 1847, under the auspices of that great and humane man Sir Henry Lawrence, and can assert that such a development of its scope would not be dissonant from the "founder's" aims and wishes. Sir Henry even advocated "hill colonization," and would have been glad to see colonies established in tho Himalayas *sub-vexillo*.

Lawrence Sunawer Asylum, established 1847.

8. Localities for such are to be found in the country of Keyonthâl—as defined in this paper—especially on its eastern boundary as far as the *Shunkun Ridge*, which is the dividing watershed of N.W. Hindostan; rivers rising on its S. and E. side fall into the Pabur, Tonse and Jumna, and so into the Ganges and Bay of Bengal; whilst those rising on its N. and W. side find their way into the Sutlej and Indus, and so to the W. ocean. This *Shunkun* ridge, in fact, which extends from Mount Huttoo to the Chôr Mountain, may be considered as the "great divide" or water-parting between the basins of the Ganges and Indus. A glance at the Map of India will show that hereabouts

The "Shunkun Ridge" the "water parting" or "great divide" of N. W. India.

a decided bend or angle occurs in the inferior Himalayas; the mountains N. and W. trending away north wards, whereas south of this point a decided turn eastwards is exhibited. The Chôr Mountain thus occupies a very important point from a geodistic point of view, as it is in fact the very pivot* of the inferior watershed from which the rivers of upper India originate. Its geological structure also is peculiar.

Affluents of the Ganges. 9. From about this point, a very decided tilt eastwards is observable in all the affluents of the Ganges, which have a decided inclination to seek year by year a more eastern channel. The following elevations of points near their debouchment from the hills will establish this.†

Seharunpore	on the Jumna,	1002	feet above sea level
Moradabad	„ Káligunga,	600	„
Goruckpore	„ Gôgra,	400	„
Rungpore	„ Kôsi,	200	„
Gwâlpára	„ Brâhmâpootrâ	112	„

The Teesta, which formerly fell into the Ganges, now falls into the Brâhmâpootrâ.

10. Beyond Phágoo eastwards, the area of the Keyonthâl extends as far as the Shunkun Ridge (7,500) which forms the western boundary and watershed line of the basins of the Giri and Pabur, the latter being the westernmost tributary of the Jumna, which it joins in the Dehra Dûn below the confluence of the Tonse. The whole course of the Giri may be traced from this point. The Pabur descends from the Burenda Pass, with a fall of 250 feet per mile, and

* In the upper or main axis of the Himalayas, the watershed may be sought in the mountains above the sources of the Ganges and Jumna (a vast knot of mountain where also the Indus and Sutlej originate) the *Kailás* (or Olympus) of Hindoo geodists. [On this subject see further on.]

† The Nepâl rivers also all trend towards the east, having an oblique dip eastwards: as proof of which the elevations of a few points on the rivers from north to south have been given above.

joins the Tonse at Timi (3000). The valleys of the Giri and Tonse—in Sirmoor territory I believe—contain fine broad river terraces of cultivation of from 200 to 400 feet in width, covered with crops. The Tonse rises in Kéderkánta (12,780). The river slopes rise 2,300 to 3,000 feet above the river bed, and are covered with deodar and pine, also sisso, olive, apricot, walnut, almond, rice, barley, poppy, tobacco, and millet. The affluents of the Jumna are peculiarly rapid; too much so for facility for floating timber to the plains, otherwise splendid forests exist in Gurhwâl and Sirmoor. The mountains on this watershed are the "Chôr" mountain about 12,000 feet elevation, and "Huttoo" (10,000), in the latter of which spring the head waters of the Giri. This conducts us beyond Keyonthâl into the basin of the Jumna, where we find the large new station of Chakrâta.

APPENDIX TO SECTION IV.

Principal Trees and Plants of the Himalayas (Sutlej Valley): with slight variations of latitude these elevations are true of the entire Himalayan ranges as far south as Nepal and Valley of the Kósi.

Hill Name.	Botanical Name.	English.	Elevation.	Remarks.
Kelu	Cedrus deodara	Deodar—H. cedar	6000 to 8000	Properly "Dewa-Daru" (God timber) identical with Cedar of Libanus
Kail	Pinus excelsa	Lofty pine	7000 „ 11000	
Chíl or Sulla	Pinus longifolia	Fir—long-leaved	1500 „ 7000	Resin used medicinally as a plaster
Neoza	Pinus gerardiana	Edible pine	5000 „ 10500	Wood not used
Rai	Abies Smithiana	Him. spruce	9000 „ 11000	The wood of these is inferior to other pines
Pindrow	Picea Webbiana	Silver fir	8000 „ 11000	
Tos or Baloot	Ilex	Evergreen oak	Very rare south	of Chumba; common in the Murree Hills & N.
Deodar	Cupressus torulosa	Cypress	6000 to 8000	Wood useful—scarce
Sewar or Sheer	Juniperus excelsa	Pencil cedar	9000 „ 12000	Wood excellent, light, and odoriferous
Pama or Talu	Juniper sqamosus	Creeping juniper	12000 „ 15000	Used as fuel on high passes
Tuna	Taxus baccata	Yew	9000 „ 10500	Wood used for bows, &c.
Paprung or Shamshad	Buxus sempervirens	Box	6000	Wood used for turning
Bán	Quercus incana	Hoary oak	5000 to 8000	Used chiefly as firewood at hill stations
Bré	Quercus ilex	Evergreen oak	8000	
Mohru	Quercus dilatata		6000 to 9000	A good heavy wood

Kursoo	Quercus semicarpifolia	Alpine oak ...	9000 „ 12000	A magnificent tree, timber much esteemed
Paharee	Populus ciliata ...	Poplar	6000	Soft wood, and paper from seed
Peepul	Populus alba ...	White poplar ...		
Akrôt	Juglans regia ...	Walnut	7000 to 9000	Wood used for gun stocks, &c.
Kunch	Alnus obtusifolia ...	Alder	4000 „ 5000	Charcoal for smelting
Knor	Pavia indica	Him. Horsechestnut	5000 „ 8000	Seeds eaten in times of scarcity
Bras	Rhododendron arborium	Rhododendron ...	6700 „ 8000	Flowers made into jelly, subacid
Bhoj-putra ...	Betula bhoj-putra ...	Birch	10000 „ 13000	Bark used for writing
Bankimu	Corylus lacera ...	Hazel	8000	Wood light, compact
	Acer lœvigetum ...	Polish maple ...	9000	Knots polished for cups
Kow or Wer ...	Olea feruginea ...	Olive	3500 to 5000	Wood similar to box
Cham, Khuruk ...	Carpinus viminea ...	Hornbeam ...	5500	Esteemed by carpenters
Rous	Cotoneaster bacillaris	Mountain ash ...	8000 to 10000	Walking sticks
Kakkar (3 varieties)	Rhus	Sumach	5000	Hard yellow wood
Tuna	Cedrela toona ...	Common toon ...	6000	Furniture
Gingaru	Cratœguscren ...	White thorn ...	3000 to 7000	Staves
	Fraxinus	Crabosk	7000	Sticks, hefts, handles
	Arundinaria	Hill Bamboo ...	4000 to 7000	South of Kumäon

Fruit Trees.

Juldárú	Armeniaca vulg. ...	Apricot	7000 to 13000	
Arú	Amygdalus persica ...	Peach	7000 „ 10000	
Januna	Cerasus cornuta ...	Bird cherry ...	7000	Simla

APPENDIX TO SECTION IV. CONTINUED.

Hill Name.	Botanical Name.	English.	Elevation.	Remarks.
Paddam	Cerasus puddam ...	Cherry	3000 to 7000	
Palu	Pyrus malus	Apple		Kunawer
Mehul	Pyrus variolosa ...	Wild pear... ...	3000 to 7000	
Trumul	Ficus macrophylla ...	Wild fig	5000	
Akrot	Juglans regia ...	Walnut	7000 to 9000	[mon
	Ribes (2 varieties) ...	Currant	11000	Asrung valley, uncom-
	R—— grossalaria ...	Gooseberry ...	10000	uncertain in ripening
Ungoor	Vitis vinifera ...	Vine	7000 to 9000	
Ré or Neoza ...	Pinus Gerardiana ...	Edible pine ...	7000 „ 10000	Common in Chini. The seeds are stored and sold at about 2 annas (3d.) a seer
Fenduk	Corylus lacerta ...	Hazel nut... ...	8000	
Nusri	Rubus flavus ...	Bramble	5000 to 7000	
	Fragaria vesca ...	Strawberry ...	7000	
Toothree	Morus paroifolia ...	Mulberry ...	4000 to 7000	
Karphul	Myrica sapida ...	Box myrtle ...	4000 „ 6000	Used for sherbet
Kūmuk or Gehu, 2 varieties	Triticum sativum ...	Wheat(red or white),	13000 „ 15000	Bearded and ownerless wheat occurs up to 15000
Ujour or Jou ...	Hordeum (2 kinds) ...	Barley	ditto	Much cultivated
China	Panicum miliacum ...	Millet	6000 to 9000	Middle region
Ogrel or Paphra ...	Fagopyrum (2 var.) ...	Buckwheat ...	13000	Much cultivated
Mundwa	Eleusina corœcena ...	Ragi	5000	Much cultivated in the Nilgherries

Bathu	Amaranthusfrumenta-	Amaranth... ...	7000	Grown in valleys
Jowar	Sorghum vulg. [cinus	Great millet ...	6000	A rain crop
Bhatwa	Chenopodium ...	Goosefoot... ...	7000	
Mash	Phaseolus (2 varieties)	Field pea	6000 to 8000	
Arud	ditto ...	Gram		
Bekla	Faber vulg.	Bean	6000	And several pulse and lentils

Economic Plants.

Bhang	Cannabis Indica ...	Indian hemp ...	3000 to 7000	Yields "churrus" and hemp
Atees (3 varieties)	Atus ferox and papillus	Wolfsbane ...		
Mowra or *Bheek* ...	Aconitum hetero ...	Poisonous aconite....	10000 „ 15000	
Moorub	Desmodium & Rumex	Sorrel	6000 „ 8000	
Bichu	Urtica peterophylla ...	Nettle	4000 „ 7000	} Yields textile fibres of much value
Purja	Bohimeria mica ...	Rhea	4000 „ 6000	

Gentian (2 varieties), cheretta (3 ditto), dandelion, bermot (meadow rue), and many medicinal herbs are found, as also wild indigo, musk, poppy, berberry, oleaster, Alpine rhododendron (up to 14000 feet), rhubarb, cummin (cultivated) and mustard; and the types of many other plants such as wild asparagus, celery, tubers, and bulbous plants of many varieties are found throughout the Himalayan Ranges.

Table taken from Government Reports—Forest Department.

SECTION V.

THE HIMALAYAN WATERSHEDS AND GANGETIC BASIN.

CHAKRATA (6,700), MUSSOORIE (6,600), AND LANDOUR (7,300). THE DEHRA DUN (2,347), AND WESTERN GURHWAL (6000 TO 10,000).

Geodesy of the Gangetic Watershed.

WE have now fairly entered into the Himalayan watershed and the fluvial basins cis-nivean, which receive its drainage into the Gangetic Valley. The sketch map will show the fluvial systems between the Jumna and Brâhmâpootrâ better than any description I can well give. These embrace all the countries of the Himalayas—Gurhwâl, Kumäon, Nepâl, Sikhim—between those extreme affluents of the Ganges, and the Alpine basins through which they escape to the plains and so into the Ganges and its delta; as also the subsidiary or cis-nivean watershed ridges which divide them. Each of these basins may be held to have its own tutelary glacier, out of which the head waters of the main stream and most of its tributaries emerge,—these glaciers are mostly found on the main axis of the Himalayan range.

This axis may be estimated at a general elevation of 20,000 feet; many of its peaks exceed 23,000 feet, and possibly a dozen are over 25,000 feet in elevation. This gigantic wall of granite and basalt must undoubtedly be regarded as the main Himalayan axis, and, though it is cut in some few places by rivers such as the Sutlej, whose sources are trans-nivean, it may be held as extending as far north-west as Cashmere before it

XVI.

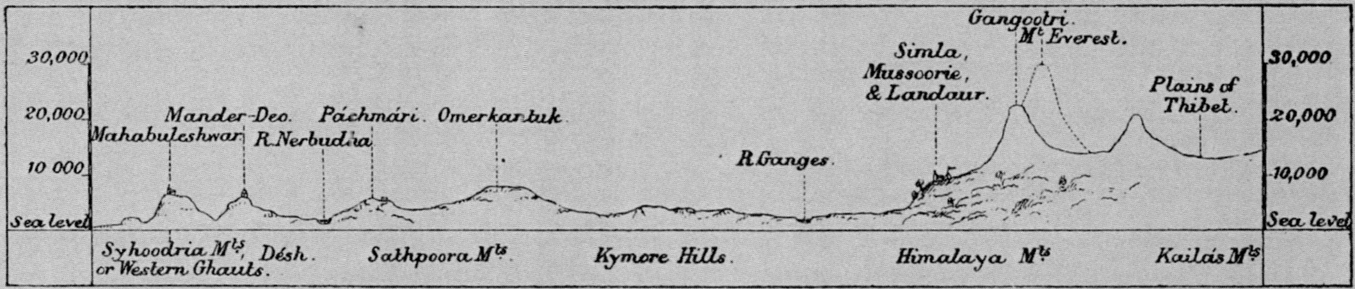

ISOMETRIC VIEW AND SECTION ACROSS INDIA. Sections IV. and V.

turns due north into the Paralang or Emodus of ancient geography. Some geodists, indeed, affect to find the Himalayan axis beyond the Passes in Thibet, near the Sampoo (Brâhmâpootrâ) watershed, and that of the Indus north-west. On an extended view of the question, however, I would suggest for consideration that the broken plateau of Great and Middle Thibet may hold the same relation to the Himalayan chain as the inner Syhoodria slopes, and the broken country of the Dekhan do to the Western Ghauts,—the ancient littoral of India before the waters of the primæval ocean had rolled "into one place" by successive cataclysms, first from the great Asian, and next from the great Indian plateau, into its present level; in other words, I hold that the Himalayan chain was the primæval littoral of Thibet,* and that the Syhoodria or Western Ghauts formed the littoral of ancient India, the modern Concan being a strip of sea beach—afterwards upheaved—formed by the receding waters of the modern Indian Ocean. I refrain from detailed arguments to support this theory, nor am I qualified for much controversy on the point, but I think there are grounds,† from geological and other existing data, to support this theory of the geodesy of the Indian peninsula, which I here only suggest as a speculative question: a diagram will, on this point also, best explain my meaning. [See Section X.., para. 6.]

Further on, marginal sketches of the profiles of the Himalayas from the "Tarai or Bhâbur" to the Cachár or juxta-nivean track will be given; this may suffice to bring us to the immediate consideration of the stations on the subsidiary ridges or watersheds named in the index of this series of papers.

---

* The outer Himalayas are mostly stratified rock, indicating water action, and although the Syhoodria range is plutonic, the flooring of the Dekhan, though primitive, indicates sub-aqueous action.

† (1) "Oolitic shells have been found in the Himalayas at an elevation of 18,000 feet."—Lyell.

(2) The Dhoon of Dehra and Sewâliks are upper miocene, and contain marine and palustral fossils.

Chakrata, a station in the basin of the Jumna.

2. Chakráta (6,700), is a station situated between the Tonse and the Jumna, on the spurs of the Deobund mountain, it has its *point d'appui* at Sahárunpore on the Punjab and Delhi Railway. Being situated within the basin of the Jumna, it belongs to that group of subsidiary spur ridges whence issue the western affluents of the Ganges. It, however, approximates in point of distance (as the crow flies) to the Cis-Sutlej or Keyonthâl base described in the last section. It thus forms a connecting link with Mussoorie and Landour across the Giri and Tonse—tributaries of the Jumna—which is crossed 23 miles below Chakráta, on the verge of the Western Dûn of Dehra.

3. The Station of Chakráta is described in Trigonometrical Series No. 48 (four miles to the inch), which gives the topography of the district, but a rough plan of the station and its environs would obviate a more detailed description. The Chakráta Cantonment is divided into three sites,* and intended to accommodate as many regiments. The sketch also shows the communication of this station with the plains *viâ* the Timlie Pass over the Sewâliks. The road crosses the Jumna at Kolsi, near the foot of the hills 23 miles from Chakráta, and so leads through the Dûn over the Timlie Pass and Asun River to Sahárunpore on the Punjab and Delhi Railway. Its present garrison (1874) is 27 officers and 875 men—Her Majesty's 8th (King's) Regiment. It occupies a fine site on a spur of the Deobund Mountain, which is about three miles from barracks, and between 9000 and 10,000 feet elevation. Another road passes through the Western Dûn of Dehra, which also forms another outlet to the plains *viâ* Dehra and the Lall Durwaza Pass to Roorkhee. The Tonse† joins the Jumna near Kolsi, and the Giri

* (1) At Gobrána site one British regiment. (2) Kailána site the Landour depôt. (3) Chilmán site one British regiment.

† The Tonse is the larger stream at the point of confluence. It rises near the source of the Jumna at an elevation of 12,784 feet.

a few miles lower down. On the tributaries of the latter is situated the site of ancient Sirmoor. The outer hills of this district are chiefly composed of slates, covered by sandstones and thick beds of limestone, intruding even into the plutonic formation of the higher peaks.

Mussoorie, Landour, and the Dehra Dun.

4. We now come to Mussoorie (6,600) with Landour (7,350). This grand group of stations dominates the Dehra Dûn, and guards the Döab as far as Allahabad. It was, I believe, the first settled of all the Himalayan Sanitaria; it is situated on the southern boundary of British Gurhwâl, on the edge of the far-famed Dehra Dûn. The Musosorie ridge constitutes, in fact, the boundary of Gurhwâl and Dehra Dûn. The Dehra Dûn is considered to contain 750 square miles up to the Sewâlik range, of which the Sewâlik forests comprise 200 square miles. The Passes are the Timlie (3,153), and Mohun (3,059). The Ganges enters the Dûn at Tupóbun. The watershed between the Eastern and Western Dûn is at Rajpore (4,500). The former is swampy, the latter dry. The wells on the watershed are deep. Inhabitants—Brahmins, Rajpoots of various castes, Rahwuts, Bisht, and Khasia, Tuars, and Goojurs. The history of the Dûn is much associated with that of Gurhwâl, of which, indeed, it formed an ancient appanage.

The Dehra Dun an appanage of Ancient Gurhwal.

Description of Gurhwal, and its historical antecedents.

5. The country of Gurhwâl—in size about 90 miles by 60, and extending from the Himalayan peaks to the plains of Dehra Dûn—comprises some of the loftiest peaks* in the whole of the Himalayan chain, but the ranges slope down into hot valleys, the country being intersected by the deep chasms of the Alaknunda, the Tonse, the Pabur, the Bhâgirutti, and many other streams which feed the great rivers Ganges and Jumna. The river Nilum (or Jáhnivi), which rises in Thibet in the district of Chungsa in Chaprang, penetrates the

* Jumnootrie, 25,669; Kédernâth, 23,062, and the average height of this part of the Himalaya range, = 20,000.

Himalaya, and joins the Bhágirutti or true Ganges. It is in fact the remotest source or feeder of the river Ganges. The Niti river, however, (or Dhauli) is sometimes considered from its size and length of course to be the principal branch of the Ganges. The Niti Pass extends along the banks of this river, and is estimated at considerably over 16,000 feet elevation; the chasms of this river gorge are stupendous, the river descending seven thousand feet in seven miles. The Burrenda Pass to the Sutlej is also over 15,000; nevertheless, armies have crossed both these lofty passes into Gurhwâl; and even entire tribes emigrating from the highlands of Middle Thibet have entered India by these lofty side doors.

Epitome of its history.

6. The ancient history of Gurhwâl is not clearly known; it is believed that the inhabitants are a cross between a rugged clan from Central Thibet and the Khasia or aboriginal women of this range; they are a stunted, poor looking race, without much spirit. The patriarchal system prevailed till about five centuries ago, when the various clans were consolidated into one Raj by an energetic spirit from the plains of India, whose posterity acquired considerable territorial power, extending over parts of Kumäon and the Dehra Dûn. In A.D. 1803—Purdooman Sah, a descendant of this worthy, being Rajah—the country was invaded by the Goorkhas, the Rajah was slain in battle in attempting to oppose them, and the entire country was subdued and overrun by the Goorkhas, who reduced the population to slavery. Sheo Durson Sah, son of the last Rajah, fled the country, but in 1815 when the British assumed the Suzerainty of the country, he was reinstated in a portion of the territory of his ancestors, the Dehra Dûn and Eastern Gurhwâl falling to the British.

7. Landour (7,350), crowning the ridge and containing a convalescent depôt of 600 men,* forms a

* It is, I believe, in contemplation to move this depôt to Chakráta.

grand position on the crest of the first range of the Himalayas, which here rise rather abruptly from the valley of Dehra Dûn. The hills thence rise gradually over successive groups of ranges and valleys inland to Gungootrie (12,000) and Jumnootrie (13,000), sources of the Ganges and Jumna. Landour in fact dominates the far-famed Dehra Dûn, also Tíri (3,400), the capital of Gurhwâl W. (4000 to 8000), and N.W. Kumäon (4000 to 7000). Landour and Mussoorie in themselves are not capable of much expansion, though guarding many sites that are so. In Dehra Dûn we have a glorious site for colonial developments, and in it and Kumäon the Indian tea interest finds one of its most important centres. The "strategic position" of Landour, after that which has been defined as the Keyonthâl refuge circle, is not only locally defensive of its dependencies, but also occupies an important site from an imperial point of view. Not only does it command its own lovely valley of the Dûn and the rich forest lands embraced by the interesting Sewâlik ranges, and the holy lands of the Ganges and Jumna, but strategically defends the "Döab" as far even as Allahabad, and supports the districts of Oude and Rohilkund. Much might be written by the Indian student and ethnologist on this interesting theme, but it falls not within the scope of this paper to enter on such subjects, nor has the history of this country any source of interest independent of the general history of *Hindoostán,** a term specially applicable to the Döab of the Ganges and Jumna, the—"Land of Brâj."

Landour & Mussoorie not capable of much expansion though guarding territory containing valuable sites for settlers.

8. Dominated by the watershed of this mountain system, lies the lovely valley called "Dehra Dûn," which

The Dehra Dun and Sewaliks: history & traditions

I infer that the want of space for the increasing demands of Mussoorie has been the chief moving cause for this.

* The term Hindoostan is more specially applied to this province of the north west, although less exactly often applied to the whole of the Indian peninsula. *Hindoosthán*, is essentially *the place of the Hindoos;* hence throughout these papers I have avoided using it as a term for *India*, of which it is a recognized province only.

is bounded on the north by the Himalayas, south by the Sewâlik range, east by the river Ganges, and west by the river Jumna. The eastern drainage is by the rivers Songh and Soosowá into the Ganges; the western by the Assun and its tributaries into the Jumna; the town of Dehra being on the ridge forming the watershed between them, and on which, as has been already stated, is also situated Rajpore at the higher end of the spur. The Sewâliks may be held to form a zone of forests, in which the wild elephant, tiger, and other heavy game roam unrestrained. Its geology and extinct fauna are well known to the paleontologist by the labours of Falconer, Cautley, etc. It is in the upper miocene, and forms a unique and highly interesting arena for investigation. Romantic and interesting points abound, and the picturesque aspects of this lovely valley are attractive in many ways.

Amongst the hills forming the north-east boundary of Dehra Dûn, seven miles from the town of Dehra, situated in a deep and romantic glen of the Songh river, are found the dropping caves of Sansadhára, where stalactites and petrifactions of remarkable character are to be seen. To the south-east extremity of the Dûn is the celebrated Hurdwâr, near to where the Ganges debouches on to the plain.

The area of the valley is about 6,738 square miles—430,000 acres—with a sparse population of about 50 to the square mile.

9. "To sum up, the prospect it holds out to the settler is this: that at an elevation of 2,300 above sea level, with a mean summer temperature of 88°, and a winter temperature of 57° (total mean 72°.5), and a yearly rainfall of 80 inches; sheltered alike from the parching blasts of an Indian hot season and the cutting cold of winter, he finds a picturesque and lovely region abounding in timber and water-power, and a fertile soil when cleared, with the pleasant and healthful hill stations of Mussoorie and Landour close at

XVII.

VIEW OF MUSSOORIE. Landaur in the distance. Section V.

XVIII.

View of part of the Snowy Range, East Gurhwal, from near Ranikhet. Section V.

hand; abundance of forage for cattle, and no lack of game for sport; excellent roads and outlets to produce: combined, however, with a doubtful tenure of land."

HISTORICAL NOTICE.

Mythic History of the Dun.

10. Of the early history of the Dûn little is known; the mythic kingdom of Kidarkūnd included the Dûn and Sewâliks (abode of Shiva), and is fabled to have been the arena of the wars of the gods and Titans, preceding the satya or golden age. Here, also, in Brahminical times, came Râma and Lutchmun to do penance for the death of Ravána, the Mohim King of Lanka. Here also came the five Pandaus on the pilgrimage to the graves of Kédernâth.* Káshyápa, the divine founder of Cashmere, is said to have feasted the gods here; also to have created the Sooswa river— or rather Nâgáchál the peak from whence it flows— on which the serpent (nâg) Bahmun did penance, and so became "lord of the Dûn." But it were tedious to enter further on the local myths of the valley. The Dûn is stated to have lain desolate for many ages, till wandering pastoral tribes — Brinjáras and others— attracted by its fertility, settled there, and subsequently it was colonized from Gurhwâl, and became an appanage of that Raj.

Its History in historical times.

11. In A.D. 1079 Sultan Ibrahim, the son of Masaood of Ghuzni, is said to have overrun the Dûn and visited Dehra. In A.D. 1658-60 Prince Suliman Sheko marched through the Dûn in progress to join his father Dára at Lahore, and took refuge with Prithee Sing, Rajah of Gurhwâl, but was delivered to Aurungzébe by the Rajah, who received a grant (or sunnud) of the Dûn in consequence. This, however, may be regarded as a gift of the recipient's own possession, as the submission of the Gurhwâl Rajah to the Emperor appears to have been merely nominal.

* Kédernâth Peak, 23,062 feet.

Futeh Sah or Sing, grandson of Prithee Sing, invaded Thibet by the Niti Pass, and exacted tribute from the Deb Rajah. In his reign the descendants of the Sikh Guru Nânak (1661) took up their abode in the Dûn, and died there; hence the Sikhs have since always gravitated towards Hurdwâr in consequence; it is to them holy ground. From about this period till A.D. 1757,* the Dûn appears to have enjoyed much prosperity, epecially under Rani Kurnaváti, "whose palace was at Nâgsidh," the (supernatural) Nâga capital already mentioned. In A.D. 1757* Nujeeb-u-dowla (or Nujeeb Khan), leader of the Rohillas of Seharunpore, invaded the Dûn and defeated Prateep Sah, who became tributary to the Rohillas. Nujeeb Khan assumed the government of the Dûn, introduced Mahomedan colonists, and "fostered all men." He died in 1770, and the chiefs of Gurhwâl soon undid his good; anarchy ensued, till at length — about 1784 — an invasion of Sikhs under Bughál Singh overran the Dûn. About this time Purdooman Sah came to the throne. The anarchy of the kingdom continued; robbers and adventurers of all sorts roaming at pleasure, looting the land, and exacting mail. The Sikhs especially extorted tribute from the Rajah. Rajpoots and Goojurs also, pouring through the Timlie and Mohun Passes, crossed the Sewâliks. The Gurhwâl Rajah began to give away jagheers and villages to escape pillage, and, in fact, about this period the whole Dûn was in this way alienated from the Gurhwâl Raj; in 1787 the Poondu Rana actually obtained the whole Dûn in fief as a forced dowry of the Rajah's daughter. In 1786 the Rohillas again invaded the Dûn, sacked Dehra, and acted the iconoclast. The Rajah Purdooman Sah allied himself to the Mahrattas; the usual results followed, and the latter plundered the country (1800), which in fact at this period belonged to none, but was freely roamed by freebooters, and the arena of

* 1744 according to other authorities.

every intrigue and outrage. At length—about 1790—the Goorkhas took Almorah, and having secured themselves in Kumäon, advanced westwards into Gurhwâl, and finally overran the Dûn in A.D. 1803.

The Goorkhas took Almorah (1790).

12. As regards the united country of Gurhwâl, it is stated that in the time of Purdooman Sah, the last Rajah, who fell in battle against the Goorkhas, it had been divided into 22 pergunnahs for more than 3,700 years—each independent of the other—till, consolidated by an energetic Rajpoot of Ahmedabad, named Bhâg-Dhúnt, who united them into one kingdom under the Chandpore Rajah, and subsequently deposing him, seized the kingdom himself and assumed the title of Rajah of Gurhwâl (the country of fortresses). Other accounts state that Kanak Pal of Dhar founded the state, which consisted of 52 (instead of 22) pergunnahs. These two, however, somewhat varied accounts agree in the main fact that a branch of the great Pal family of Rajpoots reigned some 40 generations. We may approximately assign the colonization of Gurhwâl to about the 7th century B.C., and probably Scythian irruptions may have at times partially overrun or colonized its northern frontiers. At any rate Bikramajeet, the great King of Malwa, is said to have expelled an eruption of such invaders, B.C. 57, and rëestablished the Pal dynasty which had been overthrown by Sakaditya, King of Kumäon. These Indo-Scythians—fragments apparently of the ruins of ancient Media or Bactria—are stated in the "Rajah Taringini" to have conquered as far as Delhi, which together with the Dûn, long remained desolate.*

Gurhwal Raj—land of fortresses—founded by a Rajpoot.

Its early history.

* As regards the origin of the word Dehra Dûn, Ferishta states that about A.D. 1200 Sultan Ibrahim, son of Masaood, marched to a place in the hills called *Dehra*, the inhabitants of which came as fugitives originally from Khorassan, but a doubt rests on the exact identity of this with the modern Dehra, which name is moreover attributable to the fact of its being the Dehra or burying place of Gooru Rām Ray, a Lahore Saint. The word Dûn is probably identical with the Celtic "dune," "doons," or "downs."

13. As has been stated, Purdooman Sah, Rajah of Gurhwâl, who had recovered the Dûn, was defeated and slain by the Goorkhas in 1803. From that date to the war with the British in 1815, the Goorkhas converted it into a sort of depôt or reserve base for their operations westward—for which it is not badly situated. In 1815 the British, however, declared war, and soon afterwards invested the valley. They received a check at Kalinga, where Gillespie fell, but eventually prevailed. The Dûn has since remained British territory, and enjoyed that immunity from war and misfortune which constitutes no history.

Taken by the British in 1815.

From Tírí (2,278), the ancient capitol of Gurhwâl, the ridges between Mussoorie and the Bhágirutti are clothed with moroo oak. The cheer (P. longifolia) commences at Samsoo 20 miles above Tírí, and extends up to 5000 feet elevation as far as Jhála. Box, yew, and cypress, prevail at Jhála, where the river bends suddenly to the east towards Gungootrie. The great deodar forests and the red (pencil) cedar extend 24 miles; with fir and beech also up to the snow.

SECTION VI.

KUMAON, EAST GURHWAL,
(4000 to 8000) (6000 to 10,000)

AND THE GANGETIC BASIN, CONTINUED.

NAINEE-TAL (6,400), RANIKHET (7000), ALMORA (5,400), LOHARGHAT (5,500), AND PITORAGARH (6,600).

KUMAON (the land of the tortoise), associated with *East Gurhwâl* (the land of fortresses or steep places), may be considered the very nidus or cradle of Hindooism. Amidst or beyond the snowy peaks which bound it north and east is found "Kailas," the Olympus of the Hindoos, whence issue the great rivers Indus and Ganges, Sutlej and Brâhmâpootrâ; whilst on the forest-covered banks of the "Surjoo" (or Kâligunga) which rises in the same mountain tract was enacted the prelude of the drama of the war of Râmâ with Râwun the giant king of Ceylon, as related in that great epic the "Rámáyáná," the very text-book of Hindooism. *Gungootri*, *Jumnootri*, *Kêdar-nâth*, *Boodrinâth*, *Trisool*, *Pindri*, are all glacier-peaks of this holy land, but the fables attached to these sacred resorts are too multiform to be entered on here. These peaks are mostly subtended by temple shrines and places of pilgrimage, which enjoy large revenues,* but can only be touched on in this section as they affect topographically the districts treated of. The holy name of the entire country embraced by the Ganges to the Kâli is *Ootera-Kûnd*, which may be translated "the cardinal points" (of the compass), "the Kibla," or macrocosm of Hindooism. The area of this province is not less than 7000 square miles, but its

---

* As an instance the Rawul of *Boodrinâth* enjoyed rent from 166 villages.

Lake system.

population scarcely exceeds 50,000. Its chief topographical features will be described further on; but some allusion may perhaps here be conveniently made to the remarkable lake system which is found in the southern acclivities of Kumäon, just within the first ranges. The small lakes enumerated below form a system of water supply which has been brought under control, and utilized for artificial "spates" to irrigate the adjacent lowlands subtending them. They are a peculiar feature of this district of the Himalayas, which, as a range, is singularly deficient in lake scenery. Their origin is partly attributable to glacial, and partly perhaps to volcanic action also, but more especially to landslips which have closed the gorges of the valleys, thus enclosing the waters of the surrounding drainage in valley basins. "Mulwan-Tal" is an instance of such a formation within the memory of man; and legends attribute the formation of "Bheem-Tal" and others, to the agency of the Pandaus, which is equivalent to assigning them an origin such as the "Pelasgian" or "Cyclopean" origin of the ancient Greek—the work of a stronger race antecedent to the present age. They may be enumerated as follows:—

(1). Naini-Tal (with Sūkh-Trikhi-Tal) was formerly a very holy lake, void of animal life, sacred to "Richóba" otherwise "Naini-Devi;" *Naini* being the equivalent of *Naik* or patrol—an *Outpost*—(of the Gangetic waters)* elevation 6,410 feet, length one and half mile by width of half mile, 96 feet deep; described further on in para. 13.

(2). Bheem-Tal, 4,270 feet elevation, 5,580 feet long, by 1,490 feet wide, is stated to have been made by "Bheema," the fourth Pandau, and may be partly artificial. It has a sluice to the low country. There is here a temple sacred to Mahadeo, called Bhimesir.

(3). "Nuldamutti-Tal," so named from Raja "Nul,"

* Such was the explanation given me by a Brahmin reader of Almora.

and his wife "Damnuti," a pair of worthies who dwelt there.

(4). "Sâth-Rikhi-Tal," merely a small tarn in the mountain above the last. These two lakes drain into Bheem-Tal.

(5). "Mulwun-Tal," elevation 3,400 feet, length 4,480 feet, by 1,830 feet wide, depth 127 feet, is of recent formation; being caused by a landslip which partly dammed up the course of the Kulsa river, a tributary of the Gôla, which still runs through it. It is surrounded by a steep amphitheatre of hills, which enclose it as in a cauldron. It has an overfall and sluice towards the low country at Bér.

(6). "Nau-Kuttia-Tal" (nine-cornered lake), 4000 feet elevation—122 feet deep—of an irregular polygon shape, of considerable size and depth, with a sluice to the low country. Absurd fables are attached to this spot, and legends which need not be entered on.

These lakes, as has been stated, form a fine water system for the irrigation of the lowlands. In their vicinity is some excellent level ground at elevations of 3,500 to 4,500 feet or more, most of which is available for agricultural settlement, as well as pasturage for cattle, etc. Higher up are slopes as well suited for tea as any in Kumäon, and rising to altitudes elevated above the zone of malaria, to afford sites for planters' habitations.

Râmpore (6,700), a place midway between Nainee-Tal and Almora, where a Goorkha corps—the old Nusseree battalion were formerly cantoned — dominates this tract, and appears to me a good military post—healthy— sufficiently elevated above malaria — and capable of some expansion for industrial development.

The Kumaon group of Hill Stations as a refuge or reserve circle.

2. Our onward progress has now led us by a not very long step to the group of Kumäon stations represented by Nainee-Tal (6,400), Almora (5,400), and Ránikhét (7000), perhaps strategically valuable as commanding Rohilkund, Oude, and—so long as Nepâl

remains politically what it is—important as a possible refuge in time of trouble. To this end I would suggest that the equilateral triangle, of which Nainee-Tal, Ránikhét, and Almora constitute the angles, should be in a way fortified as a refuge, the base--about 24 miles--being on the side of Râmpore and Rânibâgh towards Bareilly. The sketch map will roughly show the topographical and strategic conditions of this position, on the left flank of which stands Almora, which may be considered the British capitol of Kumäon, and calculated to form the chief "military circle" or "refuge" of the district.

Its capital, Almora, described: its historical aspects.

3. Almora is an interesting town of very sacred character, inhabited by "Brahmins of the Brahmins." It was formerly one of the great refuges to which Hindoo fugitives from the plains, escaping from Mahomedan usurpation, gravitated. It is flanked by two forts, one called "Fort Moira," and the other the site of the palace of the ancient kings of Kumäon. The only action fought between the Goorkhas and British during the war of 1815 occurred near Almora, at Sitowlie and Simtollah, ending in the repulse and dislodgment of the former from the heights which crown the Hawilbagh Valley—now a large tea district.

The geology of this district consists of slates, on which the sandstones and limestones of the red sandstone epoch are superimposed with carboniferous beds extending into the plutonic formation of the upper regions. Almora stands on loose micacious schist.

The Sub-Himalayan and longitudinal valleys are common to the entire ranges of Himalayas as far as Khâtmándoo; beyond that, to the east, a distinct geological formation is found, evidencing fusion, whereas lacustrine and, perhaps, glacial influences must account for the Sub-Himalayan basins west of Khâtmándoo.

4. Always closely associated with Gurhwâl, we find Kumäon now entirely a British province, incorporated

XIX.

General View of Almora from Sitowlie. Section VI.

XX.

View of "Cheena," and the Lake of Naini-Tal, looking north-west, showing the site of the great landslip of 1880. Section VI.

with Eastern Gurhwâl. Some of the grandest glaciers of the whole Himalayan range are visible on this range, and several of the best passes into Thibet issue from it. They are, however, mostly very high. The Niti Pass, is above 16,000 feet, the Byánsi 15,000 feet, the Mána 20,000 feet. The glaciers overhanging them present stupendous altitudes and gorges, sublime in the extreme. Nanda Devi reaches 25,700 feet; many others exceed 23,000 feet; and it is calculated that in the snowy wall of Thibet bounding Kumäon there are thirty-four peaks rising above 18,000 feet in elevation. **Mountain Passes.**

5. This country is intersected by deep valleys following the courses of the numerous mountain rivers which fall into the Ganges. Of these the great chasm of the Alaknunda may be considered to hold the most important tributary. Here, in Kumäon, is the head-quarters of the great tea industry, and numerous tea estates stud the valleys at elevations from 3000 to 6000 feet; Almora, the capital of Kumäon, being the centre of the tea-producing lands. The convention by which the Nepâlese evacuated Kumäon, gave the country into British occupation, I believe by lapse of heirs-male to the guddee of the ancient kings.* **Rivers.**

6. To revert to the ancient history of Kumäon. Previous to the middle of the 14th century its history is uncertain. In A.D. 1379 Feroze Togluk invaded Kumäon, and reduced 23,000 inhabitants to slavery; and in 1402 Timour—during his invasion of Hindoostan—made an incursion and located some Mahomedan families there. Akbar sent an army into Kumäon which besieged Almora, but was defeated by the Rajah Rudra, who, following up his success, advanced into the plains and conquered part of the Dehra Dûn. **Ancient History of Kumaon.**

* Fable relates that Gurhwâl and Kumäon were first occupied by the Pandaus, whose descendant, Kuttoch Rajah, was defeated and his progeny destroyed by Anook Pal of Nepâl, who came by Seul and at Bhâghésir defeated the Gurhwâllies, advanced and planted his standards at Bûdrinâth, where he set up a stone pillar to commemorate the event.

Military History continued.

Akbar seems to have been content to let Rajah Rudra hold the country in fief, and empowered him to coin money in his own name. That Emperor's policy of conciliation, rather than want of means to subdue this small hill principality, may probably account for this leniency. In 1791 the Goorchâlis made an attempt on Kumäon, and seem to have, from that date until 1814—when the war with the British broke out—been continually vexing the frontiers, and in 1799 actually conquered the country. In April, 1815, a British force under Colonel (afterwards Sir) Jasper Nichols advanced, and after some fighting at Sitowlie and Simtollah, as before narrated, captured Almora, and the Goorkhas then retreated within their own borders. Heirs failing, the country was annexed to British territory and incorporated as a hill province, with the reserved or eastern portion of Gurhwâl lying between the Alaknunda river and the present Nepâl frontier.

7. The Rajahs of Kumäon and Gurhwâl had been scions of the same stock. The ancient capitol of the former was at Champávat on the Kaligunga, south-east from Almora, the present capitol. The frontier posts of Loharghât and Pithóragarh, abutting on the Nepâl frontier, comprise some fertile slopes and valleys, containing several flourishing tea estates, and Pithóragarh especially seems to afford a promising locality for a subsidiary reserve (industrial) centre. The old road from Champávat and Lohargât to Bareilly led through the great sául forests at the foot of the Kumäon mountains near Brahma-Deo, and is possibly the best line of approach from the plains to Kumäon—in some respects preferable to that by Ranibâgh or Kálidūngi.

Loharghat.

Lohárghât (*not* Lohooghât) is so called from the iron ores found in the adjacent zillah of Seul, in which also Pithóragarh is situated. Hereabouts is the nidus or original seat of the ancient Kali-Kumäon. The Sub-Himalayan forests of Kumäon hereabouts, consist of sául, shissum, and toon; bahera, sun, and holdoo, are also found at low elevations to the south. The Khoee-Doon and Putlee-Doon (sául forests) embrace 200 square miles.* The author has visited these districts, and is inclined to consider them as offering unusual advantages to *individual* settlers, as well as affording a site for an industrial reserve (perhaps *native*) military circle.

8. The Kumäon Raj, however, as a distinct principality, is stated by some authorities to have been founded by an adventurer from the village of Jhansie, near Allahabad, who, about the 15th century, conquered the country.

The area of Kumäon and East Gurhwâl is about 500,000 acres; its metallic products are iron, copper, plumbago, and gold. The chief road into Thibet is by the Niti Pass, on which several roads converge. Statistical.

9. The Kumäon watershed is drained by the rivers Kâli,† Douli, Goori, Vishu, and Alaknunda, which rise at elevations of nearly 13,000 feet. The Kósila and Rámgunga originate in the lower watersheds. Topographical.

Deva-Prayâg, at the confluence of the Alaknunda with the Bhâgiráthi (or true Ganges), is twelve miles west of Srinugger (Tírí).‡ The former river before the confluence is the most considerable stream, having a breadth of 142 feet, and a depth of 46 feet, in the

---

* The Kumäon Forests may be classed as follows,—

1. Those on the Kosila
2. Grants (various)
3. Forest of Nindhoor and Surowa, Gorumma
4. Outer Ranges and Bhabur
5. On the Surjoo (Kaligunga)

(From Bengal Forest Reports.)

† Called the Surjoo in its upper waters. It rises under the peaks of Panchchooli. On its banks was enacted the prelude of the drama of the abduction of Sita, which led to the war of Râma with Ráwun, as related in the Ramayána, a beautiful epic poem of the Hindoos.

‡ There are nine intra-montane tributaries of the Bhágiráthi, in some of which gold is found interfused in the sand; also certain sacred pebbles used as charms by the Hindoos.

rainy season, above low water level. The breadth of the Bhâgiráthi is 112 feet, and it rises 40 feet in the rains. The union of these streams forms the Ganges, the breadth of which, below the junction, is 240 feet; at Hurdwar it discharges 8000 cubic feet per second. (Vide Section VIII., para. 7.)

Shrines, etc.

Other places of pilgrimage are Kédernâth, Bûdrinâth, Rûdra-Práyâg, Vishnu-Práyâg, etc.; these are mostly situated at the junctions of the main rivers. This will tend to show the sacred character of the country of Kumäon, and point its historical settlement; in fact, every stream, forest, or hill-top, has its own fabled story. The influx of devotees and Brahmins from the plains has for centuries been very great, and the present population may be held to have been formed thereby.

10. The preceding historical sketch has carried us south-east into the group of hill stations already introduced in this paper, and which we have defined as the group dominating Rohilcund and Oude.

Almora described

11. Almora (5,400) has already been mentioned in paragraph 3, as the modern capital of Kumäon. It stands on the ridge of a mountain in the midst of a bleak and naked country, and is approached by a long and steep zigzag road from the river, a path which a few resolute men might defend against an army. It was taken by the Goorkhas in 1790, and by the British in 1815. A new citadel called "Fort Moira," is built on the western extremity of the plateau; it occupies a strong position, but is in disrepair. This, as a citadel or refuge for Europeans, with the other old native fort at the east end of the ridge, appears to me to constitute ample defence for the capitol town, which, with the exception of a few earthworks, requires no further defensive works. I regard it as an excellent military position, and a support for our frontier posts, Pithór-agarh, etc., towards Nepâl. It is capable of much expansion especially along the Bhinsir ridge, and it commands valuable tea lands. It is bare, but seems

above the zone of malaria, and healthy, except that its sanitation has been neglected, and high crops allowed to intrude too closely on the station. Its climate is not so cool as Ránikhét (which is visible from the ridge across the valley of the Kósila) or even as Nainee-Tal, from which it is distant 24 miles; but I should consider it to enjoy a better climate than the latter, and I could have wished the sanitary depôt there located could be removed to Almora, if for no other than sanitary reasons alone; for I cannot but regard it as one of the worst hill climates I have visited; its military position is inferior, and I distrust the slopes of detritus and slatey conglomerates on which many of the houses of Nainee-Tal are built.*

The town of Almora consists of one long street three-quarters of a mile long, with a natural pavement of rock, and a gate at each end. It is a town of very sacred character, inhabited by Brahmins of the Brahmins, and was formerly one of the great refuges to which Hindoo fugitives from the plains of India, escaping from Mahomedan usurpation, gravitated. The heat in summer is considerable, but tempered by a fine breeze; the nights are always cool. I should consider that a sanitarium for European children might here be located, as less severe than Ránikhét.

12. Ránikhét (7000), on the other hand, is a fine pine-clad plateau, where half-a-dozen British regiments might be cantoned, fairly accessible from the plains; but less valuable—to my thinking—than Almora as a military site, though a splendid location for a "reserve circle." It might also, perhaps, form an appropriate site for an "industrial circle" or "colony," such as have been proposed. **Ranikhet and its environs.**

13. This can be no more than a sketchy outline. A few touches to indicate *Nainee-Tal* (6,400), and we must leave this interesting group. The lake of Nainee- **Nainee-Tal and its environs.**

---

* This was written in 1874. Since then a destructive landslip has corroborated this opinion.

Tal—a picturesque tarn nestled in its deep rugged glen—is probably of volcanic origin, as sulphur springs are found at one extremity. It is surrounded by the slatey *skrees* of Cheena and Iapáthá, with the wooded oak-covered slopes of Sher-ka-danda, whence can be viewed (from the *Snow-seat*) a glorious panorama of the snowy range, 300 miles in stretch. Looking east the beautiful but malarious valley of the Kurnah lies at one's feet, whilst inwards to the west the picturesque church and rugged glen of Sookha-Tal, with its haunted rocks and dells, are included within the limits of the Nainee-Tal valley and station.* The detritus of several landslips, interesting as evidences of the cataclysms of former ages, their taluses abutting into the valley, many of them covered with foliage, can also hence be seen, interesting but not devoid of evil auguries. The lake, with its aquatics, forms also a great attraction, and a cheery feature of this pretty little hill station, of which we must now take leave. Though beautiful, it possesses less capabilities of expansion than almost any other, nor is its climate bracing or suitable for the *cure* of an invalid; or over well adapted for a *sanitary* depôt; albeit a charming summer resort for the pleasure seeker and lover of the "ladies of the lake," and pleasant social life.

A few elevations of points near Nainee-Tal are as follows:—

Flood level of Lake 6,410 feet, (depth 15½ fathoms), 93 feet.

Mountain—Cheena,	...	1 mile	N.,	8568
„ Iapátha,		1 „	S.W.,	7,720
„ Sher-ka-Dunda,		3 „	S.E.,	8000?
Valley of Kurnah	-			3000 to 5000
Nainee-Tal Church	-			7000
Sookha-Tal	-			6,700

14. A few words may be devoted to the outpost of

* Dwálagiri is visible, elevation 26,826, also Budrinauth 23,221; and Nanda Devi 25,700, with the range mentioned in para. 4.

XXI.

Pithoragarh. Kumaon, from the Chandag Hill, looking east. Section VI.

XXII.

Loharghat, Kumaon. Nepal Mountains in the distance. Section VI.

Pithóragarh, a native cantonment on the Nepâl frontier, where 100 Goorkhas are quartered. It forms a fine, well cultivated plain, with an elevation of 5,600 feet, and is immediately surrounded by hills rising to 8000 feet, together with the valley of Seul, it forms a fine rolling country, grassy, free from malaria, suited for European colonization. It is defended by a fort and block-house or tower. **Pithoragarh.**

Lohárghât, another outpost on the Nepâl frontier, contains a small garrison of native soldiers, and embraces a few slopes and a *terre-plein* suitable for a small European colony. Several tea estates already exist in the vicinity. **Loharghat.**

Throughout Kumäon ridges and slopes of considerable elevation suitable for individual settlers exist, and have already been availed of to a considerable extent in the tea interest. The country, however, is rather of a pastoral than agricultural character, although terraced up here and there along the rivers for local grain growing. There is much barren, rugged land, and the ridges are contorted, and valleys consequently contracted in the upper parts of Kumäon and East Gurhwâl, and on the whole the fertility of this district is not great.*

---

* The table given at the end of Section IV. includes the flora of Kumäon and East Gurhwâl, to which, however, a curious addition must be made in the *screw* pine—perhaps Pinus Sinensis or Abies Webbiana?—a tree of extraordinary character, inasmuch as *it acts as its own executioner*, by some unexplained action screwing its own head off; and it is a remarkable fact that even after it is cut down and sawn into planks, even then action goes on, and the timber warps and twists to such an extent that when used as rafters it has been known to push the roof of a house off! This extraordinary fact requires scientific explanation, which, to my knowledge, has never yet been afforded.

SECTION VII.

NEPAL

(KHATMANDOO) AND THE BASINS OF THE (1) KARNALI, (2) GANDAK, (3) COSI.

Nepal wedged in between our Himalayan Possessions, a standing menace.

A LONG hiatus now occurs, interposing some 500 miles in our imaginary perambulation of the Himalayan watershed, between Kumäon and the next step on our southward progress,—a space occupied by the independent State of *Nepâl.* This mountain kingdom absolutely commands and dominates our provinces of Southern Oude, Behár, Tirhoot, and Northern Bengal, and threatens by flank pressure the entire Gangetic Valley. The country of modern Nepâl includes the Alpine basins of the Karnáli, Gandak, and Côsi. The two last are currently believed each to receive the collected waters of seven tributaries, hence they are called *Sapt* Gandaki, *Sapt* Côsika, and together with the valley of the Gôgra (or Karnáli), constitute the modern kingdom of Nepâl. Each of these basins is bounded or dominated by its glacier peak—as shown in the sketch map—which, in fact, for the most part, contributes the headwaters which flow into it, though a few of the feeders of the main streams—such as the Arun—have their sources across the snowy range in Thibet. The offset ridges which intersect and form the natural boundaries between these basins constitute subsidiary watersheds.

The Valley of Khatmandoo.

2. The area of Nepâl has been officially estimated at 54,000 square miles, population 1,940,000, and its revenue £320,000; its seat of government is at Khât-mándoo, the Goorkha capitol. The Valley of Khât-mándoo is a fertile valley, about 50 miles in circumference, having a somewhat oval shape. It is stated to have originally—like Cashmere—formed the bed of

a lake, whose alluvial deposits formed the present fertile soil. It is a lovely valley, studded with villages and orchards and waving crops. The capitol (Khâtmándoo) was built by the Goorkhas. Pátu the ancient Newár capital was not far off. Nöa-Kôte, about 20 miles north-west of Khâtmándoo, is an important, well-built town, in the midst of a fertile valley some six miles in length, close under the snows of Dëodunga, over the shoulder of which mountain the Chinese army in A.D. 1792, passed. It is situated on the Trisoolgunga, and is a frequent residence of the Nepâl Court in consequence of its mild climate. Bhátgong is another large town of Nepâl, in the same valley of Khâtmándoo, and contains 12,000 inhabitants, chiefly Brahmins. Elám, Dhánkote, Phíkul, are also considerable towns, and capitols of districts in Eastern Nepâl. The chief shrine in the valley of Nepâl is the Temple of Sumbhoonâth, where a colossal figure of Boodh is to be seen.

Mountains and Passes.

3. The valley is surrounded by lofty mountains especially to the north, by the grand snowy range, in which occur the peaks of "Dwâlagíri" (27,600), "Gossainthán" (24,700), Sheopoori, &c.; and Garui-Sánker (29,002), or Dëodunga (Mount Everest)—the highest mountain in the world—is comprised within this range. The spurs of Kánchanjinga (28,176) also extend down along the Nepâl eastern frontier, and connect this range with that of Sikhim and south-eastern Thibet. It is not certain, however, whether the true axis of the Himalayas is to be found in the chain of Ghauts, averaging about 20,000 feet in elevation, or beyond in Thibet near the Sampoo (Brâhmâpootrâ) watershed, and that of the Indus, north-west. (Vide para. 1, Section V.)

A secondary range called the "Lâmâdangra," extends along the temperate zone of Nepâl, parallel to the Himalayan peaks, at a distance of 15 or 20 miles from the plains, at a general elevation of 6000 feet above sea level. From this subsidiary range radiate the spurs which intersect the whole country, and supply the streams which feed the main rivers.

The Passes into Thibet are (1) Taklak-har, (2) Mustang, (3) Kerung, (4) Kuli, (5) Hattia, (6) Wollung, (7) Laken—Sikhim. The Kerung Pass from Khâtmándoo leads into Thibet. In 1790 the Nepâlese crossed by this pass and sacked Shigátze. In 1857 Chinese troops threatened this frontier! The Wallanchoon Pass in East Nepâl, the Kuli in central, and Joomla Pass in West Nepâl leading into Thibet, are also quite practicable for troops, but more properly belong to Sikhim.

Rivers.

4. The rivers of Nepâl are the Karnáli, the Gandak, the Trisûl-Gunga, the Côsi, and Bhâgmutty,* having their sources at about 12,000 or 13,000 feet. The Alpine basins are as follows, (1) the Karnáli basin, (2) the Sapt (seven) Gandaki, containing the old *chowbisi* or 24 Raj's of old Nepâl, and (3) the Sapt Côsika, includes the old Rajs of Kirautis, Limbhoos, etc., the ancient dominant races. The Arûn has a trans-nivean source, and cuts the line of Ghauts. The Sampoo—now fully recognised as the upper course of the Brâhmâpootrâ—is called "Erû or Yeroo" in Thibet, which term seems synomymous with *Gunga* in India, as a generic name for *a* large river.

Duns or Maris.

5. Dûns are called "Máris" in Nepâl, and the Bhâbur or Terai subtends each fluvial basin. These are—from west to east—(1) the Sallyár-mári, (2) Gongtali-mári, (3) Chitwár-mári, (4) Mikwáni-mári, (5) Bijapûr-mári: they afford examples of quasi-dûns or valleys beyond the first ranges. As before stated, the three lower great fluvial basins of Nepâl are the Karnáli, Gandak, and Côsi, which contain all the mountain country, and receive the streams from the

Great Fluival Basins, three in number.

* The Nepâl rivers all trend towards the east, the land having an oblique dip eastwards. The Teesta, which formerly fell into the Ganges, now falls into the Brâhmâpootrâ, indicating a tilt in the land. See para. 9, Section iv.

watershed of Nepâl, it being understood that each basin includes all its remote feeders. The peaks subtended by these Alpine basins are given in para. 3. The "Cachár" is the juxta-nivean tract close along under these peaks, and extends from the Kâli to the Méchi; in short, the length of the modern kingdom of Nepâl exceeds 450 miles.

6. The products of this fine hill country are—lead, sulphur, etc., and zinc mines exist. There are also copper and iron. The Nepâlese work well in copper, much of which is imported. Very good paper is made in the country. Gold, musk, borax, rhubarb, salt, (a little silver from Thibet); horses, *pearls* and *coral*—strange to say—are also exports. The timber trade has not been developed. *Tea* is grown in the eastern or Sapt-Côsika districts, especially in Elám and Phíkul, where the author has seen it, and other valuable products. The district of Malebûm on the river Gandak, 80 miles north-west of Goorkha, produces sulphur, cinnabar, iron, copper, and zinc. It formed one of the old confederacy called "The 24 Rajs," absorbed by the Goorkhas in the last century. At least seventeen distinct varieties of rice are grown in the Nayakôte Valley and in the Biásis or low alluvial plateaux along the rivers; as also on the Tars or higher plateaux, on which, however, the higher order of grains are also grown. **Products.**

HISTORICAL NOTICE.

7. As regards the ancient history of Nepâl, it is difficult to obtain a copy of the Bansawâli or Parbuttia history of the Newár and Goorkha dynasties of Nepâl, the origin of which, moreover, is involved in considerable obscurity; but they may both probably be stated as derived from the Soorujbunsi clan of Rajpoots, and the present ruling dynasty affect to derive from the Rajpoot princes of Oodeypore; but the annals of Nepâl are, like that of most native dynasties, clouded by mythological fables. **Ancient History doubtful & clouded by fables.**

Modern Historical Events up to the War with the British in 1814-15 16.

The present reigning dynasty of Nepâl was established about A.D. 1768 by Prithivee Narain (Goorkháli), who was the ally of Runjeet Mull (son of Bhugunt Indro), whom he succeeded in 1722, the last Newár Chief of Nepâl. Called in as an ally to the aid of Runjeet Mull against the Chief of Khâtmándoo, he ultimately—like most allies—turned his arms against his employer, and after 20 years intrigue and hard fighting, gradually forced his way to supremacy, and obtained for his clan the sovereignity of Khâtmándoo, and the greater portion of the country now called Nepâl. Previous to this he had been simply chief of Goorkha, where the family is stated to have lived six generations before the conquest of the country by Prithivee Narain.

Ethnological derivation of the inhabitants of Nepal.

8. The antecedent origin of the Goorkhas is unknown, but, as before stated, they are believed to have been refugees from Rajpootana, on its conquest by the Mahomedans about the 15th century, and, as they themselves assert, are descended from the princes of Oodeypore. Prithivee Narain died shortly after his conquest, and his descendant nominally sits on the "guddee," (throne), but Chiefs of the Khus* tribe have gained the substantial power of the state, and in the person of the present Minister, "Sir Jung Bahadoor," are practically the real sovereigns of Nepâl. This strong clan of Khus seems to owe its origin to a mixed ancestry, namely, marriage of fugitive Brahmins from Hindoostan—whence they were driven by Mahomedan conquerors—with native Khasia women of the hill ranges, "Kashia" being the primitive name of the entire mountain range between Nepâl and Cashmere.

The tribes alrady mentioned—Newárs, Goorkhas, Khus, Thakoors, etc.—are of Aryan or Hindu origin.

* The Goorungs and Magars are military tribes associated with the Khass or Khus, as dominant in Nepâl. Hodgson enumerates 57 distinct tribes as inhabiting the ranges (of Nepâl) between the Brâhmâpootrâ and Ganges.

XXIII.

Fort and Valley of Elam, Eastern Nepal, from the Tongloo Ridge, with Phikul and the Lama Dongra Range in the distance. Section VII.

XXIV.

Sketch showing the true horizon of the Snowy Range from Mount Senchal near Darjeeling. Section VIII.
(Mount Everest, distant 80 miles; Thibet Peaks, distant 60 miles; Kanchanjinga, distant 40 miles.)

There are other numerous classes inhabiting Nepâl, some indigenous, others immigrant from Thibet. Amongst those of Mongolian stock may be mentioned Magars, Thappas, Goorungs, and Llamas, more or less of Mongolian type, and the ancient stock of the hill country of Nepâl. A more detailed description of these tribes can scarcely be entered on in this cursory sketch, for I find no less than 94 Brahmin and 263 subdivisional castes of the military tribes enumerated by B. Hodgson, at page 147 of his "Himalayan Papers," —Khus, Ekthanga, Thakoori, Thappa, Goorung, etc.* The reader will, perhaps, under these circumstances, be content with the synopsis given in the text on this head, and which was derived from other sources; and as I have found it corroborated by such an authority as Hodgson, it may perhaps suffice. The Chepangs and Kusundars are, I see, mentioned as wild savage tribes dwelling west of Nepâl proper.

Tribes infinitesimally divided.

Sketch of History of Nepal (1791): its aggressive character.

9. At the end of the last century the Nepâlese invaded Gurhwâl, and laid siege to Tangoor, but after it had resisted twelve months, the intelligence of a Chinese invasion raised the siege. The cause of this invasion was that in 1790 the Nepâlese had invaded Thibet and pillaged the temples; the Llamas obtained the aid of the Emperor of China, who despatched a force of 70,000 men against the Goorkhas.† The latter were defeated, and the Chinese General pressing his success, advanced into Nepâl as far as Nöokôte,‡

* Other tribes, such as Manjhes, Kumhars, Brahmes, Dunavos, and Dunes, inhabit the lowest and hottest valleys with impunity, enjoying an immunity from the effects of malaria—an extraordinary physiological fact.

† It is presumed that this force was collected in the western province of China. The distance from Pekin to Khâtmándoo, as estimated by the Nepâlese ambassador who conveyed the tribute to Pekin, was estimated at 1,268 koss, and according to the same authority one passes 607 bridges, 23 ferries, 150 lakes or tanks, 652 rivers, and 100 forts on the road.

‡ Nöokôte or Nayakote is about 7000 feet above sea level.

where he dictated terms, and reduced Nepâl to the condition of a tributary of China. The submission, however, was only temporary, the Nepâlese consenting to disgorge the plunder of the Boodhist temples of Thibet. In 1800 the legitimate King of Nepâl had been forced to seek an asylum with the British at Benares; in February, 1803, Umr Sing Thappa led an army against Sreenuggur the capital of Gurhwâl; the Rajah Purdooman Sah made a stand at Barahál, but had to fly; the Goorkhas accordingly occupied the Dûn. Purdooman Sah, however, renewed the struggle, and again gave battle at Kurbára, near Dehra, in January, 1804, but was killed in the action. The Goorkhas took possession of the country, and, as was their usual practice, cruelly harried the land, which, in fact, became literally a desert. Some of the succeeding Goorkha Governors, however, made efforts to restore the country. Their arms were extended west, and they had absorbed the hills to the Sutlej, and even besieged Kangra in 1808, during which the Dûn became a sort of reserve or base of operations. During the next few years the insolence and aggression of the Goorkhas in the direction of Tirhoot, Goruckpore, and Bareilly, and, in fact, all along the Gangetic frontier, led to hostilities with the British in 1814-15.

10. From 1792 to 1804 a treaty of commerce and alliance had existed between the British Government and Nepâl, which, however, was soon broken off, owing chiefly to the rapacity and aggressions of the latter, which at length arrived at such a pitch as to be unendurable, and eventuated in the Nepâlese war of 1814-15-16, the events of which are too generally well known to need much mention. After several repulses and losses (especially at Kalinga,* where Gillespie fell) the conduct of affairs was entrusted to Sir David Ochterlony, who brought the war to a successful issue, and peace was declared in March, 1816. Since that

* Three and half miles east of Dehra.

period the country — though at times the prey of anarchy, intrigue, and no common atrocities — has remained friendly, though exclusive, and the supremacy of Jung Bahadoor, the Regent Minister, is the best guarantee of peace. Of late years, under the strong rule of Jung Bahadoor, the menacing position of Nepâl has become less pronounced, and its attitude at present wholly quiescent, so as to escape much public attention. Let not, however, the fact of its former relations with us be ignored or forgotten! Its sting is much weakened, but still exists.*

11. In a time of profound peace it were futile to vaticinate the future of this fine hill country, containing as it does some of the best sites in every point of view for military settlements throughout the land. *Were it ours* I would name the *Valley of Khâtmándoo* as a site suitable for the *fourth* grand "Himalayan Refuge" or "Military Reserve Circle;"—the others being as before stated (1) Cashmere, (2) Keyonthâl (Simla group), (3) Mussoorie and the Dehra Dûn, or the Kumäon group of subsidiary stations, described in Section VI.

12. Failing Nepâl, we must seek our fourth Himalayan Refuge elsewhere, and passing south-eastwards may perhaps, in the country of British Sikhim find a fair substitute near the fine hill station of Darjeeling.

13. Immediately west of Nepâl was formerly the "country of the 24 Rajs," being as many petty states **The 24 Rajs.** unconnected by any common origin or system of defence, which may account for their subjugation or absorption by the Goorkhas. They mostly acknowledged, however, in some degree, the superiority of the Rajah of Jemlah. They may be enumerated as follows:—1 Goorkha, 2 Tannahung, 3 Palpa, 4 Rising,

* The author having made an official tour of the Nepâl eastern frontier may, perhaps, add in an appendix the prominent features of his report made on that occasion. (Vide Section VIII.)

5 Ghiring, 6 Goojarkote, 7 Dhor, 8 Bhirkote, 9 Ghorahung, 10 Nayakote, 11 Satahung, 12 Poin, 13 Lamjun, 14 Kaski, 15 Malebûm, 16 Galkot, 17 Gulmi, 18 Mussakot, 19 Tarki, 20 Khachi, 21 Argha, 22 Dhurkote, 23 Isma, 24 Rytahir.

Some of these chiefs had entered into leagues for mutual defence; and some were connected by common descent, such as the *atha*-bhaie or *eight*-brothers; and the *sath*-bhaie or *seven*-brothers.

Jemlah.

Jemlah is in the western district of Nepâl; its capitol was Chenâchin, built in a plain stated to be as large as that of Khâtmándoo, as well cultivated, and as populous, but higher above sea level, and its climate more severe. It was a great emporium for salt, musk, horses, and other products from Thibet. I should suppose that this fine hill plain with that of Pithóragarh across the Kâli, and Khâtmándoo on its other flank, were a fine locality for a hill settlement.

The 22 Rajs.

Another agglomeration of chiefships west of the river Rapti, was the region of the 22 Rajahs, one of whom—the Rajah of Jemlah—seems to have held some sort of feudal suzerainty over the rest, till absorbed by the Goorkha dynasty of Nepâl.

Jemlah, Chilli, Dang, Soliana, Malameta, Satatala, Jahari, Dharma, Kolpa, Rugun, Duti, Messikot, Gujal, Bangphi, Jajarkot, were amongst the chief of these petty states.

On the eastern district of Nepâl are several fine valleys, such as those of the Sun-Côsi and Arûn, close about Tumling-Tar, a town of 6000 inhabitants, situated in a plain 18 miles long by six miles wide.

The Káli Gandak, a river with a trans-nivean source, flows past the summit of Dwálagíri (26,800), probably within six to eight miles distant therefrom. The bed of the river here is a mean between Muktinâth (11,000), 22 miles *above* the pass, and Riri (1,460) 60 miles *below* it—say 6000 feet—the result being that the peak of Dwálagíri must rise sheer 20,000 feet above the river, presenting probably one of the most stupendous gorges in the world.

The route from Pokra to Tadum in Thibet follows the course of this river, and is hitherto quite unexplored by Europeans. Pokra (2,600) is at the foot of one of the Dwálagíri summits (23,000), whose horizontal distance is only 15 miles, with a direct altitude of 20,400 feet above it. These facts may tend to suggest the astonishing scenery that must here be presented. They are deduced from an inspection of trans-frontier map-sheet 9.

The route from Khâtmándoo to Darjeeling (*viâ* Darkuta and Elám) gives about 22 stages, a total distance of 250 or 260 miles.

SECTION VIII.

DARJEELING AND BRITISH SIKHIM,

PLATEAUX OF THE TEESTA, ETC.

Darjeeling and British Sikhim.

WE now come to Darjeeling, the chief station in British Sikhim, where there is a Convalescent Depôt of 200 men, and a battery of Royal Artillery armed with some four small mountain train post-guns. This fine station would, in the event of rupture with Nepâl, form the *Refuge* of the whole district, and in its present strength might be much pushed to maintain itself, for I may say that by converging roads on our Frontier Post No. 17, from the Nepâlese fort of Elám — which is within 20 miles of Darjeeling — a hostile force might be, in the course of one long moonlight night, thrown across our communications with the plains *viâ* Kursiong, etc. Such an eventuality is scarcely probable, I only indicate its possibility; but in view of the importance of this position, should complications arise, I think that the garrison of Jullapahar (the burnt mountain), on which the barracks are situated, should be strengthened by a few pieces of heavy ordnance, etc., so as to enable a portion of the garrison to take the field if necessary, and operate on the "line of least resistance" leading into our territory.*

Area and Topographical features

2. The actual area of British Sikhim is not above 740 square miles, or as has been estimated by Government 250,000 acres for British Sikhim (including the ceded Döars east of the Teesta), to which may be added a like acreage for Independent Sikhim, or a total of 500,000 acres. British Sikhim, situated in 27° north latitude, 88° east longitude, is bounded on the

* See Report at end of this Section.

XXV.

General View of the Mass of Kanchanj nga above the clouds. From a photograph.
Section VIII.

XXVI.

View of Kanchanjinga from the Barracks, Jullapahar Cantonment, Darjeeling.
Section VIII.

north by the rivers Rummaun and Great Rungeet; east by the Teesta; west by Singaleela, Tongloo, and the river Mêchi; south indefinite. In the upper regions are found juniper, cypress, cedar, larch, yew, box, poplar, willow, and walnut. In the middle zone, birch, holly, oak, chestnut, magnolia, laurels, rhododendrons (scarlet, white, and pink), pear, cherry, thorns, elm, hornbeams, maple, tree-ferns, and palms. In the lower, or "morung," as the Sikhim *terai* is called, saul, sissoo, sémul (the cotton tree), pinus longifolia, figs, peepul, and acacias. The area of this last region of terai (spurs and forests) called the "morung," between the Mêchi and Teesta, is about 4000 square miles, with a population of 36,000 (Mechis, Dhoonds, Koochees, and a few Mahomedans). The soil consists of vegetable moulds passing into loam and gravel; rather sandy to east, clayey to west; its products being cotton, rice, hemp, oil-seeds, and tea.

3. The tea interest is here highly developed, and cinchôna is also grown. It has been estimated that the average out-turn of an acre of tea in the Sikhim district is as follows, *viz.*— Produce.

Of an acre	3	years old—	1	maund =	80lbs.
„	4	„	2	„	160 „
„	5	„	3	„	240 „
„	6	„	4	„	320 „

This may be considered a low estimate, the figures might probably stand at 100, 200, 300, 400lb., or even more as the out-turn. The highlands are pastoral. The sheep stock of this country cis-Thibetan, are three, *viz.*—(1) The Barhwál, a large horned white sheep with fair wool. (2) The Phéda, a black-faced horned sheep, are bred at high elevations, near the snows, the wool is fine. (3) An entirely black breed (horned), fine wool, bred at high elevations. There is still a fourth variety trans-Thibetan, a small hornless black-faced sheep, with very fine wool. This is a promising industry of this region. The cows of Sikhim (called the "Sher-gau,") are fine animals, mostly red, white, or spotted, and with no hump: the other—the Nepâl or Parbuttia—are smaller, and usually black or brindled. Pigs and poultry are fine and plentiful, and would form excellent stock for an industrial colony or colonies, such as are especially advocated for this district. Geese and ducks also thrive well.

Picturesque aspects of British Sikhim.

4. Of the aspects of nature in these grand mountains I need not speak. Who that has witnessed "Kanchanjinga," its peaks lighted up by the sinking sun, whilst the grey shadows of night are stealing over the lower mountains, can ever forget a sight almost unique in the world! The magnificent forests contain a flora quite distinct from that of the Northern Himalayas, and approach a sub-tropical or Malayan type, with tree-ferns and waving orchids, aruns, and ferns. The grand river scenery impending over the bright flashing waters of the Rungeet and its tributaries from the western watershed, with the deep green flood of the Teesta—semi-tropical foliage clothing its margin and lateral glens—certainly present glorious objects of admiration to the lover of the picturesque.

5. I am not here writing a guide book, and can scarcely in this place touch on the interesting Boodhistic localities, and Goompahs (Monasteries), which are found throughout Sikhim, at Pemiánchi, Toomlong (the capital of Independent Sikhim), Rumtik, etc. Innumerable *Harrs* or *Mendongs* (walls having slabs inscribed with the mystic "*Om-'om-máni-pémi-'om,*"*) also stud the upland spurs.

---

* This invocation is generally given as "Om-mani-*padmi*-om," but in the Sikhim district it differs, and is as in the text, *viz.*, "Om-om-mani-*pémi*-om." Scholars have translated the former, "Hail to the dweller in the lotus, amen!" My rendering of the latter is "Hail to (God) the all preserving the all punishing!" The word *pémi* clearly refers to the punitive attribute of Deity. I was most particular in my questions on this point to the second Llama of Pemiánchi (*Yar Bomboo* by name), who repeatedly denied the word *pémi* to have any reference to the Lotus. The Lepcha invocation may

XXVII.

Kanchanjinga (28,176), with Pemianchi Monastery, etc., from Kullock. Section VIII.

XXIX.

The Cinchona Grounds, Valley of the Rungbee, British Sikhim. Section VIII.

The inhabitants of Sikhim are divided into about eight different races, *viz.*— **Ethnological.**

(a) "Lepchas," these are of two clans—Kong and Khamboo—both having within the last two centuries immigrated from Thibet, the latter from the province of Kham (a district of Thibet next to China) seven generations ago. They are Boodhists, omnivorous, drink tea and murwah (millet beer), are partially nomadic in their habits. They wear the long straight knife called "Bân." **Tribes.**

(b) "Limboos," a Nepâl tribe, but found also in Sikhim. The name is a corruption of "Ek-thomba;" it includes the sub-tribes of Kerautis, Eakas, and Rais; they are said to have come from "Chung," a province of Thibet; they wear the "kookerie" or curved knife of Nepâl. Religion half Boodhist, half Hindoo. They are not ruddy like the Lepchas, eyes smaller, and nose also, but higher in the bridge than the Lepchas. They bravely defended their country against the Goorkhas.

(c) "Mechis." Inhabitants of the Terai—a belt of jungle of the lower hills—from Nepâl to the Brâhmâpootrâ; cast of face strongly Mongolian, closely allied **Terai.**

---

therefore differ from the orthodox liturgy of Boodhists, and may perhaps be a corrupted form, but assuredly no reference to the lotus is involved in it. The following were the *Llamas of Pemiánchi*—1 Durtzie Loben, 2 Yar Bomboo, 3 Rechú (son of Chibboo Llama), and 108 others, when visited by me 24th November, 1873. Besides the Goompahs (monasteries) already mentioned, there are as many as seven on the spurs of Kanchanjinga alone, forming with Pemiánchi itself a sort of holy land;—these are (1) Chángáchilling, (2) Tassading (Phándogat, Catsupperri), (3) Doobdie, (4) Sunnook, (5) Dholing, (6) Raklong, (7) Pemiánchi. There is also (8) a monastery near Mount Maimon on the Raklang Pass, on the watershed between the Teesta and Great Rungeet. Here the Lepchas made a stand against the Nepâlese in 1787. (9) *Mon Lepcha* was the original seat of the Lepchas after their immigration from Thibet. (10) The Kay sing mondong or Harr is 200 yards long with nearly 700 slabs. A monastery is called a *goompah*, a mausoleum a *chort*, a wall of slabs a *harr* or *mendong*. Phadung and Phazung are two of the monasteries closely adjacent to the capitol—Toomlong. The whole country is full of interest, strange to India.

to the "Mhugs" and "Burmese." No caste; omnivorous except as regards the elephant. They worship "Kâli," (the Earth Goddess). The Terai malaria does not affect them; they are a healthy race; they manufacture a red silk spun by the silkworm of the castor-oil plant. They have no written language.

(d) Haioos, a distinct tribe inhabiting the lower ranges of East Nepâl; worship Ráwun; in face Mongolian, bridge of nose not raised; stature short, cheek bones flat and very high.

(e) Moormees, a Nepâl tribe, but found in Sikhim as far east as the Teesta, a pastoral tribe rearing flocks at a great elevation; they ordinarily settle on mountain *tops* (whereas the Lepchas affect the hill-*sides*). Boodhists, language a dialect of Thibetan, but understood by the Bhootiahs; bury their dead on hill-tops; non-military.

(f) Bhootiahs, originally from Thibet; language a dialect of Thibetan. A very strong and robust tribe, carry enormous weights; closely allied to the Chinese in nature, and do not possess the light and cheerful nature of the Lepchas; can carry as much as six maunds *(say 500lbs.) 30 miles in a day!* The word Bhootiah is sometimes rendered "porters" or "carriers," as a generic term.

(g) Nepâlese, a light, nimble people of the poorer classes, much employed on tea gardens as agricultural labourers. They are Hindoos. The Nepâlese Government does not allow their families to leave Nepâl, hence they continue to regard themselves as Nepâlese subjects, though many of them smuggle their families across the frontier.

(h) Sheebahs, a mixed tribe—half Nepâlese, half Bhootiah—chiefly coolies or porters. There are a few other subdivisions of tribes not requiring special notice.

Mountains. 6. The whole country is mountainous in a high degree, the Darjeeling hill itself being 7,166 feet, whilst *Jullapahar*—the site of the barracks—is 7,800 feet. Senchåll exceeds 8000 feet; Singaleela—the spur of Kánchanjinga forming the Western frontier of Sikhim—10,000 to 12,000; whilst the highest peak of the great mountain Kánchanjinga rises to 28,178 feet above sea level. The mountain is considered a *month's march* to circumambulate, and includes many peaks exceeding 20,000.—The general level of the country being near 8000 feet. The following are a few further altitudes in Sikhim and basins of the Teesta and Arûn:—

Kánchanjinga 28,178. The Wallanchoon Pass (into Thibet) 16,750. The Núbra Peak 24,000. Junnoo Peak 25,312. Donkria 23,176. Chola 17,320. Nursing 19,139. Chumalhári 23,929. Mount Maimon 11,000. Mount Tendong 8,663. Mon Lepcha 13,080 (original seat of Lepchas after migration). Peak of Pindum 22,000. Kutera 24,005. Kanglanámoo Pass 15,000. Choonjerna Pass 15,260. Nango Pass 15,770. Kangláchar Pass 16,000 (thence three marches to Tashirukpa). The Catsuperai Lake, near Pémiánchi 6,040, and about 500 yards in diameter. The Chólahámoo Lakes (sources of the Láchen) 17,000. Siklo Donkria (sources of the Lachoong) 22,582. Paling Pass under Kánchanjinga 16,000. Peak of Donkria 21,870, Pass 18,450.

7. The Côsi, or Arûn (which enters the Ganges at Colgong), drains the watershed between Kánchanjinga and Gossein-thân. The Rutong, the chief head or tributary of the Great Rungeet, is *the* river of Kánchanjinga, *par excellence*, originating in its southern slopes. The Kullait, Little Rungeet, and Rummaum are tributaries of the Great Rungeet—all issuing from the watershed Spur of Kánchanjinga between Nepâl and Sikhim, which forms the boundary of British Sikhim. At the junction the Great Rungeet turns due east, and forms the boundary of British Sikhim, and ultimately falls into the Teesta towards Damsong and the ceded Döars. The *Teesta*—called above Singtam Rivers.

"The Lachen," or "Lachoong,"—is formed from two affluents of those names which unite at Chongtám 20 miles higher up. The Lachen rises in the Cholámoo Lakes, 17,000. The Lachoong rises from Donkria (Siklo), 22,582. The Ryott, Ruttoo, and Rungnoo, are tributaries of the Teesta above its junction with the Rungeet. These, with the Rungphoo, drain the subsidiary watersheds of the Great Rungeet and Teesta basins.*

The Lachen rises in the Cholámoo Lakes (17,000), and flows round the northern base of Kánchanjinga to the Kongra-Lama Pass. From the Donkria Pass, near Kiangtam, the axis or watershed of the Himalayan range is visible. Its southern drainage is into the Arûn, and its northern into the Yaru, Sampoo or Brâhmâpootrâ.

Passes. 8. The Wallanchoon Pass from Nepâl into Thibet—16,750. The route by the Kanglécheen Pass 16,000. The Nango, Kombácheen and Kánglanámoo Passes to Jongri in Sikhim, are open from April till November. The circuit of Kánchanjinga by the nearest route could not be accomplished under a month. The Paling Plains under Kánchanjinga 16,000 feet elevation. On the east the Chôla Pass, *viâ* Kabée, Pomunting, Laghep (10,423), is not less than 14,925, the Yakla Pass—15,600. These passes lead from East Sikhim through the Chumbi Valley, on to Gialze and Llássa: as far as I have had opportunity of examining them, they seem unusually easy and practicable for traffic. There are some rather interesting small lakes in this vicinity, especially near the Yekla Pass route. A fine view is

---

* As a comparison it may be stated that at Chongtám, the junction:

The Lachen	...	discharges	4,420	cubic feet per second
,, Lachoong	...	,,	5,700	,,
,, *United* Stream (or *Teesta*)		,,	10,120	,,
,, The Ganges at Hurdwar		,,	8,000	,,

and is 80 feet wide at Tupobun gorge, whereas the Lachen is 68 feet wide at the junction: the Lachoong 95 feet. The former being, however, the more rapid stream.

XXVIII.

Looking down the Teesta from the junction of the Great Rungeet, Sikhim. Sect. VIII.

obtained of the Chumbi Valley across the axis, from the Yezlep Pass (14,000). There is still a fourth pass from the south frontier to Chumbi—the Gnatissla Pass, near the Nemitzoo Lake,* but I have not seen it.

9. There are some fine plateaux across the Teesta, in this district, which would, in my judgment, form excellent localities for Industrial—or even Military—Circles such as have been advocated. Should trade relations ever be opened with Thibet they would form appropriate depôts or marts for commerce. I would mention the plateau of Dámsong and the bluffs of the Kalling-pong ridge. Here indiarubber and shellac are found; gypsum crops out of the hillside. Land very fertile, and a distinctly Alpine flora is found at a general elevation of 6000 feet.

10. On the whole, this may be considered a very favourable district for the establishment of an "experimental military reserve circle," such as have been advocated. There are several splendid plateaux, both in British Sikhim and across the Teesta, excellently adapted for the purpose; and it is further believed that an arrangement could be made with the "Durbar" of Independent Sikhim, whereby in consideration of a pension or money gratuity, the country up to the frontier might be acquired by us, and the Sikhim Raj revert to its original cradle across the passes—Choombi in Thibet—where, indeed, half its territory at present lies, across the Chôla pass. The country up to the granite walls of Thibet would then be ours, and available for settlement; and I scarcely know of any country more calculated to form a refuge or "military circle" such as I have suggested. In this fine hill district, then,—since Nepâl and the Valley of Khâtmándoo cannot be availed of—I would suggest the establishment of a Grand Southern Military Reserve Circle for Bengal.

11. The writer has made many trips in this district,

---

* Sir R. Temple's Report.

but an appendix would be necessary to show the details. Across the Teesta the Kallapong and Dámsong plateaux are found most favourable for settlements. Could water be obtained at the bluff I should consider the Dámsong plateau especially, the most favourable for military settlement in the whole of this range. With reference to the opening out of trade routes into Thibet, they should, I think, be traced *viâ* Titalya, Julpigorée, and Dálinkote, on the *left* bank of the Teesta to Dámsong and the Chôla, thus turning the intra-montane rivers Rungeet and Teesta. The spur between the Kánjûlia outpost on the Nepâl road, and Gôke on the Sikhim road, may be also noted as a favourable locality for an industrial settlement; and I think Government would do well to possess themselves of "Lebong" whilst in the market for a sanitarium, for which it is more suitable than Jullaphar. The latter might then become a cantonment for regular troops—say a wing of a British regiment, or more, with a battery of Royal Artillery. I think the railway terminus should be near Titalya, with branches to Julpigorée and Silligoree, for Darjeeling and Kursiong.

Trade Routes, and Sites for Settlements.

12. For a further general physical description of the topography of these hills, "Hooker's" Himalayan journals may be consulted. Dense bamboo forests clothe the western frontier or ridge of Tongloo, and form an effectual barrier to an invader, except by the converging roads on Post 17—from Elám—already mentioned in para. 1. The frontier road is cut through these forests from post to post, and forms the only pathway.

Topographical.

I must conclude this very brief notice of a most interesting locality, by saying that the position of Darjeeling is even at present of considerable strategic value, and under certain contingencies might become much more so. It commands—or should command if developed as has been proposed—Southern Tirhoot and north-east Bengal up to the Brâhmâpootrâ, and it is believed that when the railway, now in course of construction, shall have been carried to the foot of these fine hills, not only will an increased outlet for commerce—especially tea—be thereby afforded, but ultimately our trade relations with Thibet, and even China, will find through the Eastern Döars, and the Yekla and Chôla Passes, their legitimate development: we may then anticipate a still "brighter" future for this "bright spot."* There is a volunteer corps in this district, with one centre or company at Darjeeling, and the other at Kursiong 18 or 20 miles distant, on the Calcutta road, and as this is a country where a handful of men skilfully handled might hold in check or defeat hosts, I cannot see why, with the small additional resources I have indicated, this district should not hold its own, and, indeed, form a refuge for outlying settlers in times of peril.

HISTORICAL NOTICE.

13. The history of British Sikhim is briefly as follows:—Darjeeling having been established about 1835 by the cession of a small tract of land by the Rajah of Sikhim for the purposes of a sanitarium, was gradually— under the able superintendence of Dr. Campbell from 1839 to 1861—settled, and rendered prosperous. In 1849 Drs. Campbell and Hooker, being on a botanical tour in Sikhim, were imprisoned by the Rajah, and the first rupture with the State took place. As a punishment for this outrage the British Government resumed the land, now called British Sikhim, that had formerly been bestowed on the Sikhim Raj as a reward for alliance in the Nepâl war of 1815-16. In 1860 the Sikhim Court having countenanced kidnapping our subjects, and generally displaying insolence, an expedition under Dr. Campbell went out into the north-west district to Rinchinpoong, but after a temporary occupation of that frontier was dislodged and

* Darjeeling or "Darjegling" means "bright or holy spot."

utterly dispersed by the Sikhim Bootiahs, and its one gun captured: early in 1861, however, a force under Lieut.-Colonel Gawler, H.M.'s 73rd Foot, consisting of two howitzers, with a detachment of artillery, 300 of H.M.'s Royal, and about as many Sikhs and sappers, crossed the river Rungeet into Independent Sikhim on the 2nd February, 1861, and after some slight resistance occupied Toomlong, the capital town, on the 9th March, when the young Rajah surrendered, and a treaty of peace was signed on the 28th March of the same year. Since then Sikhim down to the present time has been quiescent and civil, but distant. In June, 1873, a visit of the Rajah and his family to the representative of Her Majesty—Sir George Campbell, Lieut.-Governor of Bengal—took place at Darjeeling, and this may probably be viewed as the first step in a new order of things, pointing to opening out trade relations with Thibet *viâ* the north-east passes.

APPENDIX TO SECTION VIII.

Extracts from Reports on the Military Defences of Darjeeling, by Colonel D. J. F. Newall, R.A., commanding:—

Darjeeling, 4th January, 1873.

Defence of Darjeeling, No. 2. Sir,—Having in accordance with the intentions expressed in my "Report on the Defences of Darjeeling," dated 1st of August, 1872, completed a Military Inspection of the frontiers of British Sikhim, I have now the honour to submit the following remarks as a sequel thereto, and solicit the favour of your laying them before His Excellency the Commander-in-Chief at an early convenient opportunity.

(1) My Report, dated 1st August, 1872, pointed merely to a defence of the Town and Station of Darjeeling, but inasmuch as much valuable property is included within the district, I have deemed it expedient to acquire a knowledge of the frontiers where it is possible an enemy might be met with advantage, so as, if possible, to keep him at arm's length, out of the district altogether.

(2) It is doubtless well known to His Excellency that a

XXX.

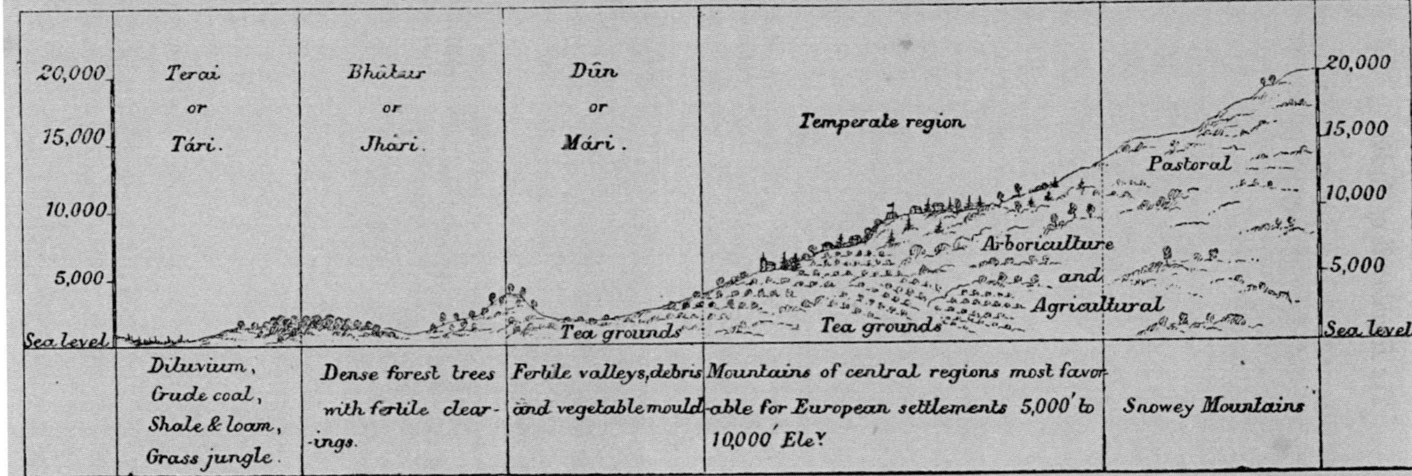

IMAGINARY SECTIONAL VIEW OR PROFILE OF THE HIMALAYA MOUNTAINS. Sections IV. to VIII.

belt of dense bamboo forest clothes the crest of the hills bounding the Western or Nepâl Frontier, which forms a very effectual barrier to any possible invasion from that quarter in force, but there is one weak point which attracted my notice, and which I consider it right to mention, as bearing on the subject of this Report.

(3) Behind the ridge forming our boundary—called, I believe, "Tongloo"—exists the Fort of "Elam" in Nepâl, some eight miles from the frontier, dominating a fertile valley; here the Nepâlese government possesses a considerable garrison, with granaries, store houses, and, as I am informed, several field guns. This fortress is about eight hours or less from our frontier pillar or post No. 17, which is situated at the point where our boundary line of road turns north along the Nepâl frontier, and which is itself about equidistant from our own position at Jullapahar, by an easy, level road. From this Fort of Elam (3) three roads converge on Pillar 17, so that—granting the desire of aggression on the part of the Nepâlese Government, and that they could have the address to conceal their preparations till the last moment—I can see nothing to prevent their marching by these converging roads on the point indicated, and in the course of one long night throwing a force of 5000 or 6000 men, with a couple of mountain batteries, right across our communications with the plains; in other words occupying the ridge from "Lepchajuggut" to "Senchál," the key of Darjeeling, by an army twenty or thirty times the strength of the garrison.

(4). The garrison of Post 17, at present, consists of one police constable.

(5). It would not become me to vaticinate, or to point to possible political complications, or venture on suggestions beyond my immediate province, but I cannot help stating that I think a Block-house calculated to hold, on an emergency, from 50 to 100 native levies or police, should be quietly constructed at this point. Were the garrison at Jullapahar sufficiently strong to detach, I would select this point to occupy in strength, there to meet the enemy on the frontier, and prevent his debouching on the basin valley of Darjeeling, where much valuable property would be at his mercy for plunder; but the numerical strength of the present garrison would not admit of detaching any sufficient force of regular troops, who would be amply occupied in the defence of the town and suburbs of Darjeeling. More could not be attempted. The Post No. 17 in question could perhaps, however, be held by police or volunteers placed in telegraphic communication with the main position of Jullapahar, and would form a valuable outpost on *the line of least resistance* into our territory. If unable to hold the block-house suggested, the garrison might retire on ambuscades or other strong positions previously prepared by the regular troops in rear. Should, moreover, the British garrison of Jullapahar ever reach 300 men, it is believed that half that number—including a portion of the artillery with guns—might be safely detached towards the outpost named for the above purpose.

(7). In view, however, of the importance which a successful effort on the part of the enemy would confer on the position of Senchál, and the ridge south-west if in his possession, I would propose to modify the scale of ordnance recommended for the defence of this station in my Report of 1st August, 1872, and instead of the howitzers named, would incline to prefer two additional 40-pounder Armstrongs, as—from their longer range—better calculated to dislodge an enemy who had gained possession of the ridge named. The ordnance therefore recommended would be as marginally noted. I consider these essential to the adequate defence of this station under circumstances that might occur in the future; and I would earnestly and respectfully urge that the supply of this ordnance be considered of.

Four 40pr. Armstrongs,
Two 10in. mortars,
Four light brass 5·5 inch or 4·4 inch ditto,
beside the four mountain guns already here.

(8). It occurs to me to remark that several very promising plateaux for sites for "military colonies" or "reserve circles," such as have at times been advocated as a means of frontier defence, exist in this district; such are found at "Dámsong," "Kalingpoong," on the Bhootan frontier to the east across the Teesta; the long ridge spur between the Kanjûliá and Gôke outposts on north-west, besides the Lebong spur in the immediate vicinity of Darjeeling.

(9). The Military Communications of this district appear generally good, but a Report on the Frontier Defences of the district would be incomplete without some allusion to the Passes south of Post 17 from Nepâl leading towards Kursiong,

Pankabarrie, &c., and the lower hills towards the Terái; especially that from Phíkul in Nepâl *viâ* the sources of the Méchi, Mirig, &c. This road, as ascertained by personal inspection, is fairly good, and quite practicable for native troops. The district of Phíkul is singularly fertile, and commands resources available to an enemy in event of aggression from that quarter. It is not above six or seven miles from Elam. In the event of invasion thence the garrison of Darjeeling, when numerically increased, might perhaps detach as far as Kursiong, not further!

Paras. 10 and 11 advocate formation of a *volunteer rifle corps.*

(12). Concluding remarks.

I have the honour, &c., &c., &c.,

D. J. F. NEWALL, Colonel R.A.,
Commanding at Darjeeling.

SECTION IX.

THE KHASIA HILLS,

WITH ASSAM, SILHET, CACHAR, & MUNIPOOR.

SHILLONG (6,500), CHERRAPOONJEE (5,600), ETC.

Khasia & Cachar Hills and Stations

OF Shillong and the Khásia Hills I am scarcely qualified to speak from personal knowledge, and must therefore advance my opinions with some diffidence, and borrow largely from other travellers. Although of slight importance in a strategic point of view, they—with Munipoor—nevertheless form an outpost against Burmah, and probably contain excellent sites for settlements of *individual* colonists, and offer small sanitaria for the adjacent tea lands of Assam, so well known as the most productive centre of that rising industry. Although they form a section of the "Highlands of India," I cannot indicate them as a promising locality for a "military reserve circle," nor would they find scope for mention here, did they not indirectly influence our north-east frontier, and form a lever against Burmah and quasi-Chinese pressure, Bengalwards. Perhaps their importance in this respect may hereafter increase.

2. The access to Shillong is by water, ordinarily by rail to Kooshtea, and so by Dacca up the Brâhmâpootrâ, Megna, and Soormah Rivers to Cherrapoonjee and Shillong. The Soormah drains the Cachár, Jyntia, Khásia, and Garrow Hills; in the rains it forms a vast jheel or shallow sea, having an area of not less than 10,000 square miles. It rises on the Munipoor frontier. Contrary to all expectation this is a healthy district, and free from the malaria of higher and more wooded

districts, and on the whole I may perhaps modify what has been said above in favour of the *southern* aspects of the Khásia Hills as a site for colonization.

Topographical, Flora, etc.

3. From Cuttack, on the Soormah, the Khásia hills appear as a long flat-topped range, running east and west, 4000 to 5000 feet high, steep towards the jheels. About 12 miles distant the waterfalls of Moasmai are seen falling over "the cliffs with a bright green mass of foliage that seems to creep halfway up their flanks." This place—as the jheels generally—is extraordinarily healthy, being, like Cachár and Silhet generally, free from malaria. The products are oranges, potatoes, coal, lime, and timber. The Soormah rises 50 feet in the rains; the Northern Terái of the Khásia hills, however, at this period, is most deadly. The flora of the Khásia forests differs from that of the Himalayas, consisting of bright green evergreens and palms, whereas the former are chiefly large forests of deciduous trees; the laurel and betel-nut are found, oaks, oranges, bamboo, gamboge, plantains, and vines, with palms and cocoa-nuts, present a tropical flora of a Malayan character: orchids, ferns, and mosses, and grasses also abound. Fifty grasses and twenty sedges were found by Hooker in this district. On the road to Cherrapoonjee one passes the valley of Möasmai, where "several beautiful cascades rolling over the table top of the hills, broken into foam, throw a veil of silvery gauze over the gulf of evergreen" vegetation 2000 feet below. To give some idea of the exuberance of the flora of the Khásia hills, it may be stated that Hooker enumerates 2000 flowering plants within 10 miles of Cherrapoonjee, 15 bamboos, 150 grasses, 150 ferns, 250 orchids, and many mosses, etc. This great variety is attributable to the varied nature of the soil and climate, which embraces the stony plateau and the steaming forest.

Cherrapoonjee. The Moasmai Cascade.

4. Cherrapoonjee is on the high road from Silhet and Gowhatty, the capitol of Assam, on the Brâhmâpootrâ.

The view from the plateau of Cherrapoonjee is magnificent; 4000 feet below are valleys carpeted as with green wheat, from "which rise tall palms, tree ferns with spreading crowns, and rattans shooting their pointed heads surrounded with feathery foliage, as with ostrich plumes, far above the great trees. Beyond are the jheels, looking like a broad shallow sea with the tide half out, bounded in the blue distance by the low hills of Tippera. To the right and left are the scarped red rocks, and roaring waterfalls shooting far across the cliffs, and then arching their necks as they expand in feathery foam, over which rainbows float, forming and dissolving as the wind sways the curtain of spray from side to side."—(Hooker.)

Panoramic Views inland.

5. Inland at about 5000 feet, the country is open and bare, till the valleys of the Kálapáni and Bógúpáni* are crossed. Beyond this the Bhotân Himalayas may be seen at the astonishing distance of 160 or 200 miles. Môflog, on the axis of this range, is 6,062, with a splendid view of Bhotân, but from Shillong (6,600)—the highest point of the Khásia range—a truly magnificent panoramic view is obtained of an area of 340 miles. The view embraces nearly an entire circle. To the north are the rolling Khásia hills and the entire Assam valley, 70 miles wide—100 miles distant—and the great river Brâhmâpootrâ winding through it—50 miles distant—reduced to a thread. The first ranges of the Himalayas are 100 to 200 miles from Shillong. These snowy mountains are below the horizon of the observer, and occupy 60° of the horizon = 250 miles. To the west are the Garrow hills—40 miles distant—and eastwards the loftier Cachár hills (4000 feet) 70 miles off. To the south the Tippera hills, 100 miles distant, bound the horizon, whilst to the south-west lies the sea-like Gangetic delta. Fully 20,000 square

---

* This river disembouches into the Jheels at Chóla west of Cheerra, forming rapids below this point.

XXXI.

[Falls of Moasmai, Khasia Hills. Section IX.

XXXII.

Cherrapoonji. Khasia Hills. Section IX.

XXXIII.

The Kullong Rock on the Moflog Plateau, Khasia Hills. Section IX.

miles are encircled in this area. The products are cinnamon, potatoes, iron, timber, cherries, etc.

6. The following are a few local features of these interesting hills:— Physical Features Altitudes, etc.

(a) From the West are (1) the "Garrow" Hills, (2) the Khásias proper, (3) the Jyntiah Hills, (4) Cachár and Nâgas as far as Munipoor. Ascending from the jheels towards Möasmai and the plateau of Cherrapoonjee we traverse first low wooded hills about 200 feet in height, rounded and beautifully wooded; then we find an abrupt precipice—3,500 feet—rising by successive gradients to 5000 or 6000. On the North, the hills suddenly drop at Munglew upwards of 2000 feet, and then gradually sink to the valley of the Brâhmâpootrâ.

(b) The "Kullong" Rock, a curious dome on the Môflog plateau—600 feet in elevation above the *terre-plein*—is of crystalline granite; the plateau itself is metamorphic, but contains greenstones and nummalitic limestones, the presence of "faults," and the intrusion of granite is found; elevation 4,500 to 5000 feet above sea level.

(c) The Cherrapoonjee plateau attains 4,200 feet in elevation. The rainfall in 24 hours has at times equalled 2 feet 6 inches!* a whole year's rain in Europe! and 600 inches of rain during the year is not an excessive quantity in the southern exposure of these hills. The denuding force of such is of course remarkable, and is evident in many parts. From Myrong, Chumaléri, and Donkria in Sikhim may be seen. The Eastern Khásia Mountains reach the Valley of the Kálapáni *viâ* Nokreen and Pomrang, thence enter the Jyntea Hills *viâ* the Valley of the Oongkoot. Hence are seen

---

* "Yule" states that "in August, 1841, at Cherrapoonjee, 264 inches fell = 22½ feet. 500 or 600 inches is no unfrequent annual fall at Cherrapoonjee, whilst at Silhet 30 miles distant it is under 100; in Assam at Gowhatty 80; at Shillong (20 miles inland from Cherrapoonjee) 200; at Darjeeling 110."

the Cachár Mountains with a general elevation of about 4000 feet. The following points being Amunee (3000), Joowje (4000), the hill capitol, Nurting (4178), the watershed of the Jyntea range 4500.

(d) The following are a few of the altitudes of these mountains, *viz:*—Cherrapoonjee 4,118, Lailankot 5,703, Bogapani 4,451, Pomrang 4,748, Jasper Beds 2,384, Myrung 5,537, Kálapáni Ridge 5,300, Fossil Beach Bed 2,974, Sohrung 5,355, Top of Waterfall N. of C.P. 4,860, Kullong Rock (top) 5,684, Top of Greenstone Manloh 3,200. Archæological remains are to be found in the vicinity of Nurting, bearing close resemblance to Celtic (so called Druid) circles, with stones 30 feet high. Pomrang, Syong, Nunklow, Baijaree, are important villages of this district.

Ethnological.

7. The tribes inhabiting this range are the Khásias and Garrows, who are of Indo-Chinese race, and are a muscular but rude and sulky race. The sister's son inherits, like some tribes of the western seaboard; omnivorous; dislike milk; believe in a Supreme Being and in "deities of the grove," cave, and stream; good cultivators, keep bees. The rainfall at some seasons in these hills amounts to 200 inches, and the climate of Assam, on the northern slopes of the Khásia hills, is so deadly as to form an additional objection to their colonization by British settlers, though probably private settlers of independent means may be able in a measure to baffle the climate.

As regards the land tenures of this province the sunnuds or grants show the dates of conquest, and are very varied. (1) The oldest tribes are Dhrumpals of Barmootan lands extending as far back as the 11th century. (2) Next come the grants of the Kings of Delhi, and the Mahomedan Governors of Bengal. (3) By the Ahôms to 1744, especially down to Rajah Sib Sing. The worship of *Sib* was the especial religion of ancient Kamroop. Some holdings are "lakraj" or free, some in fief, others freehold (pyka), on capitation or poll tax and hearth or plough tax. Products—rice, mustard, poppy, sugarcane, betel, pawn, tea, lac, cotton, silk, tobacco, fruits, and vegetables.

The time for development across the Brâhmâpootrâ, on our north-east frontier has scarcely arrived, but perhaps when the barrier of exclusiveness of Thibet has been removed, these provinces may share in the trade which has been indicated as likely to follow the opening of the railway and roads through Sikhim and the ceded Bhotân Döars into Thibet. The principal tribes around the valley of Assam may here be conveniently enumerated as follows:—1 Bhootias, 2 Dufflas, 3 Akas, 4 Kuppah Chowahs, 5 Meerrees, 6 Bor Abors, 7 Abors, 8 Mishmees, 9 Khumpties, 10 Bor Khumpties, 11 Mooamarias, called also Muttuks, Morahs, or Noras, 12 Singphoos, 13 Murams, or Nagas, 14 Mikirs, 15 Kacharies, 16 Cossyahs, 17 Garrows, 18 Kookies.

8. The principal Döars or Passes from the borders of Assam into Bhotân territory are 1 Nâgarkote (leading into Sikhim), 2 Dâlimkote (fort taken by Captain Jones in 1773), 3 Mynagorie, 4 Chunarchie, 5 Bolaturie, Lukipoor, 6 Madarie or Phalakottu, 7 Buxadöar (pass by which Captain Turner's embassy entered Bhotân, 8 Bhulka, 9 Uldiebarie to the north of Bhulka, 10 Goomar, 11 Roopu-Ramayana, 12 Chiring, 13 Bijnee, 14 Banksa, 15 Gurkhola, 16 Killing, 17 Boorie-Goomah (held alternately by British and Bhootiahs), 18 Kooree-Parah (held by Independent Bhootiahs), 19 Chardöoar (held by British Government, paying black mail to Independent Bhootiahs, Akas, and Dufflas), 20 Naodöoar (held by black mail to Dufflas). Passes, etc.

9. In order to reach Cachár the traveller should take boat at Pundua, and crossing the jheels to the Soormah, ascend that river to Silhet. Thence 120 miles of river journey takes him to Silchar, the capital of Cachár. Here the river is 200 yards wide, with a current of two or three miles an hour. The people are a strong, bold Mahomedan race. 70 miles up the

Soormah the mountains east of Jyntea rise 4000 feet above sea level, are forest clad, and very malarious, and quite unadapted for settlers. The Tippera, and, more distantly, the Kookee Hills 12 miles north, are seen from this part of the river. During the Burmese war a force held this point, which is mentioned because thus possessing some strategic value owing to its position.

The Arracan Mountains may just be noticed here. They rise from 3000 to 5000 feet above sea level, and extend from Cape Negráis almost to the river Brâhmâpootrâ in Assam. Several passes lead across from the valley of the Irrawaddy into Arracan; the ranges on the Burmese side being generally the easier, the western slopes being more abrupt. They are called "Yomadonng" or "Anamectop" Hills by the natives, and form a well defined boundary on the side of Ava.

HISTORICAL NOTICE.

Fabulous History of Assam, the ancient Kamroop.

10. We now pass to a brief historical sketch of Assam—the ancient *Kámroop*—of which kingdom Cachár, Munipoor, and Jyntea, were probably provinces. Its ancient history is of course mythical. We find the earliest traditions to extend to about 2000 B.C., when it is stated that Nârók, the son of Prtivi (the earth) was established by Krishna, who gave him charge of the great temple of Kámakya (the Venus of the East) near Gowhatty,—*Kámroop* being, as its name implies, the "region of desire" or love. Nârók was succeeded by his son Bhâga Dutta (or Bhâgirut), who is stated to have fallen by the hands of Arjoon the Pandau, in the war of the Mâhâbhârât. According to the same

Another account.

authority —"Aeen Akbarie"—23 princes of the same family reigned in Kámroop. Opposed to the foregoing account, however, the "Jôgíni Tantro"—considered the highest authority on Kámroop — states that the god *Sib*, husband of Parbuttee, being rival of Krishna, had prophesied "or evolved from his inner perceptions," that after Nârók, in the era of Sáka (*i.e.* 100 A.D.) Sudra Kings would rule Kámroop,—the first Rajah being Débêswár, in whose time knowledge would extend. Then a Brahmin named Nâga Sunker would be king, and extend Brahminical doctrines; after him Pritivie Raj. A sequel to this fantastic legend seems to point to a prince of the great Pal family—Dharma-Pal—as extending the kingdom of Kámroop by conquest; after whose death anarchy prevailed. After this Kámroop seems to have been overcome by a northern tribe, whose chief assumed a Hindoo name—"Niloahôj"—who fostered Brahminism, and established a dynasty which lasted three generations, and still further extended the kingdom of Kámroop. This may perhaps be assigned to about the 13th century. We then find the northern frontiers invaded by successive tribes, apparently "Shâns;" and we now approach the first reliable history of the country.

About this period—12th or 13th century—a Shân Kingdom may be stated as having arisen from the immigration of clans from Thibet, Siam, and Chinese Tartary, under the pressure consequent on the victories of Genghis Khan and Kublai Khan, which overturned the Chinese dynasty, and manifested itself in the Indo-Shân provinces. The Pong Kingdom appears to have been the original Shân possession, whence the Ahôms, under "Khûntai," established themselves on the upper waters of the Brâhmâpootrâ,* gradually extending their conquests over Kámroop (Assam), Cachár, and Munipoor, where an allied or tributary branch seems to have ruled.

The name Assam did not come into use till about 1228 A.D.
1228 A.D., when "Chúkrapha, whose unrivalled" (Asâma) conquests raised him to the throne. The Ahôms—a tribe of probably a Shân origin—now come on the stage as the dominant tribe. Their origin, by

* The Yew or Sampoo of Thibet is now fully recognized and identified as the Brâhmâpootrâ.

their own accounts, is plunged in fable, more especially as the earlier Shân kings affected Hindoo genealogies, and assumed Hindoo names after their conquests. The ruling family, derived from two brothers, "Khûnlûng" and "Khûntai," who, quarrelling at the end of 14 years, Khûnlûng, the more peaceable of the two, "returned to Heaven," leaving Khântai, or Khûntai, as the founder of the Assam monarchy,* who declared himself descended from heaven (Swerga), and divided the soil of Kámroop, and the valleys of the Brâhmâpootrâ and Irrawaddy. This immigration appears to have taken place antecedent to Boodhism in those regions, as it is a curious fact that the Ahôms are the only Indo-Chinese clan in which that element is not found. The glory of the Ahôm dynasty of Assam seems to have culminated in Chukrungpha—or Rúdra Sing as he affected to be called—who, about the beginning of the 17th century, consolidated the countries of Assam and Cachár. The kingdom after this began to decline, and about the beginning of the present century we find armies of Burmese beginning to invade the country. Originally called in as allies they soon felt their strength, and finally expelled the reigning (rival) chiefs, and seized the country; and, after a time, began to evince dispositions hostile to the British. After fearful anarchy, by which Assam was devastated between 1794 and 1824, war was at length declared by the British, which ended in its absorption into British territory on 24th February, 1827, by the treaty of Yandaboo.

First Burmese War.

Cachar.

11. Cachár, and still more Munipoor, being nearer to Ava, and on the path of the numerous Burmese armies which traversed these provinces between 1809 and 1824, suffered still more than Assam, and the country was depopulated by these harrassing wars. Cachár — the ancient Hairumbo — was part of the

* Thirteen successors of Khuntai, the founder of the Ahôm Kingdom, are given; they nearly all exhibited proclivities towards Brahmanism. The Rajahs of Cooch Becha are an offshoot of this stock.

ancient kingdom of Kámroop. It first became known to the British about 1763, when Mr. Verelst led a small force into the country, which remained there; but it was not until 1809 that any decided intercourse took place with this petty state. In that year the Rajah Kishinchandra requested a small guard of British troops as guarantee for the security of his country during an intended pilgrimage. He died in 1813, and was succeeded by his son Goorúd Chándra, the only surviving descendant of "Bhím" the original founder of the family. His country was invaded by Marjeet Sing, a fugitive and rebel from Munipoor, who was followed by his brother Chorjeet Sing. Cachár from 1818 A.D.
this date became the arena on which the three Munipoor brothers contended for power. The country was harrassed by foreign troops, and ruined in these contests, and was finally absorbed by the Munipoories. Gumbeer Sing, the third brother, was finally successful; and being supported by the British Government against the Burmese, who interfered in the contest, obtained possession of Munipoor and Cachár. The Munipoor usurpers were, however, finally pensioned in 1824, and the legitimate Rajah restored to the principality of Cachár. His peaceful occupation was, however, disturbed by the various claimants and rebellions, and the British Government had to step in to support his tottering hold. He (Goorúd Chándra) was finally assassinated, and, dying without heirs, his 1830-32 A.D.
country was annexed to British territory, and has since remained a province of the British Empire.

12. Munipoor. It has been stated (para. 10) that Munipoor.
a tributary branch of the early Ahôm conquerors of Assam, ruled at Munipoor—the ancient kingdom of *Cathay*—which, however, was considered a branch of the original Shân or *Pong* Kingdom. Its history is thus involved in that of ancient *Kámroop*, and has already been given. A distinct list of kings however, 47 in number, commencing in A.D. 30 is given by

themselves; but no records of the slightest interest are recorded. An origin distinct from that of the Ahôms would thereby seem to be claimed, but they probably derive, like the Ahôms, from immigrant Indo-Chinese tribes, who, under pressure from China, gravitated westwards into the valley of the Irrawaddy in the 13th or 14th centuries. In the 15th century the States of Pong and Munipoor were united (by marriage), but the chronicles possess but little interest till comparatively modern times, when Painhïéba—
1714 A.D. better known as Rajah *Gureeb Nawâz*—succeeded to the throne, who, issuing from his mountain principality, invaded Burmah and carried his arms into the valley of the Irrawaddy, and even captured the capital city Ava. His wars and conquests extended over a period from 1725, when, having met with sudden reverses, his son Ugut-Sing, rebelled; his troops deserting him, he sought an asylum with his old enemy the King of Ava, whence, attempting to return, he was about 1753 —together with his eldest son—murdered by Ugut-Sing. The power of Munipoor culminated and sank with Rajah Gureeb Nawâz, and the chance of its becoming a dominant state passed away.

In 1755 the Burmese began to turn the tide of invasion, and to send armies to subdue Munipoor. *Alompra*, King of Burmah, invaded the valley in 1758, and occupied the capital after a sanguinary battle with its chief; but the Peguers having revolted in his absence, he had to abandon the country, and he died in 1760: nevertheless, the power of the Munipoor Rajah rested on so precarious a tenure that he (Jye Sing) applied to the British Government for aid, and a treaty offensive and defensive was in consequence negotiated with Munipoor, 14th December, 1762. Early in January,
1763. 1763, the British troops destined to relieve Munipoor marched from Chittagong, and reached the capital city of Cachár (Kaspoor) in April, where, however, they were detained owing to the setting in of the rains, and

Jye Sing failing to ratify the treaty, the force ultimately 1765.
retired. The Burmese again invaded Munipoor in 1765, expelled Jye Sing and set a stranger on the throne, but directly the Burmese retired Jye Sing returned and dispossessed the usurper. Having reorganised his power, he attracted anew the hostility of the Burmese, who again invaded the Munipoor valley; and after a desperate battle again totally defeated the Munipoories, 1765–82.
and the Rajah had to fly for his life to Assam.

Between the above dates Jye Sing had made four unsuccessful attempts to regain his throne; he then submitted, and as a vassal of Burmah reigned till 1798-9. He then set out on a pilgrimage, but died on the banks of the Ganges; his son, who succeeded him, was assassinated, and a series of treacheries and intrigues ensued until 1806, when Chorjeet Sing gained the throne. His brother Marjeet conspired against him, as also did the third brother Gumbeer Sing; a state of anarchy and intrigue ensued, Munipoor and Cachár being its arena. Marjeet foiled in two attacks on the capital, sought an asylum at Ava, where, on a promise of cession of territory and an acknowledgment of the suzerainty of Ava, he gained over the King of Burmah to his interests. In 1812 the Burmese again invaded 1812 A.D.
Munipoor, and a great battle at Kokhising ended in the defeat of Chorjeet, and Marjeet was set on the throne by the Burmese, who retired to Ava.

During the ensuing five years (1812-17) Munipoor recovered much of its former prosperity, owing chiefly to the Burmese alliance, but in 1818 Marjeet invaded Cachár but was defeated, and Chorjeet, in alliance with Gumbeer Sing, the third brother, conquered Cachár. Marjeet then quarrelled with his Ava ally, who had again invaded Munipoor, and a second battle at Kokhising ended in a victory for the Burmese; Marjeet fled to Cachár, where he finally submitted to his brother Chorjeet. The Burmese then (1822) usurped the king- 1818 A.D.
dom of Munipoor, which became greatly depopulated.

Marjeet had formally surrendered, but his nephew Pertumba Sing continued to beat up the enemy with parties of horse with varied success, until in these distracting politics, the third brother, Gumbeer Sing, again appeared on the arena, overthrew Pertumba Sing, but retreated to Cachár, where he and his brother Marjeet made some head against the elder brother Chorjeet, who fled to Silhet.

Such was the state of affairs in Munipoor and Cachár at the commencement of the Burmese war with the British: negotiations were opened in 1824, and in the war which ensued Gumbeer Sing—by far the ablest of the Munipoor brothers—co-operated as an ally of the British, at the head of a small select body of his own followers, in expelling the Burmese from Cachár, and in June, 1825, he compelled them to evacuate the Munipoor valley; and in 1826, following up his successes, he pushed them across the Ungoching Hills into their own territory. At the conclusion of peace with the Burmese, by the treaty of Yandaboo in February, 1826, Gumbeer Sing, was recognized as Rajah of Munipoor, where he ruled till 1834, when he suddenly died, and his infant son was formally acknowledged by the British Government, and a regency established. A contingent was also formed, consisting of some 3,500 regulars, chiefly cavalry, which might on an emergency perhaps be doubled. The Munipoories are good horsemen, and in the event of hostilities with Burmah, an auxiliary force of that arm would probably prove useful.

"The line of least resistance" towards Ava is clearly by the *Aeng Pass;* the two practicable passes from Cachár into the Munipoor valley are the Aquea and the Kálanága, whose balance of merit is about equal. There is a third pass by Khonjoee. The Passes into Munipoor from Assam are (1), Barak—over a pass about 6,500 feet elevation—through the Nága country *viâ* Moohong and Barphahuy to Nangara and Joorhauth (capital of Upper Assam), total distance 220 miles. (2), This route is east of the last *viâ* Barak, Kabournée, and the confluence of the Beereere and Rungna Rivers, to Naugaura, where it reunites with route No. 1. The practicable passes are the Aquea and Kálanága, both over 100 miles. (3) Across the Patkooee Mountains into Ava territory.

Singphoos and Shâns inhabit the ridges south-east of Assam, into Ava territory, but a minute topographical description of the mountains surrounding the Munipoor Valley cannot here be entered upon. Munipoor territory comprises about 8000 square miles; the valley, occupying 650 of these, was evidently—like Cashmere and Khâtmándoo in Nepâl—the bed of an ancient lake. The capital is little over 100 miles from Silchar by the two alternate routes (Aquea and Kálanága) mentioned above. The valley oval = 36 by 20 miles. Its elevation scarcely exceeds 2,500 feet, but the surrounding hills rise to about 6000 on the north, and 4000 on the south. The valley contains one sheet of water—the Leghák Lake.

SECTION X.

THE SOUTHERN HIGHLANDS.

(No. 1.)

THE NILGHERRIE PLATEAU.

OOTACAMUND (7,360), KOONOOR (5886), KOTAGHERRIE (6,500), ETC.

Nilgherries.

WE now proceed to the sanitaria of the southern or Madras Provinces. Supereminent amongst these stands the grand Nilgherrie plateau, which was first occupied by us in 1822. The chief stations are Ootacamund, Koonoor, and Kótagherrie, and in the immediate vicinity of Koonoor is the large convalescent depôt of Wellington (or Jackatála) accommodating some 600 invalids. The general features of this plateau are eminently suggestive of military and other colonization; here, if anywhere in India, might a "grand refuge" or "reserve circle" be inaugurated. Here we find a noble plateau, well over 7000 feet above sea level, with miles of rolling downs, recalling to mind the pastoral hills of Wales or Southern Scotland, over which a pack of hounds can hunt, and where, whilst galloping over the rich orchid and flower-spangled turf, larks will dart into the air from your very horse's feet, and commence their song; such features combine to present a noble site for a British colony. The *terre-plein* of this elevated region, averaging over 7000 feet above the sea, is not level, but appears like a rolling park-like plain, intersected by wooded spurs and valleys, and like most mountain plateaux is surrounded by an elevated buttress ridge or edge, called locally the "Koondahs." Some of the peaks attain elevations exceeding 8000 feet above sea level as follows, *viz.*—Dóda-betta (8,760), Koodiakád (8,502), Bevy-betta (8,330), Kimdal Peak (8,353), and

The "Koondahs."

XXXIV.

View of the Nilgherries from Ootacamund, looking west. The "Koondahs" in the distance. Section X.

XXXV.

South-east Edge of the Nilgherrie Plateau from near Kotagherrie. Distant view of the Annamallay Mountains. Section X.

Kumdamya (7,816), Ootacamund Peak (7,360), Tambur-betta (7,292), Hokubetta (7,267), Urbetta (6,915), Kótagherrie (6,571), Koonoor (5886.) **Altitudes.**

Such are a few of the principal altitudes of this fine plateau, from whose watershed streams originate and flow in every direction. Following, therefore, the somewhat fanciful theory enunciated in this series of papers, that as a rule the watershed of a country is its tactical objective base, it follows that the strategic energy of this block of mountain can really operate on all sides. To carry this out practically, we have about six chief ghauts or passes into the lower country, one of which (the Seegoor) leading to Mysore and Bangalore, is fit for cart traffic, and others are being sloped off with similar success, such as the Sispara, Koonoor, etc.

2. Instead of the cramped ridges and nicks in the hillsides, such as the roads in most Himalayan stations may be termed, we have here miles of driving roads, many of them adjacent to the pretty semi-artificial lake, with its willow-bunds and pleasant marginal sites. Hence you see the distant blue peaks of the surrounding "Koondahs," the bounding *enceinte* of this fine plateau. The eye ranges over waving "shôlas" and exotic foliage—Eucalyptus and flowering shrubs. These shôlas are small woods or groves occupying clefts or basins in the hills, a peculiar feature of Nilgherrie scenery; they are often very densely filled with ancient knarled trees **Physical features and Topography.**

> "Bearded with moss, and with garments green,
> indistinct in the twilight."

They often hold game, sometimes even a stray tiger from the low country; and herds of buffaloes range over the *terre-plein*. An *ensemble* is thus presented of unusual character and combination at Indian hill stations; which—coupled with its accessibility and central position—certainly confers an immense advantage in many respects, and must always render these hills a popular resort. I must class it as "A1,"

K2

for a "Military Reserve Circle," and as calculated to become one of the great "refuges"—*propugnacula imperii*—of India!

Out Stations, chiefly on the edges of the plateau.

3. It would take long to do justice to this subject, or to fully dwell on the capabilities and resources of this grand mountain plateau. To take the reader with me to all the surrounding outposts and points of interest would occupy too long a space. I may mention (1) Kôtgurh or Kotagherrie, a civil station elevated 6,500 feet, to the south-east, a fine position whence you can see in the blue horizon the Palnay and *Annamallay* Mountains; it is on the south-east edge of the plateau furthest from the sea. (2) On the south west *Avalanche* and *Sispára*—haunts of the sambur—with their green shôlas and interesting grassy downs, sloping from the koondahs, suggestive of sheepwalks and pasturage. (3) Neddiwuttan, whence you look down on the "Wynaad" and its rolling forests, varied by the clearings of the coffee plantations, here greatly developed. (4) On the North Buckrâta and its cascade, whence you have an outlook over the rolling Mysore table-land, which here rises to 3,500 feet, narrowing to some 15 miles in width at its blending in with the mass of the Nilgherries. (5) Lastly, one may climb Dôdabetta (8,760), that fine peak to the north-east of Ooty, which grandly towers over the lowlands of the Carnatic.

As I write, these and many other charming "outings" rise on my "storied memory." Starting after an early breakfast—sketch book and "tiffin" in wallet—one can easily ride from Ooty to any part of the buttress edge of the plateau, gaze on the country subtending it, and return by nightfall; but he must have a good horse under him to do this, as he will have to cover upwards of 50 miles during the day.* Only occasional

* The vision of a certain raw-boned old "Dekkani" roan occurs to me, from whose back I certainly beheld some glorious scenery in this district—a dangerous runaway brute scarcely controllable—but I forgave him this in consideration of his unwearied services. He tried

game is to be found on the plateau, but the forest-clothed sides of the great mountain block of the Nilgherries swarm with every description of heavy game known to the Indian sportsman, whilst the surrounding koondahs are the rocky haunt of the "muntjak"—the small ibex—and the sambur. The presence of "sport" certainly does not lessen the attractive character of this region as a locality for a British settlement. On this plateau many regiments could be readily cantoned, and a grand "reserve circle" for the whole of Southern India established. At present it affords—besides the sanitarium at Wellington, and a small *Lawrence Asylum* at Ooty—a home resort for many retired officers and their families; and it may safely be said that its social aspects are attractive in no ordinary degree. It is some years since the author visited this charming region, and he is scarcely aware to what extent "progress" may have affected it; but it is surmised that its central position, its proximity to the seaboard—both east and west—will always tend to classify it as amongst the most important of our hill possessions.

Resources and Products.

4. Sheep farming has been tried, but I believe without success, though this is most certainly a promising *looking* site for such, and I am not convinced it would not succeed under further experiment. I am inclined to think that, with careful selection of hardy breeds and housing of the stock, combined with personal superintendence of small flocks such as an individual farmer could command, success would reward the enterprising settler, and assured fortune follow rapidly. Botanical experiments have been largely introduced, and it may be said that an exotic flora has been established on these hills — chiefly

---

all he could to break his heart by violent going, and though in his own interest trying hard to spare him, I fear that at length he accomplished it for himself. After a long 64 miles one day he certainly seemed considerably "beat."

Australasian. The Botanical Gardens at Ootacamund form a delightful resort; here the development of foreign flora has been fostered and introduced broadcast. Eucalyptus, cinchôna, etc., have been naturalized before planting out. The very hedges of the stations on the plateau abound in fuschia, verbena, goodia, besides roses, honeysuckle, etc., whilst ground and other orchids carpet the *terre-plein* or flutter from the forest trees. *Gold* has been found under these mountains to the west, near Makúrty Peak, and will be touched on further on in Section 12, "Coorg and Wynaad." Stock rearing and some slight arboriculture has been tried. Coffee, cinchôna, tea, silk, potatoes, wheat, barley grow freely, and hides, wax, opium, damma, and resin, are exported from this region. Fields of amaranth are also cultivated by the burghers on the upper terraces at elevations of 4,500 feet.

Climate & Rainfall.

5. The general climate of this plateau is equable as to temperature, averaging perhaps 54° to 60°. It is rather wet *(Scottice "dreeping")* at times; but very healthy to the organically sound: its characteristics may be considered prohibitory, rather than recuperative, of disease. The rainfall at Sispára on the extreme south-west escarpment of the koondahs = 250 inches; it is less on the actual plateau, which is protected from the south-west and south-east monsoons, and in places is under 100 inches. It is only about 60 inches at Ootacamund, 55 at Koonoor, 50 at Kotagherrie, which is at the east edge of the plateau furthest from the sea.

Geological.

6. The Nilgherrie plateau* — formerly supposed of plutonic origin — has recently been pronounced schistose or metamorphic. The principal rock is gneiss; though basaltic dykes and quartz veins occur; no trace of granite is found, and the chief minerals are quartz, hornblende, felspar, garnet, magnetic-iron, hœmatite, graphite, with a little mica and laterite.

* 48 miles long by 20 miles broad.

Towards the coast, on the western "koondahs," the laterite appears in detached masses and disintegrated, pointing the distinctive features of the Western Ghauts, of which they are the offset. They add much to the picturesqueness. Near Coimbatore the limestone and gneiss crop up in most fantastic forms, and the escarpment of the south-west such as "Makúrty" Peak, assimilates to the rocky headlands. The writer, pursuing his theory of a primæval ocean covering the whole Indian peninsula,* thinks he recognises evidence of marine action even on, or close under, the elevated plateau of the Nilgherries, which he would thus regard as an ancient denuded island (or headland) half awash by the waters of the antique ocean he supposes to have covered all but the veritable "Highlands of India."

7. The tribes inhabiting this block of mountain, enumerating them from the base, are as follows:—(1) The Erulars, 22 villages, estimated at 1000; a wild tribe. (2) Koroomburs, estimated at 1000, wild men of the woods, uncivilized. (3) Kŏhotars, six villages, estimated at 2000; handicraftsmen. (4) Burghurs, 84 villages, estimated at 10,000; Hindoos, worshippers of Siva; an industrious agricultural clan inhabiting the higher slopes and terraces of the mountains, and the lower inclines of the upper *terre-plein.* (5) Tódars (or Tonwars) are divided into two clans or families, but now scarcely exceed 600 in number. They inhabit the *terre-plein* of the plateau, and are herdsmen of the buffalo, on the milk of which they subsist. They are a peculiar and fine race physically, with long curling hair, and sometimes blue eyes. They have been lately described by an able writer on the ethnology of these provinces (Marshall); he considers them Aryans, and possibly they may be the descendants of some Aryan tribe who have wandered south in early times; for myself, I have always considered them to Ethnological.

---

* Vide Section V., para. 1.

assimilate more closely to the Polynesian rather than the Aryan or Turanian type. Granting the validity of the conjecture conveyed in para. 6, the aborigines would naturally be found on the highest mountain summits, and perchance the Polynesian affinities here suggested of the Tódars may be explained by the theory stated.

All these tribes enjoy that complete exemption from history which is said to constitute happiness. They have absolutely no history, nor even traditions or genealogical fables of any kind; and if the life of the savage, traversing the dense forests of a wild mountain block, can be called happy, they may be said to enjoy happiness to perfection. The storms of war which from early ages have swept over the Carnatic, have never affected these savage uplands, nor has any ambitious potentate ever considered it worth his while to assail the forests and cliffs of its wild *enceinte*. These indigenes may perhaps have roamed their pastoral glens a thousand years undisturbed, herding their half-wild buffaloes, almost unknown to civilized man; their very existence scarcely recognized by even their semi-barbarous neighbours. Now, however, we may reasonably assert that the rugged home of these savages may, in the dim future, assume considerable strategic and other influences on the circumjacent provinces, and become the home of a conquering race, destined to hold the southern part of the great Indian peninsula against a world in arms. I anticipate that ultimately an Australasian population will probably gravitate, and perhaps possess these fine mountain regions of Southern India.

Adjacent ranges. 8. Two small ranges called "Villingherry" and "Paulghaut" Hills connect these mountains with the Annamallays, presently to be described, but they scarcely deserve special notice, as they seldom rise beyond 1,500 or 2000 feet in elevation. North-east of the Nilgherries, however, is a range of primitive trap

XXXVI.

South-east Edge of Nilgherrie Plateau from Kotagherrie. Distant View of the Paulghat and Shervaroy Hills. Section X.

XXXVII.

The Coffee Grounds at Neddiwuttan.

Sample of rounded gneiss hills, seen also on the Shervaroys and elsewhere in Southern Highlands. Section X.

XXXVIII.

Example of gneiss and limestone cropping out of Hill near Coimbatore. Section X.

hills called the "Cauvery" chain, forming the southern part of the Eastern Ghauts, and extending eastwards from the Nilgherries; they attain 4000 feet elevation, but are bare and illsuited for settlement. The Jawádi Mountains may also be mentioned. The Shervaroys are described further on. The Potchewally and Collewally Hills and offsets attain 5000 or 6000 feet elevation. The Shervaroys rise to a plateau averaging 4,500 feet, and the highest peak of the block 5,260 feet.* Here the rounded gneiss hills which crown its summit are covered with coffee plantations. They present an appearance exactly similar to the Nilgherrie plateau at Neddiwuttan.

---

* I have taken these altitudes from Government Survey Reports, but they are not corroborated by my own observation; I conjecture them to be considerably less, *viz.* 2,500 feet for the rounded plateau and 3,500 for the highest peak. I remained three days, and found the heat, even in November, very great.

SECTION XI.

THE SOUTHERN HIGHLANDS

(No. 2).

THE ANNAMALLAYS (ANI-MALAYA); THE PULNEYS OR PALNAYS (PALANI); THE TRAVANCORE MOUNTAINS; SHERVAROY AND COILAMALLAY HILLS; ETC. ETC.

The Annamallays and Pulneys.

THE group of mountains now about to be considered may be regarded as a prolongation south of the Western Ghauts, across that remarkable gap of "Ponany" or "Coimbatore," which leads to Beypûr harbour on the west coast from Madras and the plains of the south Carnatic. They are of similar geological structure, and attain to about the same altitude as the Nilgherries—themselves simply an abutment inland of the Western Ghauts. Their fauna and natural flora—slightly modified as they trend some 180 miles to the south—is for the most part similar. They are sometimes called the Travancore Mountains, being chiefly situated within that principality, and to the southern portion, which ends in a bold headland at Cape Comorin, the term "Cardamon" Mountains is sometimes applied.

The following are a few elevations of this region,—Mount Permaul, north-west of Dindigul, has been found=7,364; Mâhendrâghirri (20 miles north of Cape Comorin)=5000; Annay Moody=8,835, the highest summit in South India. It has even been asserted that the highest peaks attain the snow-line, but this is doubtful.

2. In passing along the line of railway to the western coast, through the gap of "Ponany," shortly after passing the Shervaroy hills, the Annamallays are viewed rising abruptly to the south, where they culminate in the great peak of Annay-Moody (8,835),

from which point their axes radiate east and west (65 miles) as also to the south, where they blend in with the Pulneys. The highest peaks are visible from Kotagherrie on the Nilgherries, whence viewed they appeared to the author as a blue outline in the far horizon. They are still wild and unsettled, but at least two grand sites for stations or camps, at elevations of 5000 or 6000 feet, are known to sportsmen and others, who have sought these forest-covered mountains in search of game. These forest ranges are in fact the paradise of the hunter and European sportsman, as containing in profusion most of the heavy game to be found throughout the Indian peninsula. There is a town of Annamallay, 24 miles south-east of Paulghaut on the river Alima, but it is doubtful whether it or the mountain of Annay-Moody or "Annamallay" (elephant hill) gives its name to the range.

Local description of the Annamallays.

3. The Annamallay Plateau contains about 80 or 100 square miles.* The distance from the foot of the hills to "Appia-Mallay," nine miles, and on to "Michael's Valley," 11 miles further, total—20 miles; elevation 5,900 feet. Above this, at an elevation of 7,500 feet, is the plateau of "Timukka," length about five or six miles, average width one and half miles. There is a smaller plateau south-west called "Coomârikul-Mallay," on the "Ungneeâd" road, but inferior as a site to "Michael's Valley." Easy gradients lead up to the Coomârikul-Mallay, where the scenery is most grand; but the most extensive plateau on these mountains appears to be that under the "Annay-Moody" (elephant's forehead) Mountain. This plain is about the same elevation as Ootacamund (7,360), and is about seven by four and half miles in extent. It is watered by two perennial streams, and a lake could be formed from one of them. It is about 15 miles from Kâta-Mallay. The access to this block is rather difficult. No. 1 track leads by Kootûr, up the valley of Jooraca-

* Vide Hamilton's Report for 1856.

darû to "Michael's Valley,"—20 miles. No. 2 from Dhullee on the north-east, over the Appia-Mallay ridge. No. 3, from south-east *viâ* the valley of Ungeenâd, on to the Coomârikul plateau. On Nos. 1 and 3 the gradients are easy, and could be adapted for wheeled traffic. No. 2 is valuable as it leads by a short road straight to a ridge (Appia-Mallay) well raised above malaria.

4. These hill ranges abound in the smaller ibex, and the lower spurs and forests contain all the usual game of Southern India. The climate is favourable and healthy. The rainfall is not greater than on the Nilgherries. Thousands of acres adapted for the growth of coffee, tea, or cinchôna, are available on these lovely hills. The government forest and timber agent delivers wood at the foot of these hills at 5as. (8d.) per cubic foot; this points to an available industry. In these regions the coffee interest supplants that of tea, though this product is also grown, as well as cinchôna and cereals.

5. I have spoken of the strategic value of the Nilgherrie plateau as guarding the lowlands of the Carnatic, but I can offer no opinion as to how far these mountains share it. I have not personally visited them, though having passed in their close vicinity, I have superficially viewed them, and should consider their probable chief value in the future to be their adaptibility as local refuges from the heat of the plains, a value which they share with the Pulneys (Paláni), which will now be described.

6 The Pulneys or Palánis (from the word "pal" fruit), between 9° and 10°20′ north latitude, occupy a considerable surface, and attain considerable altitudes. These mountains properly extend only about 54 miles east to west, with a medium breadth of about 15 miles; comprising about 231 square miles in the Travancore State, though the total area = 798 square miles, of which 427 is government land and avail-

Pulneys or Palnays.

able for settlers. Many of the summits reach 7000 feet. The average elevation consists of an undulating bleak table-land covered with coarse grass, with trees, however, in the "shôlas" or dells. Towards the east the plateau dips to 4000 feet, and then to 1000 feet on the lower slopes. The climate of these beautiful but malarious valleys is very similar to that of the Shervaroys, and enjoys an average summer temperature of about 70°. The climate of the upper plateau, however, is drier and more equable even than that of the Nilgherries, and may be termed the "land of grass;" whereas the latter is more diversified by water and wood. The Anna-Mallays may be termed the "land of forests." The soil of these mountains is virgin soil; though during the 16th and 17th centuries some attempts at sparse colonization were made by the "Polygars" (or landholders) of Madura and the adjacent plains, but no relics of antiquity exist, and these mountains may be justly termed *virgin soil.*

7. Kôdi-kânâl is the chief station or settlement of these hills, where there are some dozen or twenty European officers' houses, chiefly residents of Madura, in which district it is situated. There is a small lake at "Kōdy," and about 12 miles south-west there is a large lake, but whether natural or artificial is doubtful; by damming up its waters a fine lake not less than 15 miles in circumference might be formed; elevation about 7000 feet. This is the "land of ferns," more than 100 varieties having been classified. The products are nutmeg, cinnamon, pepper (grow wild), coffee, perhaps tea, cinchôna, etc., and various fruits, (some authorities even derive the name "Paláni" from "pal" = fruit); plantains of peculiar excellence are found. Such products growing in valleys bathed in perpetual spring, with a bountiful soil and climate, are no doubt attractive features of this fine range, and its adjacent or tributary offsets. **Local description**

8. Some writers—as has been stated—term the **Offsets of the Pulneys.**

whole of this range the *Cardamon* Mountains, even down to Cape Comorin, near which the "Ariangáwul" Ghaut leads from Tinevelli to Quilon on the west coast, north of which the mountains reach the shore, and impinge on the salt lakes or "breakwaters," as they are termed, which intervene between their base and the sea, and form a most remarkable and picturesque feature of that coast.

The Aligherrie Mountains south-west of Madura = 4,219 feet elevation, are offsets of the Pulneys, and are covered with forest trees—chiefly teak—also pepper and cardamons; they are traversed by the "Ambōli" Ghaut, 20 miles from Cape Comorin. Doubtless progress may have penetrated into these interesting ranges, so lately all but a *terra incognita* to English in India. Probably new settlements may have arisen within these hills since the notes on which these observations are framed were taken, and the state of things depicted therein may be more applicable to 15 or 20 years ago than to the present day.*

Geological. 9. The top of this range is chiefly syenite, and the mountains were long supposed to be of Plutonic origin, but I believe that the most recent geological surveys pronounce them to be *metamorphic;* though in places "faults" occur in which basalt, trap, and veins of granite and other igneous rock intrude: when I mention that in one district alone were found three granites, twelve iron ores, four quartz, 25 other minerals, together with 320 more specimens throughout the

---

* Since writing the above I have had the opportunity of reading Col. James Welsh's Journal—"Forty Years' Military Reminiscences of Actual Service in the East Indies," (an old work now out of print)—and I find mentioned therein a "bungalow" on the mountains near Cape Comorin belonging to my kinsman and namesake, Colonel David Newall, of the Madras Army, at that time (1825) Resident of Travancore. The author (Welsh) states it to be the only point he had seen in the Indian peninsula whence one could "behold the sun both rise and sink in the open blue ocean." The text must therefore be modified as to these hills having been altogether *terra incognita* to the last generation of British in India.

XXXIX.

The Amboli Ghaut. Section XI.

XL.

Laterite Cliffs near Wurkully, Coromandel Coast. Section XI.

XLI.

View on the "Backwater," Travancore. Section XI.

district, perhaps the non-professional reader will forgive me for abstaining from a detailed description of the geology of these and other contiguous ranges.

10. This group of mountains is almost uninhabited, but in the Annamallays, on the north and north-west, are found a tribe called "Pooliars," not more than 200 in number. There is another clan called "Moodoô-wars," chiefly herdsmen. No history, of course, attaches to these wild regions of forest and mountain, on either flank of which, however, the ancient kingdoms of Madura and Travancore possess interesting histories, too long to be entered upon in this cursory notice. Doubtless population will follow the gradual settlement of Europeans in these mountains, for which, like the Nilgherries, I would anticipate a bright future, and a development somewhat similar to that already forecast in Section X. of this work. **Ethnological.**

11. Several ranges, subsidiary or detached from these mountains, some also offsets of the Southern Ghauts, may here be conveniently noticed as amongst the ranges of Southern India. **Subsidiary spurs, offset ranges, and other mountains of the Southern & Eastern Ghauts.**

(a) Amongst these a small isolated block called the "Shervaroy" Hills demand mention. They are crowned to their summits, which scarcely exceed 3000 feet, with coffee plantations; but north of Salem the peak of Mount "Mūtu" (4,935) dominates a rounded table-land seven by three miles, which might form a pleasing retreat from the heat of the plains in summer, and might even serve as a local refuge in times of peril. **Shervaroys.**

(b) West of Salem, near the river Cauveri, we find the peak of "Paula-mallay" (4,950), chief peak of the range, with less fertile soil, however, than the Shervaroys; probably an offset of the Southern Ghauts. **Paula-mallays.**

(c) The hills called "Coilla-mallays" are of very similar characteristics, and their altitude being 4,500 feet, they are perhaps above the zone of malaria, which has been estimated in most parts of India to ascend to about 4000 feet, and in exceptional localities **Coilla-mallays.**

to even a higher altitude. In all these ranges the rock is of a red syenite and gneiss, with granite extruding at places.

Nella-mallays. (d) To the East also we find the "Nella-mallay" Mountains, as a portion of the Eastern Ghauts between 78° and 79° east longitude, where they are nearly 80 miles across, and at their highest (near 13°30′ north latitude), may attain an elevation of 3,500 or 4000 feet above the sea. They consist of a number of ridges running parallel to each other. They are very stony, arid, and unfit for agriculture, but their mineral wealth is considerable, even diamonds are found in parts such as at Kondapillay and Kolconda, and on the banks of the Krishna. The axis of this range lies south of the Krishna, between that river and the Godávery, in which direction their offsets are of inconsiderable altitude, and cease altogether on approaching the delta of that river.

Marmedi Hills. (e) North of the Godávery the "Marmédi" Hills rise to about 4000 feet. They are situated about 70 miles (as the crow flies) from the seaboard, due east from Coconada, or Koringa harbour on the coast. These hills, from the influence of the sea-breeze, enjoy a temperature in the hot season of 68° to 85°. They are not settled, and are only pointed out as a possible refuge under any scheme of general European colonization such as has at times been mooted. The approach to them lies from the Godávery up the Sewny river. They are limited in extent—about seven by three miles, with ridges three by one miles—rocky, and water scarce; soil adapted for coffee, cinchôna, etc., and possibly might be utilized as a local retreat.

Thoamool Hills. (f) The "Thöamool" Hills in the Eastern Ghauts may also here be mentioned. The "Indrâvâtti," a large affluent of the Godávery, rises in these hills; the approach to which naturally lies along its course. They are a fine extended range 110 miles from the sea; about 3,500 feet in elevation. The country is undulating and well watered. They are better adapted for settlement than the Marmédi Hills, having plateaux and sites for building.

Mardi-Abaj Hills and Bailadila range.

(g) In this vicinity also are the "Mardi-Abaj" Hills, which are, however, believed to be highly malarious: but proceeding, on south of the Indrâvâtti we find a range called "Bailadila," terminating in a grand collection of granite peaks, the highest of which, called "Nandiraj," attains 4000 feet elevation. South of these peaks we strike the edge of the plateau which juts out to the south-west, and forms one continuous mountain system with the Eastern Ghauts. The view from Nandiraj is very grand.*

* Holdich's Survey of the Mardian hills and lower Indrâvâtti.

SECTION XII.

SOUTHERN INDIA.

THE BALAGHAUT—

(1) MYSORE TABLE-LAND, (2) COORG, WITH WYNAAD, (3) CANARA, (4) MALABAR, WITH A NOTICE OF THE "DROOGS" OF MYSORE.

Balaghaut; its constituents—Mysore, Coorg, Canara, and part of Malabar.

THE districts named above may be grouped as comprising the chief districts of the *Bálághaut*, which comprehended also the so-called Eastern Ghauts, and constituted the ancient empire of "Kârnâtâ," *no part of which was below the Eastern Ghauts.* The country now called the *Carnatic* is, therefore, a misnomer and a misapplied term. The rivers Toomboodra and Krishna* may be considered its northern limit. Its ancient capital was "Bijáya-nugger" on the Toomboodra; and it was conterminous or "marched with" the province of "Mâhârâshtâ," which will be treated of in Section 13 of this work. Although these districts comprise a fine table-land with ridges at elevations rising from 2000 to 5000 feet and more, where they blend in with the Western Ghauts and Nilgherrie Mountains, it is to be feared that—Mysore especially—they scarcely rise above the zone of endemic cholera or epidemic fevers, although presenting a temperate climate. In other respects they contain appropriate sites for settlements of considerable strategic value as dominating the lowlands of the Carnatic, as also through Coorg and Canara, the seaboard of Malabar subtending the Western Ghauts.

Mysore.

2. The area of Mysore = about 30,886 square *miles*, with a population of 3,000,000, and enjoys a revenue of £800,000 per annum, of which £245,000 is paid to the British Government; and a force of 2,700 irregular

---

* Sometimes termed Kistnah.

cavalry is maintained as a contingent.* It is an extensive plateau at a general elevation of 2,500 feet, and is represented in the Parliamentary Report of 1861 as producing wool, coffee, cotton, etc.; scarcely adapted for permanent settlement by Europeans, though a few high points such as "Baba-Boodeen," "Coody-Moolah," "Gunga-Moolah," etc., from their elevation, are available as residences and partial settlement by capitalists.

Table land varies in elevation, and rises to peaks.

3. Assuming, therefore, the country of Mysore to be about 250 by 230 miles in extent, the table-land varies in elevation from about 2000 feet at Bangalore, to 2,513 feet at Mysore, and 3,500 feet at "Gindlapetta," where the country rises into a junction with the Nilgherrie plateau. The highest point in the province of Mysore is probably the conical mountain of "Shivagunga," which forms the northern extremity of the range of wooded hills which stretch across Mysore between Bangalore and Seringapatam. It is a conspicuous object for many miles. "Severn-droog," "Chittel-droog," Kishnagherrie, and Nandi-droog, are strong rock fortresses of Mysore, mostly situated on spurs of the "Chinragna-konda" Hills, in which the (south) "Penaar" and (north) Palaar Rivers take their source, and on the west side of which the Cauvery and Toomboodra Rivers also rise; this is probably the watershed of the country south of the Krishna. "Austra-droog" is on the northern termination of this range. These *Droogs*, or isolated rocks, ordinarily crowned with a fortress as the name implies, are a curious feature of the Mysoro country; they rise abruptly some 1000 or 1,500 feet above the surface of the plain of Mysore, which has been already fixed as at an average elevation of 2,500 feet above sea-level. A few of these "droogs" will be described further on at the end of this section,—they are mostly of syenite.

Passes and Mountains.

4. The "Koombetarin" Peak in the Southern

* Sir M. Cubbon's Report of 18th November, 1859, gives the area of Mysore as 2,644,306 *acres*.

Ghauts = 5,548 feet. The Pass of "Gâzâlhâthi," leading from the plains of the Carnatic on to the Mysore table-land, across the valley of the Mayom River is not above 2,500 feet elevation. On the left bank of this river are seen the ruins of the old fort of Gâzâlhâthi. The river separates Mysore from the mass of the Nilgherries, which here rise abrupt from its chasm more than 4000 feet, presenting a noble buttress. The highest point near Bangalore = 3,026 feet, Kolar 2,900 feet, Seringapatam 2,412 feet, etc. The chief passes from Mysore, across Canara and the Coorg country, over the Western Ghauts to the seaboard, forming the outlets to the products westwards, are—taking them from the north—(1) From Bednore over the "Hussoo-Angadi" or Hyderghur, (2) The Bisli, due east of Bangalore, north of Mount Soobramâni, (3) The Yelláni, leading down from Merkâra, the capitol of Coorg, to the seacoast, (4) The Munzerabad, south of No. 2, through Coorg and the Wynaad. There are other passes, such as the "Kodadibol" to Mangalore, west of Mount "Balaryn-droog," 5000 feet. The Hingri or Hugalla to Cannanore, a bad pass, very steep, and the Manantódi Pass *viâ* Seringapatam, through the Wynaad to Telicherry. The outlet of Coorg is chiefly through Canara by Munzerabad and Soompanch Ghauts, but the Wynaad routes are much easier to Malabar.

Coorg. 5. Coorg—from Kôdâgu or Kôdûma, signifying the *steep mountain*—first mentioned in history by Ferishta, *circa* 1582 A.D., is situated between 12° and 13° north latitude, is a mountainous tract to the west of Mysore, extending into the Western Ghauts, containing (including the Wynaad) about 2,400 square miles. Assuming its area to be about 60 by 40 miles, it is bounded on the north by South Canara and the Brâhmâgiri Mountains, east by Mysore and the Cauvery, west by South Canara and Malabar. In 1861 the entire population was estimated at not more than

168,312, of which 26,389 only were Coorgs. The highest points in Coorg are Todiandamut, near Viragundrapet, on the Western Ghauts, which has an elevation of 5,682 feet. The Subrámáni Peak, north of Coorg = 5,611 feet; and the general average of the country may be estimated at 5000 feet. The Brâhmâgiri range or table-land of Coorg = 4,500 feet, is essentially the watershed of the Ghauts south-west; the waters divided by it flowing diversely both into the Indian Ocean westwards, and into the Bay of Bengal eastwards. The Tambacherrie Pass on the south, to the river Hemavâti on the north, may be considered the limits of Coorg, which comprises a succession of hills and valleys, abounding with all sorts of game, especially that thick forest extending from Sonawarpet to Merkâra (the capitol of Coorg) 20 miles, round which the hills form an amphitheatre into which the different roads enter through gateways across an old line and ditch extending along the tops of the ridges; a Coorg Rajah, before the country was subdued by Hyder, having made a hedge and ditch along the whole extent of his dominions.

6. The principal rivers of Coorg are the Cauvery **Topographical.** (Kâveri), the Lucksmântirah, the Surmavâti, and Hemavâti. None of these rivers are navigable within the district, their waters are utilized chiefly in irrigation; and a great deal of wood is floated down the Cauvery in the rainy season from the Madras Government forests, through which it runs, thereby effecting a great saving in its carriage. After leaving Coorg in the country of Mysore, it forms some beautiful cascades on to the level of the table-land: these falls may be best approached from a point on the Mysore and Bangalore road 30 miles from the latter. Although the Cauvery has its source in Coorg, among the Bababoodeen Hills, so near the Western Ocean, where also the river Toomboodra originates, nevertheless these two great streams belong to the drainage basins

of the inner Bálághaut Mountains, and find their final issue into the Bay of Bengal.

Climate v. Elements of Value, Military, etc.

7. The climate of Coorg is exceedingly damp; the rainfall averaging 120 inches, and most inimical to the constitution of Europeans. Jungle fever is very prevalent, and, in fact, may be considered endemic; Coorg cannot, therefore, be looked upon as a good site for a colony, although a few planters brave the deadly effects of the climate year after year with the indomitable perseverance of Britons wheresoever an opening is feasible. They direct their energies towards coffee planting, and also of late *cinchona.* The other principal products are rice, sugar, plantains, oranges, tobacco, grain; the chief woods are teak, blackwood, and sandal,—the sale of the latter is a government monopoly. Coorg, however, may be considered as slightly valuable in a military point of view; and should the long mooted scheme of connecting Bangalore with the town of Mysore by a railway, with a branch from Toomkoor—45 miles from the former—be carried out, it would become much more so.

The "Coorgs," a brave, hardy, and loyal race of mountaineers, appear to present elements of good soldiers, and might perhaps with advantage be enlisted into our regular service as local militia; as a class they are agricultural and foresters, and—like the Goorkhas—delight in field sports. The strategic position of Coorg, lying between Mysore and Malabar, is valuable; troops could march from Merkâra to Mysore in three days, and from Virájapet to the coast in two days.

Wynaad products Gold, Coffee, Cinchona, etc.

8. The *Wynaad* may be regarded as a district of Coorg. It was formerly ruled over, as a fief, by a younger branch of the Verma family. It is only estimated at 1,250 square miles, and as viewed from Neddiwuttan on the Nilgherries, appears a rolling country of forests, amidst which coffee clearings are dotted in patches of lighter green.

Lately *gold* has been found in all parts of Coorg—

XLII.

The Makurty Peak, Nilgherries, north-west. Sections X. and XII. Below this peak, on the west side, gold is found.

especially in the Wynaad—at elevations varying from 500 to 8000 feet; on the Seetaputtee River, in the drift and alluvial deposits; again at Karambaut, in the gravels and quartz (in parts 30 feet thick); below Eddakurra in the tertiary strata and laterite in the south; near Nellakotta on the north; at Vyteri on the west; and at Bolingbroke on the east; that is to say, covering an area of 500 square miles. The reefs are numerous, and gradiate from 500 to 8000 feet above sea level. Near Devâla, especially, the proportion of gold for the washings is large, and eventually "there "can be no doubt that sooner or later gold-mining will "be established as an important industry of Southern "India, but forethought and industry in conducting "operations will be essential."* The rocks are quartz, hornblende, magnetic iron (extruding through gneiss), with granular quartz in places, also alluvial deposits.

9. North of Coorg we find the so-called country of *Canara*, a corruption apparently of "Kârnâtâ." It extends 180 miles along the seaboard, which fact con- **Canara.** stitutes its sole importance, as it is otherwise a wild and mountainous country, with an estimated population of only 600,000, and an area of 73,800 square miles; of which only 2,758—above the Ghauts—can properly be called *highlands*, although offsets or rocky spurs extend to the seaboard; and in many places the Western Ghauts themselves approach the sea. This province may be considered as enjoying the same climate and physical characteristics as Coorg. The name Canara is altogether a misnomer as applied to the Indian province of "Tuláva," which commenced north of the river Châdrâgiri, the northernmost boundary of Malabar. Haiga, which was the seaboard section of Canara, is fabled to have been part of the territory of the mythic Ravâna, King of Lanka (or Ceylon).

Canara was subdued by Hyder in A.D. 1763, and was transferred to the British in 1799. South Canara,

* *Vide* Brough Smith's Government Reports.

north of the river Chândrâgiri, where Malabar ends, is called "Tulâva" by the Hindoos. Its products are sandal-wood, teak, sugar-cane, cinnamon, nutmegs, pepper, and coffee. Tribes of singular habits people it, such as Moplahs (Mahomedans), Nairs, Jains, and others whose ethnological peculiarities it were too long to enter on in this work.

South Canara escaped Mahomedan conquest until invaded by Hyder A.D. 1765-6. Cannanore, Mangalore, etc., are ports of Canara or Malabar, and share with Beypore (the harbour terminus of the G.S.I.P. railway) value as *points d'appui* over the Western Ghauts from the highlands of Bálághaut, or the upper districts of Coorg and Mysore, as outlets for produce.

Topographical features of Balaghaut, Altitudes, etc.

10. Before proceeding to an historical notice of these countries, a few altitudes as points bearing more or less directly on that wide subject, "The Highlands of India," may here be noted, *viz.*—

Periapatam—on the borders of Coorg—and the Fort of Bettâdapoor, 15 miles distant, are not less than 6000 feet above the sea level.

Dévakôti, 20 miles distant, is the chief centre of the sandal-wood district, the traffic in which has been stated to be a government monopoly.

Subramâni (5,611 feet), is a peak in the Western Ghauts, between the Jellanir and Bissoli Passes in Canara,—a remarkable mountain.

As a curious feature of Canara, the Falls of the Surnavâti, at "Giarsuppah," may be mentioned. These are amongst the most wonderful cascades in the world. The chief fall = 880 feet in perpendicular altitude. Another—"The Roarer"—plunges into a deep cavern behind the grand fall; and "The Rocket" and "Dame Blanche" are adjacent cascades: the whole forming an *ensemble* almost unique in waterfalls. The Falls of the "Tadree," from the same watershed in Canara, are also remarkable cascades. Whilst on the subject the cataract of the "Gâtpoorba," a tributary of the Toomboodra River near "Gokauk," may also here be mentioned as a wonderful sight of South-West India.

Though not in the provinces under review, it may here be stated that "Cuddapah" (1,900), Gooty (1,182), Bellary (1,488), Dharwar (2,352), and Hyderabad (1,696), are all included in the old territorial district of Bálághaut south of the Toomboodra. "Adóni," a district of Bálághaut, is perhaps as well adapted for individual capitalists as any in the South of India. From the Adoni-hill a noble plain of black soil ("regur") bearing most valuable cultivation, may be seen stretching away north-west and south-east from Gooty to the Toomboodra, with an area of 15 by 20 miles. This country was conquered by Hyder between 1766-80, and in 1800 was, by treaty with the Nizam, ceded to the British: it possesses very great resources for army supplies in cattle and grain.

The so-called "Golconda" diamonds are mostly derived from this district; the matrix is usually the sandstone breccia of the clay-slate formation, and those found in the alluvial soil are produced from the *débris* of this rock. Natives of India have a belief that the diamond is always growing and increasing in bulk.

HISTORICAL NOTICE.

Historical—ancient fabulous.

11. It now only remains to give a short historical sketch of the provinces treated of in the foregoing paragraphs of this section—Mysore, Coorg (including Wynaad), Canara, Malabar, and their associated ranges.

Going back to mythic times they may be regarded as constituting the ancient Kingdom of "Sugriva," whose minister or general, "Hunúmân,"—now worshipped by the Hindoos as the monkey demi-god—took part in the war of Râma against Râwan, the Giant-King of Lanka (Ceylon). We may regard these fables of the *Rámáyán* as of about the same historical value as Homer's Iliad or "Siege of Troy;" they are, in fact, as likely as not, diverse traditions of the same historical myth, the fair *causa belli* being Helen or Sita, according as narrated by the Greek Homer or the Indian "Kálidâsa," their *vates sacer.*

Modern History. Coming into demi-historical times, we find the "Chalûka" and "Cadumba" dynasties successively ruling the country, but no authentic history can be said to exist till about A.D. 1310, when the Mahomedans first appeared on this arena, and several invasions ensued. In A.D. 1326 Togluk III. overran the country and destroyed the capitol, hence the modern "Bednore." In A.D. 1336 the "Harihar" Kings founded a new capital on the banks of the Toomboodra, called "Vijáya-nugger"—city of victory—and absorbed nearly the whole of the country now called Mysore. In A.D. 1564 their descendant, Rajah Râm, having provoked the Mussulman powers of the Dekhan, a coalition of the States of Beejapore, Ahmednugger, Bédur, and Golconda, was formed against him, and the united armies utterly defeated him at the great battle of "Talikát in A.D. 1565. The king fell in the battle, and his capital was sacked and destroyed. The chief feudatory or "polygar" of Mysore then made a bid for power, and raised a principality on the ruins of the "Harihar" kingdom, and in A.D. 1610 a successor, Rajah Wudeyár, established a dynasty and kingdom, having its capitol at Seringapatam, and extended his sway over the whole table-land of Mysore. Chiki-Déva, Rajah, was the chief prince of this dynasty; he died in A.D. 1704. His feeble successors, however, soon forfeited their heritage by their imbecility. They were, in 1731, overthrown by a minister—"Deo Raj,"—who set up for himself, and in A.D. 1737 defeated a large Mahomedan army sent against him. He held his own till about 1749-50, when Hyder Ali commenced his predatory career. It is not the object of this historical notice to follow the career of Hyder Ali—itself a history—except as bearing on the Mysore

State. Commencing as an officer in the army of Mysore, he gradually fought and intrigued his way to power, and in A.D. 1760 virtually became sovereign of Mysore; and after fluctuating fortunes he sacked Bednore, obtaining thereby it is said as great a treasure as twelve millions (£12,000,000) of money. During the course of his rise to power, Hyder always affected to regard the legitimate heir as king—a pageant of mock authority. In 1769 Hyder invaded the Carnatic, and dictated terms at the very gates of Madras. In 1770 the Mahrattas overran Mysore, beseiged Hyder in Seringapatam, and obtained some success; but from 1773 Hyder, with his son Tippoo, successively invaded and annexed Coorg, the Wynaad, and much of the Malabar littoral, and ultimately wrested the whole of their conquests in Mysore territory from the Mahrattas. About this time (1768) the pageant titular King of Mysore died, and the succession failing, Hyder adopted a curious method of establishing a successor, by a selection from amongst the children of the principal branch of the royal house. This ceremony, whose details need scarcely be given, ended in the selection of "Chám Raja," who was the father of the Rajah who was placed on the throne of Mysore by the British on the overthrow of Tippoo in 1799. This feeble prince, however, being unable to maintain order in his state, the Mysore country was absorbed into the British system of government in 1832, and the Rajah pensioned in 1847. The Raj has since, however, been restored.

Historical Notice of Coorg.

12. Coorg is first mentioned by Ferishta (*circa* 1582), as ruled by native princes. In the 16th century "Viraráj" of the "Nuggurs" settled in Coorg and founded the "Holéri" dynasty of Coorg, which lasted till 1834, when the country was resumed by the British. "Chik-Virájappa" V. repulsed Hyder Ali's invasion of 1765, but in 1772 was conquered, and died a prisoner at Seringapatam. A Mahomedan governor was appointed, who, however, was driven out by the Coorgs in 1782.

The country was nearly depopulated by Tippoo, and the young Rajah imprisoned at Mysore. In 1789, however, "Vir Rajendra" escaped from Periapatam, the ancient capitol, and returned to Coorg; he there raised a revolt. He succeeded in expelling the Mahomedans, and even invaded Mysore. He was aided by the British, and became an ally of Cornwallis in 1790, and assisted at the seige of Seringapatam. "Vir Rajendra," the patriotic Coorg, died in 1809, bequeathing to his son and successor his insane temper without his talents, so that eventually the last prince—"Chik-Vir Rajendra"—was deposed after some resistance, and ultimately died in England.

General Remarks 13. Doubtless there are many sites at present undeveloped in the vast mountain tracts of the Bálághaut, forming the watershed of the south of the great Indian peninsula, that in the future will become better known, and perhaps rise to importance in some of the points of view noted: but I must leave these interesting regions—interesting moreover in an ethnological point of view. Many of the tribes inhabiting these diversified tracts of mountain and forest are well worth study; but I must "move on" Northwards into Mâhârâshtrâ and the northern reaches of the Western Ghauts—or Syhoodria Mountains—which, with the ranges radiating from the Central India plateau, forming the basins of the Nerbudda and Tapti, are mostly within the limits of the Bombay Presidency. These comprise the next strategic step it is proposed to take; but before passing across the Toomboodra into Section XIII. of this work, a few words of description of the "Droogs" or hill forts of the "Carnatic," seems called for as a branch of the interesting subject treated of. These "islands of the plain," as they have been called, are numerous in the Mysore country, and a brief description of a few of the more prominent will now here be given.

These curious peaks are mostly of syenite, extruding their denuded heads and shoulders out from the plutonic and slatey flooring of the *terre-plein* some 1000 or even 1,500 feet in height. Their summits may, therefore (assuming the general elevation of the Mysore table-land in the Bálághaut province to be 2,500 feet) attain an elevation of 3000 or 3,500 feet above sea level; not beyond the zone of malaria, which in this work has been assumed to be about 4000 feet, but meriting passing notice in a work treating of the "Highlands of India," as—at least some of them—presenting a cool restorative retreat from the heats of the plains subtending them.

THE "DROOGS" OF SOUTHERN INDIA.

The Droogs of Mysore. Severndroog.

14. (a) The first of these hill fortresses here to be noticed is *Severn-droog* (the golden fortress) situated in the Mysore country, about 20 miles south-west of Bangalore. This vast mountain is not less than from 12 to 20 miles in circumference at the base, from which it rises with a granite peak to an almost perpendicular altitude of 3,500 feet. The mountain is divided by a chasm into two separate peaks, called respectively the "white" and "black" forts, forming two citadels, each with its defences capable of being maintained indopendent of the lower works which crown the connecting ridge. Although this stupendous fortress well defended would be well nigh impregnable, it was taken by assault by the British in 1791 without the loss of a single man, the garrison being panic struck at the advance of the British under Cornwallis in person. The fort is in the midst of thick bamboo jungle, which—whilst strengthening its defences—renders it an unhealthy residence. This is not to be confounded with another fortress of the same name on a rocky islet of the Concan Coast, formerly the stronghold of the pirate "Angria," and which has been used as a convalescent depôt for sick European soldiers from Bombay.

Chittel-droog.

(b) *Chittel-droog* is another rocky fortress of the

Mysore country, on a bluff sometimes called the "Cháhtta (umbrella) of the Chittel-droog hills. It attains an elevation of near 2,800 feet above sea level, but does not rise over 800 feet over the subtending *terre-plein.* This position has been occupied as a military station by British troops, and is famous for its fruits and vegetables. The fortress owes its strength to the precipitous nature of the hill on which it is built, as also to the extraordinary labyrinth of works defending it, consisting of six successive gateways, all winding irregularly from rock to rock to the summit. The ascent is partly by steps, and partly by mere notches cut in the steep or smooth surface of the rock, the whole crowned with batteries and good walls, and magazines cut in the live rock. On the whole, Chittel-droog probably presents the most elaborate specimen extant of the fortified "droog" of Southern India. Chittel-droog owes its strength not so much to its elevation as to the steepness of the acclivity on which it stands; and such is the intricacy of the works, that an enemy might be master of the outer walls and yet not materially advanced towards the reduction of the "droog." Here are still to be seen the ruins of the buildings in which General Matthews and the other English prisoners were confined in 1783 by Hyder Ali. It is one of those points selected—and noted on the map—as of some strategic value, as guarding the defensive line of the Southern Ghauts of the Bálághaut. Its elevation above sea level is about 2,800 feet.

Nundy-droog.

(c) *Nundy-droog* is another strong hill-fort of Mysore, about 30 miles north-east of Bangalore. The fort is built on the top of a mountain 1,600 feet above the plain, and is nearly 3000 feet above sea level. Nearly three-fourths of the circumference is inaccessible, and the remainder is approached by a steep and slippery path, mostly cut in steps out of the rock, about one and half miles in length. It was reckoned inferior to, but next in rank to Severn-droog and

XLIII.

Kurmul-Droog, sample of a southern Hill Fort. Section XI.

XLIV.

Distant View of Nundy-Droog, Mysore. Section XII.

XLV.

Hyder's Drop, Mysore. Section XII.

XLVI.

Sunkery-Droog; gneiss hill pierced by granite in foreground. Section XII.

Chittel-droog, and was stormed in 1791 by the British after a resistance of three weeks. Whilst under the Mahrattas it resisted Hyder for three years, and was taken by a blockade. This is the watershed of the South-east Ghaut district. The Pennaar River rising in the hills close adjacent, runs to the north, and the Palar, which flows south, also rises near Nundy-droog. These hills may therefore be regarded as the highest part of the country in the centre of the land South of the Krishna.

The sources of the Cauvery and Toomboodra on the west must, however, be regarded as higher. The shape of the Nundy-droog mountain is peculiar, and has been compared to that of a "tadpole," or perhaps that of a recumbent figure of *Nandi* the attendant bull of Siva, whence it derives its name.

(d) *Kistnagherry* (Krishna-gírí) is another isolated Kistnagherry. rock fortress of the Mysore country of very considerable strength. The rock on which the fortress stands is over 700 feet in perpendicular height, its summit being near 2,500 feet above sea level. It is so bare and steep as never to have been taken by direct assault. Here in 1791 the British were repulsed with much loss. The fort is now a ruin, and in its vicinity are many rocky insulated mountains of a similar character. It bears about 100 miles east of Seringapatam.

(e) *Ry-droog* may be next named as a fortress of Ry-droog. the same system, 170 miles north-east of Seringapatam, on the summit of a stupendous mass of granite rock, which rises to the extraordinary height of 1,200 feet above the *terre-plein* (3,200 feet above sea level). A low ridge of mountain connects this mass with that of Chittel-droog. This is rather a sacred place, and contains several interesting ruins and temples, and one monolith pillar 40 feet in height. It is rather better built than most hill fortresses.

(f) In the Bálághaut, though scarcely in the district Rawan-droog. treated of, on the Sundoor Hills, we have an instance of an ironstone (*not* granite) hill called *Rawan-droog* (a sanitarium), at an elevation of about 3,400 feet above sea level. Length of the range about 15 miles, south-east from Hospet, where shales, sandstone, iron-pyrites, appear *in situ*. Subtending this, the plain consists of the "regur" or black soil so famous in the growth of cotton and other products. Bejanugger is 18 miles west of this group, and is on granite.

Sunkery-droog. (g) Near this "droog" the granite vein pierces the gneiss hill, and crops out in prismatic shaped cubes, a striking instance of plutonic rock extruding through the tertiary flooring of the *terre-plein*.

General Remarks 15. Many other rock fortresses of Mysore and of the Bálághaut district might be named, such as Astra-droog, Hooliar-droog (35 miles north-east of Seringapatam), and many others.

As one approaches the Western Ghauts, hill fortresses abound, many of them of great natural strength, but a description of one nearly applies to all. The characteristic "droog," however (or doorga)—an insulated peak rising abrupt from the *terre-plein* to the altitude of 1000, 1,200, or even 1,500 feet—is not found further north than the Toomboodra. They then give place to the flat-topped plateaux and buttressed rocks of the Dekhan (to be described further on). Doubtless such points of vantage early attracted the notice of the savage aborigines inhabiting these lands. The "Vâna-pootras" (children of the forest), followed by the hordes of Aryans, Mahrattas, and Mahomedans—even Hánumân himself, the demi-god monkey king—may have scaled these precipitous peaks and offered sacrifices to to the earth-goddess "Dūrga." Originally points of veneration, they must soon have offered the additional attraction of military security to the inhabitants, and from time to time chiefs seized upon them as the centres of their predatory warfare, each adding defensive works; perhaps before the dawn of the Christian era most of these points may have been occupied by belligerent tribes. The Mahrattas siezed on many of them, added to and strengthened their works, and were in fact dominant throughout Mysore and the Bálághaut till the rise of Hyder Ali in the 18th century. That leader doubtless expugnated them from many, and the British coming after, completely effected their subjugation. Most of them are now deserted and in ruins, and exhibit a sample of a state of things passed away for ever. They merely deserve passing notice in a work professing to treat of the "Highlands of India," though a few summits possess a pleasant climate, afford soil for the growth of fruits, and may be mentioned as *pieds-de-terre* or "refuges," affording relief from the lassitude of the heats of the adjoining plains; but few rise beyond the zone of malaria, noted in this work as about 4000 feet above sea level; and this must suffice for illustration of the "Droogs" or rock-fortresses of the Bálághaut.

SECTION XIII.

MAHARASHTRA.

THE WESTERN GHAUTS OR "SYHOODRIA" MOUNTAINS.

(1) MAHABULESHWAR, (2) MATHERAN, (3) THE WATERSHED OF THE GODAVERY AND KRISHNA, (4) THE SMALLER SANITARIA OF THE BOMBAY PRESIDENCY, MANDER DEO, ETC.; WITH A NOTICE OF THE HILL FORTS OF THE DEKHAN.

Maharashtra or the Dekhan; the Land of Sivajee.

MAHARASHTRA, the land of Sivajee and the Mahrattas, conjures up vivid scenes of romantic history such as the writer of picturesque annals might well turn to account for an historical romance; but the nature of this work scarcely admits of long dwelling on such an enticing theme. The rise of Sivajee (the Mountain Rat) is in fact the history of the highland ridges and hill forts of Mâhârâshtrâ within historical times. I will endeavour, before leaving this section of the work, to touch on the "Hill Forts of the Dekhan" somewhat at length. It has been estimated that the country of the Dekhan included in the term "Mâhârâshtrâ" from the Tapti to the Toomboodra, contains not less than one thousand hill forts, though, of course, of this large number, many are deserted, and contain little deserving notice except their names. In the Poona division alone 140 forts are officially registered, though most of them are noted as "deserted," in short, Mâhârâshtrâ may be termed with propriety the *Land of Forts.*

The linguistic limits of Mâhârâshtrâ would be included in lines drawn across the peninsula through Oojein on the north, and Bejapore south; this would

XLVII.

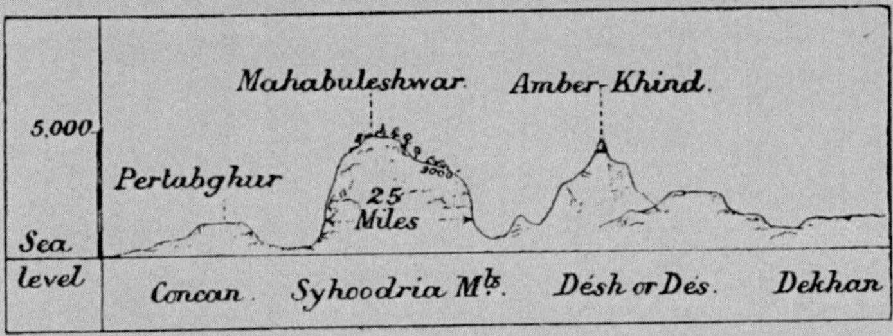

Section Across Maharashtra. (Area 100,000 square miles. Population 7,000,000.)
Section XIII.

XLVIII.

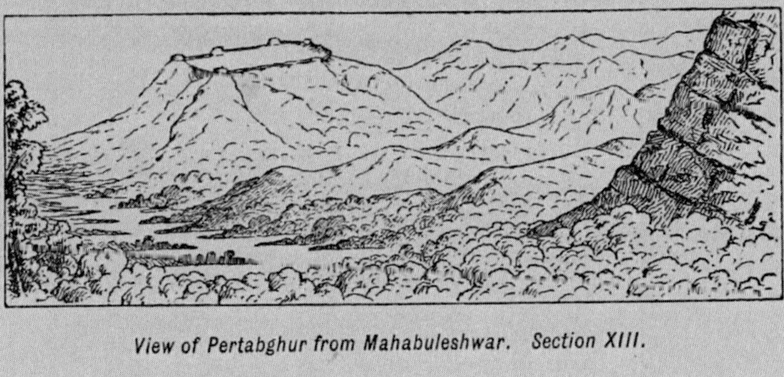

View of Pertabghur from Mahabuleshwar. Section XIII.

include the Mahratta speaking races; but its geographical limits may be considered for our purpose as—On the north the Sáthpoora Mountains; south, the Toomboodra; east, the Wurda River; and west, the Syhoodria Mountains. It is the last of these that it is proposed first to introduce.

2. The Syhoodria or Sáhyádri Mountain axis was perhaps the littoral of a primæval continent at an epoch when the level of the ancient Indian Ocean had receded from the Central-Indian elevated plateau, and (as was suggested in the preamble of this work) possibly it might be regarded as bearing the same relation thereto as the "Himalayan axis" may have done to the great primæval continent of Thibet and Central Asia—*the crown of the world*—before the waters of chaos had been "gathered together into one place." The Syhoodria Mountains or Western Ghauts, therefore, represent the true mountain littoral of an elevated tract of which the Vindhya and Sáthpoora ranges may be termed the northern buttresses. Its great rivers, as the Nerbudda and the Tapti—which rise in the Omerkântuk plateau—running through valleys, formerly a chain of lakes, which have formed the present alluvial deltas, containing the coal measures to be found on their course to the sea. The Godávery also rises in the Chandpore Mountains near Nassick, and the Krishna in the Western Ghauts close to Máhâbulêshwár, and their upper basins are within the limits of this mountain system. These mountains are plutonic—porhaps also partly metamorphic, as they trend southwards—but black basaltic rock and disintegrated laterite are amongst the most striking features of their western aspects. I know not whether the sheet-rock of the flooring of the Dekhan has been recognised as stratified rock, or whether—as my slight idea of geology would lead me to suppose—it is attributable to igneous, but sub-aqueous action. The whole geology of these regions seems to require exact investigation.

The Syhoodria or Sahyadri Mountains, usually called the Western Ghauts.

Mahabuleshwar.

3. Máhâbulêshwár (4,700 feet)—mighty parent of strength and power—thy forest rides and "tiger walks," and black basaltic cliffs deserve remembrance! The station is situated somewhat scattered on the reverse or eastern slope of the Western Ghauts or Syhoodria Mountains, which here jutting out into bleak precipices and salient bluffs, look down sheer 3000 feet or more on to the cocoa-palm covered slopes of the Concan. Such "points of vantage" whence one gazes down these vast crags are very striking, and glorious sunsets reward the visitor who observes them at even towards the Indian Ocean. Rolling spurs crowned by flat-topped summits often holding a fortress, (such as Pertâbghur from Horseshoe Point) also appear subtending the base of this giant buttress of the Concan.* Máhâbulêshwár and Mátheran are both situated on these Western Ghauts which, as have been stated, are usually termed by Hindoo geographers the *Sáhyádri* Mountains. They commence some 60 miles north of Bombay, and extend parallel with the coast to the gap of "Ponamy" or "Coimbatore" in north latitude 11°30′, where they blend in with the elevated mass of the Nilgherries, to whose altitude they gradually attain as they trend south. This grand extended buttress of Western India must needs contain elevated summits, and even plateaux suitable for sanitary occupation; accordingly we shall find within its axis, or its offsets, most of the sanitary sites to be touched on in this section.

Description of Vicinity.

Ascent.

The ascent to the Máhâbulêshwár plateau is by the "Pussurni" Ghaut to Pánchgunny and Máhâbulêshwár. The road commands some very fine views of the valley of the Krishna, which, rising in a small pool at the village of Máhâbulêshwár on the reverse slope of the Western Ghauts runs through a beautifully wooded

---

* Pertâbghur was the scene of the "Wâgnuk" murder by Sivajee of Afzool-Khan in 1659. It is visible from the "Horseshoe Point," Máhâbulêshwár.

and cultivated valley to "Waee," where are seen the celebrated temples so often described as not to require further mention here, even were the subject within the scope of this work. The Krishna then passes on southward to fulfil its destiny of watering a vast tract of country, to its debouchment into the Indian Ocean on the Coramandel coast. The hill of "Pandooghur," adjacent to "Waee," is celebrated as the place of residence of the erratic "Pandaus" of whom we have so many traces in the Himalayas and other parts of India.

Rivers originating near Mahabuleshwar.

4. The Temple of Máhâbulêshwár—whence the name of the hill or sanitarium is derived—is to the north-east of the station, some two or three miles distant, on the reverse of the bluff. The spring-head of the great river Krishna is enclosed within its precincts; nor is it the only spring-head in this pre-eminently sacred watershed. No less than five streams here originate, *viz.*—(1) The Krishna, (2) The Yêna, (3) Kayâna, (4) Sewâtri, (5) Gäootri, and on the north near Nassick the great river Godávery rushes from the Chandpore hills towards the south.

General Features

The Máhâbulêshwâr Hill as a site for settlement may be regarded as a plateau some 15 miles in length by 8 or 12 in breadth. It is during tho rainy season cut off by rivers and torrents from the surrounding country. The annual rainfall considerably exceeds 200 inches. The station is at the north-west corner of the plateau, about 30 miles from Satára, in which territory it lies. It is the oldest established sanitarium in the west of India, having been selected by Sir John Malcolm in 1828, solely from sanitary considerations. Cereals and tubers—especially the potato—are freely cultivated, and largely exported, and are famous in Western India. The flora is peculiar and striking, but not exuberant.

Strategic value nil.

On the whole the *strategic* value of this settlement must be pronounced absolutely *nil*, and as not suitable for a "reserve circle," though possibly capable of holding a small colony of settlers sufficiently acclimatized to endure the excessive rainfall, and to hold their own when cut off, as they would be, by rising rivers and floods, between May and September. This station is peculiar, but scarcely so interesting as most of the sanitaria of India. A few deer and jungle fowl may be picked up by the sportsman, and there is no lack of heavy game in the lowlands of the Concan which subtend the precipitous bluff of Máhâbulêshwár.

Wassotah.

5. In the Western Ghauts, and exactly at a similar distance (30 miles) south-west of Satâra, is found the fortress of Wassôtah, formerly a strong position of vantage. It towers above the Concan, a sheer perpendicular cliff 2,500 or 3000 feet elevation. Well defended, it might become, like so many hill-forts of the Dekhan, practically impregnable; though in this instance its inward or east face is enfiladed by the fort of "old Wassôtah," over a chasm 1,500 feet in depth. Wassôtah was taken in 1818, the garrison being frightened into surrender by mortar practice. Near Satâra also are the Hill Forts of Chundun-Wundun, Nangherry, Wyrátgherry, Pandoghur, Hummulgurh, Kalinga, and others. Satâra itself is midway between the Krishna and Torna Ghaut. The plateau above it is seven miles in length, and not less than 4000 feet elevation above sea level; but like that of Máhâbulêshwár, cut off by floods and torrents in the monsoon.

Amber-Khind and Mander-Deo.

6. The above remarks, however, scarcely apply to the small plateaux of "Amber-Khind" and "Mander-Deo" (4000 feet), in the close vicinity—a plateau nine miles from Waee and 24 from Máhâbulêshwár, but more inland. Their strategic site is good as commanding the passes such as the Warrenda Ghaut, which runs close under its base, leading to the seaboard, through the Syhoodria range to Mhar on the coast. They are situated also on the hither side of the river Krishna and other streams of the west watershed which so hamper the Satâra plateau.

"Mander-Deo" is nine miles from Waee and 24 from Máhâbulêshwár. It possesses most of the advantages of the latter as to elevation and soil, with the additional ones of accessibility and freedom from its excessive rainfall.

At "Amber-Khind," close to Mander-Deo, are extensive water tanks, but less room for building purposes. There is a temple on the summit of Amber-Khind (elevation 4,500 feet) commanding a view of Poorundhur, Singhur, Rájghur, Torna (and Máhâbulêshwár), which hill forts may be mentioned here as satisfactory sanitaria for Europeans. The rainfall does not, on an average, exceed 50 inches, whereas that of the Syhoodria or Western Ghaut exposure exceeds 200 inches, and forms an appropriate residence for the hot months only, ending with May.

"Panchgunny" is another plateau of these regions, which may be mentioned as adapted for a European settlement. It is 14 miles from Máhâbulêshwár, with an elevation of 4000 feet. It is, or has been, a sanitarium for British soldiers of the Poona garrison. **Panchgunny.**

On the whole, I may indicate this group of plateaux and hill forts as possessing considerable value in a strategic point of view as a Military Circle for a *Reserve;* or for such of the garrison of the South Mahratta country and Dekhan as can be spared by the Bombay government.

7. To the north of Máhâbulêshwár, and in the same (Tonga) range which buttresses in the Indian mainland opposite Bassein, we find the pretty hill station of Máhteran not over 2,500 feet elevation, but possessing a fresh, restoring climate after the heat of Bombay—looking out over Bombay harbour and reversely to Bassein. The coast line may be traced as far as the Bálasore roads, a lovely island-studded littoral of tufted bluffs, bays, islands, and palm-crowned promontories. It possesses much the same formation as Máhâbulêshwár, though here detached laterite and **Mahteran.**

other rocks crop out like pyramids, and form fantastic gables towards the setting sun,—a weird sight when the grey evening shadows are creeping over the scene, and the fiery ball of the sun is sinking behind the flat-topped hills of the Concan into the Indian Ocean. A detachment of convalescents from Bombay might perhaps with advantage be located here in the summer heats, or a small trading colony might be established; but the position is too restricted to be of much importance or strategic value, except as an outlet (or rather support) to the port of Bombay. If it be true that the "proximity of ocean" is essential to the prosperity of "social bantlings," such as infant colonies have been termed, we have it here, and no doubt Máhteran in some points of view, were we less masters of the ocean than we are, might even rise to importance as a development of the suburbs of our great western port of Bombay.

A few pleasant days has the writer spent there years ago, when the spangled jungle fowl could be shot from the path-side, and an occasional crack at a "kákúr" deer rewarded the early sportsman.

Khandala. 8. Khándála (2000 feet), in this same range, occupies perhaps a better strategic position than either Máhteran or Máhâbulêshwár, as it commands the G.I.P. Railway and approaches from Bombay and the low levels, on to the table-land by the Bhóri Ghaut. It has been selected, I hear, as a sanitarium for British troops, which are aligned also along the crests of the same range to the north. It is 42 miles from Bombay. Near it is a very grand cataract, descending in four successive falls as much as 1,200 feet into the Concan, whence the stream flows into the sea at Tanna, near Calliân.

Deolalie. The Deolálie Camp, on the Nassick table-land above the Thal Ghaut, sometimes contains as many as 800 or 1000 men, and forms a strong military support to Bombay, but is under 2000 feet elevation above the sea.

XLIX.

View from Mahteran, showing the denuded laterite peaks. Section XIII.

L.

Chandore Range, from near Deolalie. Section XIII.

LI.

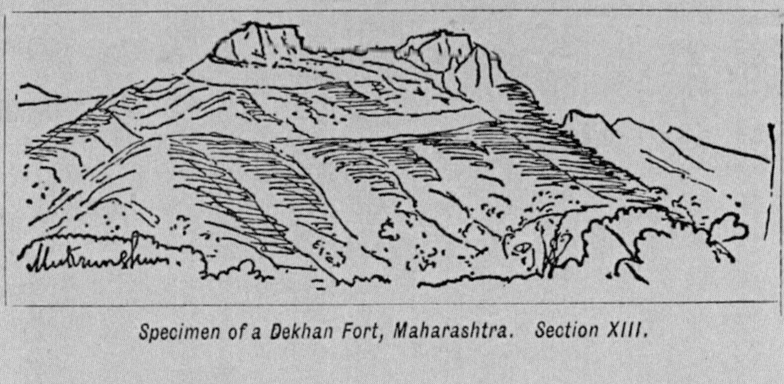

Specimen of a Dekhan Fort, Maharashtra. Section XIII.

The fine artificial Lake of Vihár is below these two passes; it supplies Bombay with pure water. When visited by the author some years ago, it was 17 miles in circumference, with a depth of 50 feet or more; a grand reservoir for the water supply of Bombay. It is formed by damming up the gorge of a valley in the low hills subtending the Tonga offsets of the Syhoodria; and it were to be wished that more such useful works existed throughout the land for purposes of irrigation. The ruins of splendid dams or "bunds" of this description are to be found throughout the Indian peninsula —in Rajpootana, and especially in the South, and many in Ceylon—a fact which would almost seem to reproach us with a retrogade policy or supineness in that particular. **Vihar Lake.**

9. Other small Sanitaria of Western India may be enumerated as Khándala, Lanauli, Singhur, Poorundhur, Punâka, Panchgunny, and Mander-Deo already mentioned.* **Small Sanitariums of Western India.**

The scenery of this coast is highly picturesque. The Tonga range, as has been mentioned, buttresses in the Indian mainland opposite Bassein, and dominates the Northern Concan, "the leek-green watery lowlands "studded with brown ravines and dotted with rich "groves, the hills and mountains of a warm red laterite ". . . . . contrasting with the verdigris of the 'jambu' "tree, and the Riornic sea-arm reflects the pale blue "sky."† **Scenery.**

10. With respect to the term "Concan," which has been frequently introduced in the above paragraphs: in its more extended (or Hindoo) acceptation it has been held to include the whole mountainous littoral of **The Concan and its Forts.**

---

* Kalsa Baiee, in the Syhoodria range, might perhaps be named as a high point of this region, its elevation being 5,409 feet above sea level.

† I am indebted for this picture to Mrs. J. Burton's *A.E.I.*, Chap. XIII., to whose work I would refer the reader for information on this special subject; methinks it was an artist's hand that penned the paragraph quoted; a vivid and true picture indeed!

the old Bejapore and Aurungabad provinces; which comprised North and South Concan. This area included a most surprising number of Hill Forts, Fortified Heights, and Plateaux; many of which have been destroyed since its occupation by the British in 1818. The names of the following may be mentioned as supplementary to those of Mâhârâshtrâ; a description of which will be attempted in the next section:—

On the sea coast Bassein, Arnalla, Kolir, Mahim, Sirigaom, Tariapoor (close to the sea shore), Cheooboon, Dhaow, Omergong, and others. These forts were mostly on the seaboard, as a protection against the pirates of this coast.

The principal fortified heights are Gumbheerghur, Seigwât, Asséwol, Bhóputgurh, Purbhool, varying in perpendicular height from 700 to 1,200 feet, and many others.

Inland, the forts of Gotowra, Tookmoorkh, Gójì, Vilkeetghur, Mullunghur, Asúree, etc., whilst *on* the Ghauts or Syhoodria Mountains may be enumerated Byránghur, Garuckghur, Kôtulgurh, Singhur (commanding the Gareedhari Pass), and others, which may be held as comprised in the "land of forts," a term suitably applied to the whole of Mâhârâshtrâ, the land of the Mahrattas.* It has, indeed, been already (page 162) estimated that the country of the Dekhan included in the term Mâhârâshtrâ—from the Tapti to the Toomboodra—contains not less than one thousand forts; though of course most of this large number are deserted, and contain little deserving notice but their names. In the Poona division alone 140 forts are officially registered—most of them as "deserted."

The Mountain Chain of Maharashtra.

11. I have termed Mâhârâshtrâ the "land of forts;" it is further emphatically the land of "mountain chains." It is in fact intersected by four such chains, besides the

---

* The author has visited but few of these sites, and the list is taken from *Hamilton's E.I. Gazeteer.*

Western Ghauts; these are the Sathpoora, Chandore, Ahmednugger, and Mahádeo Hills, which mostly run east and west, and divide the country into three sections. These—mostly flat-topped—hills are, I believe, of primitive rock. Plutonic fusion—probably sub-aqueous—was the origin of their peculiar structure. Laterite, basalt, porphyry, and tufa, and the other ingredients of volcanic action in varied combination, are found to be their chief constituents; and *upheaval* rather than subsidence of strata has apparently marked their emergence from the flooring of the primitive ocean. (See page 135.) Geological Remarks.

The red cliffs of the Western Ghauts, so observable at Máhâbulêshwár, Máhteran, and elsewhere, most certainly evince denudation from atmospheric influences; and the action of the severe weather prevailing along that coast during the "monsoon," may account for much of the fantastic formation observable.

12. Five great rivers traverse this region, *viz.*—The Nerbudda, Tapti, Godávery, Deenah, and Krishna. The Nerbudda rises in the table-land of "Omerkântuk," in Nagpore territory, in a "khoond" or pool built up as a tank, such as are also seen at the sources of the "Sône" and Wynegunga, which rise in the same range. The Máhánuddy also rises in pools of considerable size and depth; so that from this elevated watershed the waters escape eastwards into the Gangetic valley and the Bay of Bengal, and westwards through Mâhârâshtrâ to the Indian Ocean. Natural lakes exist in this plateau; especially to east of the Wynegunga, such as the "Nogong-bund," 24 miles in circumference; and the "Seoni-bund" is six miles or more. The watershed of this region drains south into the Godávery to the Coromandel Coast. The Nerbudda, after a westerly course over the plateau of Omerkântuk, is precipitated over its western declivity near Mundlah; thence through gorges, amongst which are the celebrated "marble rocks" near Jubbulpore (1,458 feet), near Rivers. The Nerbudda.

which it also forms a cataract at Bedaghur. At Hussungabad it is 900 yards wide, and is navigable to Chiculda, below which it narrows from 1,200 to 200 yards, and forms rapids where the Vindhya spurs impinge on its banks. Below this it enters the plains of Guzerat, where it again becomes navigable—its total course being about 600 miles. The valley of the Nerbudda contains coal, and was probably originally a chain of lakes. "The measures extend along the "southern side from Baitool and Seoni to near Jubbul-"pore. They form a long narrow strip resembling an "old sea beach extending along the base of the "'Páchmári Hills.'

The Basin of the Nerbudda. "The geological formations of the Nerbudda Valley "are interesting, and abounding in iron ores; but iron "and coal are nowhere found together. The tracts "may be classed as follows:—1st, The Vindhya sand-"stones; 2nd, the great schist formation; 3rd, the coal "measures (Burdoán group); 4th, the Mahadeo rocks; "5th, the cretacean rocks of Bang. The sites of the "iron ores are—1st The Bang (caves); 2nd, Burwai "(mines); 3rd, Nandia; 4th, Chandgurh and Makerbom "(higher up the valley), Dhurmpoor, Agaria, and "Juoli. Coal is found also at Sônádah, Sukher River, Mopári, Sper River, and Senáta Ghaut."*

The Toomboodra the southern limit of Maharashtra. I have dwelt on the Valley of the Nerbudda because that river—the northern boundary of Mâhârâshtrâ—drains and intersects so many ranges and "Highlands of India," noted in this work. The southern boundary of Mâhârâshtrâ—our present subject—may be considered the River Toomboodra. It is only so called after the junction, at Huli-Onore, of the rivers Tungha and Bhâdrá. The former rises near Bednore in the Western Ghauts, and the Bhâdrá in the Baba-Boodeen Mountains opposite Mangalore. On the banks of this stream are situated the vast ruins of "Bijanagur" or

* Bo. Government Geological Surveyor's Reports—No. xliv. of 1857.

"Annagoondy," 24 miles in circumference on both banks. They include an immense mass of temples to most of the deities of the Hindoo Pantheon. The city was built by Aka Hurryhur and Buka Hurryhur (brothers), about 1336-43 A.D., whose minister was Madhâna Achárya.

Ethnological.

13. A word as to the inhabitants of the Syhoodria Mountains, and valleys of these hilly regions.

Mawullies, etc.

The Mahrattas of course constitute the bulk of the inhabitants of Mâhârâshtrâ. The hill country is specially called (1) the *Concan;* (2) *Ghaut-Mâhta;* (3) *Désa-Désa;* and the Mahratta inhabitants of the table-lands of the Ghauts and Syhoodria ranges (or "Mâwuls") are called "Mâwullies." They are a brave and hardy race; and under Sivajee (the mountain rat) founder of the great Mahratta kingdom of the 16th century, made excellent soldiers, and to their bravery he mainly owed his rise. They are much enlisted as soldiers in our service, and form the staple of the Bombay army to the present day.

Other hill tribes of the Sáhyádri Mountains are the "Kâtkáris" (makers of the kât or cathechu), Kolis, Walis, Thâkūrs, and Dángurs. The Thâkurs are a superior race; the Dángurs are purely a pastoral forest tribe; the Kâtkáris are evident aborigines, and allied to the Sánthál or Kólè tribes of the central and eastern provinces.* Others might be mentioned, but it is to the Mâwullies that we have chiefly to refer as the dominant and martial highlanders of Mâhârâshtrâ.

HISTORICAL.

THE HILL FORTS OF THE DEKHAN.

Historical—The Hill Forts of Maharashtra and the Dekhan.

14. The Hill Forts of Mâhârâshtrâ contain, in fact, the history of this people, which cannot here be fully

---

* I refer the reader to Mrs. J. Burton's work *A.E.I.*, Chapter XIV., on this particular subject.

entered on. The wars waged by them against the Mahomedans in the 16th and 17th centuries, and against the British in the 18th, would alone form a volume. In lieu of an historical sketch, therefore, a description of the hill forts forming their military strength will now be attempted.

The summits of the hills in which they live are frequently crowned with huge basaltic rocks, forming natural fortresses of great strength. Many of them (as Poorunda, Singhur, Torna, etc.) are fortified by art, and very strong and numerous. It has, in fact, been already stated that the country of the Dekhan included in the term "Mâhârâshtrâ" from the Tapti to the Toomboodra, contains not less than 1000 forts. Mâhârâshtrâ has been termed the "land of forts," and its inhabitants may be credited with possessing that sense of independence which the feeling of security and pride imparted by such a condition of things can confer.

"Sivajee," the great founder of the Mahratta nation, was essentially a man of forts; born in a fort, mostly living in a fort, he died in a fort, and made or strengthened forts innumerable during his stormy career. Under him forts became the terror of India, and the cradle of his nation. They are identical with the "Highlands of Western India," but it is scarcely within the scope of this work to describe minutely the "Forts of the Dekhan." Plans and profiles of the various localities would be necessary to do justice to them as "refuges" and posts of vantage. There seems, however, to be a general generic resemblance between them.

The approach by the sloping hillside, ribbed with bands of rock, steeper and steeper as it rises to the summit on which the mass of porphyry rock—as at Poorundhur—scarped to 100 or even 200 feet, on the verge of which the walls of the fortress usually appear; sometimes massive gates, in others precipitous steps, or even nothing but the embrasure for a rope ladder, or a bamboo drawbridge can be seen; over all, the "bála-killa" or citadel, the last resort of the beleagured garrison! In some, the red columnar laterite cliffs stand forth like giant walls of some Cyclopean fortress of the mythic ages. "When primitive man began to "crawl and quarrel on the surface of this fair earth he "found these strange islands in a sea of hills, which "gave him security from the hand of his fellow-man "and from the wild beasts of early times; he cut steps "up the scarps, climbed to their summits, and was safe; "and it is probable that ever since the first dispersion "of our race these forts have been places of the greatest "importance to the security of the inhabitants. Some-"times they rise amid the plains, but more frequently "in chains like the series of forts built by Sivajee, on "the caps of a line of hills, running from 'Tataowra,' "near the 'Salpi' Ghaut, to 'Panálla,' by which the "valley of the Krishna is defended; or like that still more "remarkable line of forts which crown the range of "mountains dividing the Dekhan from Khandeish and "the 'Gungatherra,' or Vale of the Godávery, from that "of the Tapti. These hills are called the 'Chándore' "Range, and are from 600 to 1,100 feet above the plain; "rising again above which is a series of abrupt preci-"pices of from 80 to 100 feet higher, so wonderfully "scarped that only the great number of them—more "than is necessary for the defence of the country—"prevents one at first sight from supposing them the "work of the chisel. Almost all are supplied with "good water on their summits, and possess little more "of fortification than a flight of steps cut on or through "the solid rock, and a number of intricate gateways. "This strange line of inaccessible and—if well defended "—impregnable forts, stand like giant sentinels athwart "the northern invader's path. . . ."

From the peak of "Kulsa-baiee" (5,409 feet) may be seen not only the great chain just described, but to Views from Kulsa-baiee.

the northward the Rocks of Trimbuck, Anjineer, and Hursh, at the source of the Godávery, Nassick, above and beyond which the great Chándore range extends across the horizon, each of its forts—the "Septa Sring" (or seven horns)—"tipped with sunlit gold; beginning "at that nearest the Sáhyádri Ghauts, Ackla, then "Junta, Markundeh, Rowleh-Jowleh, Dorumb Doráos, "the celebrated Rajgheir, and Irdnge, successively "lifting their peaks against the morning sky; and, be- "yond Chándore, the well-known twin-forts with the "curious name of 'Unkye-Tunkye,' which command "the road between Nugger and Malligaum."

On the Kalsa-baiee range itself another series of strongholds, beginning near the Ghauts with Aurung, Koorung, Muddunghur, Bitunghur, and the better known forts of Ounda, Putta, and Arr.

To the south, along the line of the Ghauts, rising amidst dense jungle, there are several more forts, chiefest of which is "Hurrichundrágurh; and beyond, to the south and west, lies the Concan, and resting upon it the great fort of "Mowlee." Further to the south the Máhteran range is dimly visible like islands floating in a sea of wave-like hills. As examples of these fortresses the following, such as Singhur, Torna, etc., already noticed, have been selected for slightly detailed description.

Torna.

(a) *Torna* has been well called the "Cradle of Mâhârâshtrâ." It is visible from Poona. It was thence that Sivajee, having launched forth on his adventurous and stormy career, stretched his arms across the mountain chains of the Dekhan. First having scaled the great mountain "Mârbûdh," three miles to the west, he constructed on it the vast and inaccessible fortress of

Raj-ghur.

(b) *Râjghur*, which he adopted as his residence, and the construction of which gained for him from Aurungzebe the appellation of the "Mountain Rat." "In "the troubled times of 1857 the Commissioner of

LII.

Torna from Singhur, Dekhan. Section XIII.

LIII.

Fort of Raighur in the Concan, from the Western Ghauts. Section XIII.

"Poona went up and threw over an old gun or two "that remained, and which might have tempted some "one to fix on this wild crag, so full of historic associ-"ations, as a haunt, from which dislodgment, while "provisions lasted, would have been simply impossible." The elevation of this great stronghold is not much less than 4,500 feet above sea-level. *Râj*ghur has been sometimes confounded with *Rai*ghur, a very different place, and which merits some description, though strictly speaking it is not a Dekhan but a Concan fort. "When Sivajee began to rise into almost imperial "power, Rajgurh became too small for his retinue, and "in 1662-3 he selected a mountain called formerly "'Rairee,' situated on the edge of the Ghauts not far "from Râjghur."

(c) On its flat summit a mile and a half in length **Raighur.** and half a mile broad, and well supplied with water, he erected his seat of empire, *Raighur*, and transferred thither his great offices of state. Here Sivajee was crowned, and from hence he issued his coinage, and here he died in 1680 A.D.

"*Raighur* was soon after taken by the Moghuls. "Sivajee's son's wife and infant son were captured in "it. The celebrated sword 'Bhowâni,' and that also "which Sivajee had taken from Afzool-Khan, were "conveyed thence to Aurungzébe, who long after "restored them to the heir of his ancient foe."

The three forts just named—Torna, Râjghur, and Raighur—may well be instanced as highland forts of Mâhârâshtrâ:—the very nidus and centre of the Mahratta Highlands.

(d) There are, of course, many other forts, such as **Lingana.** Lingâna, close to Râjghur on the Ghauts, built by Sivajee at the same time as Tála, Góssâla, another Rairee, to secure his hold on the Concan. The way to these lies from Poona by "Singhur," over the Pábek-Khind near Torna, down the Asanalli Ghaut, past Raighur; or by the Nishnee Ghaut south.

N

Hurrichandra-ghur.

(e) "Hurrichândrághur" is perhaps the most remarkably situated fortress of the Dekhan, and is said to present the sublimest scenery in the whole range of the Western Ghauts. "The top of the mountain is of "considerable extent (4000 feet) and it has a small but "very comfortable set of caves for residence, and a "reputation for bears enough to allure the sportsman. . . ." It has a scarp of 3000 feet of nearly perpendicular height, and is 4000 feet above the Concan immediately below it. It enjoys a fine climate, and is well worthy of a place in any work treating of the "Highlands of India." "I wonder," says an author to whom I am much indebted for this portion of my work,* "this cool and lovely solitude is not oftener "visited;" but it seems to be subject to violent blasts of wind at times.

Sewnere.

(f) Near Hurrichândrághur is the fort of Sewnere near Jooneer, a fief of Sivajee's grandfather, "Máloji-Bhonsla," and here (1627 A.D.) was born the great Sivajee himself. This fort commands the Nána and Malsej Ghauts, the former a *point d'appui* from the Dekhan.

Pertabghur.

(g) Pertábghur, already mentioned (page 164) as visible from Máhâbulêshwár, is interesting as connected with the rise of Sivajee, being the scene of the notorious "Wâgnuk murder" of Afzool-Khan of Beejapore, by Sivajee in 1659; a deed not to be palliated of its treachery and baseness, but viewed perhaps by Sivajee as a great duty to his country and religion, and one that assuredly did more than perhaps any other deed of his to the establishment of his ascendancy and escape from the power of the Moghuls.

Trimbuk.

(h) Trimbuk is a strong and interesting fort amongst the Chándore mountains, 20 miles south-west of Nassick.

---

* *Vide* a lecture delivered before the U.S. Institute of Western India at Poona by Rev. F. Gell, to which I am greatly indebted for much valuable information on the subject of this section.

It is a spot of great religious importance; perhaps the most sacred to Hindoos in Western India. From its rocks rise the fountains of the great river Godávery. "Here great detached pillars of rock, 200 feet high, "stand round the little valley like giant sentinels." It was surrendered to the British in 1818, after having repulsed one assault.

General Remarks

Nature has done much, art but little, for these strongholds; many of them all but impregnable if well defended. Escalade or treachery has been the most common mode of their capture. Ofttimes has the garrison—as in the case of Trimbuk—been frightened into surrender, even after an unsuccessful assault.

The Duke of Wellington, speaking of these fortresses, says he always attempted to blow open the gates, but seldom succeeded; he adds, "I have always taken "them by escalade;" which, however, he adds, "is un-"certain in its issue unless the attack can be made on "more points than one at the same time, and the "advance covered by musketry, and by enfilading the "parts attacked!"

It may be added to this, however, that a number of forts were captured by Sivajee by surprise, such as Kangoorie, Toong, Teekóna, Köaree, Bhoorûp Lohurgur, Rajmûchee, and the escalade by night of the great fort of Singhur by Tannaji-Maloosré and his son, with 1000 Mâwullies from Torna, is a well known instance of early Mahratta courage, and adds one more instance to the proverb that "fortune favours the brave."

On the fall of Trimbuk, the strongest and most sacred fort in the country, 30 other forts—each if well defended capable of defying an army—were (according to Lake) surrendered to us almost immediately without a blow, "and the vast Mahratta empire which had "overshadowed all the East, soon became an example "of the instability of thrones, the foundations of which "are not laid in the affections of the people.

"We naturally ask why are these forts now of such

Military Aspects. "small account compared with what they once were? "Without pretending to go into all the military questions involved in the answers, I may call attention to "the pregnant words of the 'Great Duke.' 'In fact,' "he says, 'no fortress is an impediment to the operations "'of a hostile army in this country except it lies immediately in the line on which the army must "'necessarily march; or excepting it is provided with "'a garrison of such strength and activity as to afford "'detachments to operate upon the line of communi-"'cation of the hostile army with its own country.'

"For various and perhaps sufficient reasons, orders "have been given out to dismantle many of these "fortresses. It is difficult to help regretting it, how-"ever necessary and expedient it may be. Is it im-"possible that the time may come when India will be "emptied of troops by the urgent needs of some great "European struggle with which we shall sympathise "too much, not gladly to make every sacrifice? Then "we, a handful of men amid angry populations, may "again wish for strongholds of security to fly to till "the storm be over: who can tell?"

To the above words of wisdom quoted, the author would humbly add his earnest endorsement. The want of "refuges" and posts of vantage, chiefly in the "Highlands of India," has for years been the key note of his military views. Long before the Mutiny broke out he pointed at the possibility of such a thing, and in his then very subordinate capacity, urged upon authority to spare several points, which almost immediately afterwards *did* become of the first importance as "refuges" in the perilous times of 1857-9—*e.g.* Mooltan old fort. The author has never believed in the foresight or forecast of the British official mind. Prompt to face danger, it seems deficient in the sense of eventuality which foresees it, and the above few words of warning—the words of the wise man sitting in a corner—so chime in with his own convictions, that he has quoted them *in extenso,* as expressive of his own long cherished conviction.

Picturesque Aspects.

"Of late years indeed, changes in the mode of war-"fare have shorn the forts of their honours. As living "powers in the country they are now comparatively "unimportant. We are no longer afraid of them. The "descendants of their former owners have ceased to "put any trust in them. They are things of the past. "It is not impossible, indeed, that they may some day "be again manned with warriors, and play their stir-"ring part in future struggles of their country. But "now they lie neglected and forsaken, or put to uses "quite other than those for which they were erected. "But I am not sure that the pleasure of living in the "past rather than in the present, together with the "sympathy one feels with fallen greatness and dimmed "glories, has not added a charm of which they could "not otherwise have been possessed; and one loves "the giant crags and rude and crumbling fortifications "none the less because they have been distanced in "the race, and are now decidedly behind the age, and "because they stand amid their highland summits and "fern-clad hills with a melancholy grandeur, no longer "what they were. The world has swept by them; "'civilization' declines to acknowledge them; and the "busy nineteenth century knows them not.

"Once they were everything; the active centres of "political life, and the great nurseries of military spirit; "the keys, and keepers too, of the surrounding countries; "the refuge in every hostile storm of invasion; the "founts from whence, like lava from mighty craters, "flowed forth the fiery hordes which desolated India. "They were the receptacles of wealth and wisdom, the "much desired prize for which each conqueror strove; "the suppressed premiss in every negotiation; the "seats of government; the schools of youth; the re-"source of a dignified old age. Undoubtedly too, they "were the foster-mother of Mahratta nationality, and "interwoven with every element of the national great-"ness. They reared the hardy tribes which have been "called the Goths of India. If a time of prosperity "came, it was spent in strengthening their fortifications; "if adversity, in defending them to the death; it was "only disaster when they had to be given up. On "their summits treaties were framed, and terms were "signed with the luxurious princes of the plains of "India; to their subterranean chambers were carried "the plunder of great cities in all parts of Asia; and "in their dungeons—still horrible to behold—were "confined the captives (male and female) torn from "the homes of the enemies of their country. Ah! and "many a dark and thrilling deed of blood and cruelty "has been perpetrated in those now silent recesses. "Along their proud ramparts troops of richly dressed "and well armed men were ever moving. Bright silken "ensigns threw broad folds over their towers; and the "numerous cannon of their bristling battlements woke "up ever and anon the echoes of the surrounding "mountains. It was a gay and gallant scene.

"Alas! they are nothing now. In a very few of "them a havildar and a few sipahis still keep the gate; "but hundreds of them—by far the larger number—"are marked in the lists of the quarter-master-general "as 'deserted' or 'destroyed.' They are all silent now; "witnessing indeed to later times, and to degenerate "races, of the great deeds of their forefathers, of self-"sacrificing heroism, and desperate courage, and high "hopes, which seem as if they have for ever mouldered "cold and low."

With these extracts I approach the end of my slight chronicle of the "Hill Forts of the Dekhan," as a subsidiary offset of the general subject—"Highlands of India."

Concluding remarks.

At the time I write (1875) India is *quiet*—"as quiet as gunpowder,"—and we war not at present so much against man as against the climate and powers of natural evil evolved from miasm and disease. If it can be proved that any of these mountain summits and plateaux contain, from their position and elevation, an exemption from those dire enemies, malaria, tropical heat, and the consequent lassitude and disease, then assuredly we may class them amongst the points of vantage and "refuges" so often insisted on in this present work, and their garrisons might be even perhaps concentrated into a "Military Circle" such as has been advocated; beyond this, I fear we cannot contemplate them in the light of agricultural industrial circles, such as military colonization would take cognizance of, as their essential features are stony and rocky solitudes, perched amidst dense jungle and scrub, and surrounded with arid plains, where sheet-rock and tracts of half reclaimed desert and sand nourished vegetation alternate with strips of fertility taken up by the exuberant populations of Mâhârâshtrâ.

Their strategic position for those who hold the seaboard is but little; though *tactically* as points of vantage, good. Let us rather contemplate them here under their romantic aspects, so pleasantly put before us by the able author quoted from,* and I venture to think from the comparatively slight experience I have undergone in viewing them, that much of interest attaches to these grand old solitary eeries of the past age of Mâhârâshtrâ, and of the mountain plateaux they defended.

The foregoing sketch of Mâhârâshtrâ, with the vivid picture of its thousand forts and posts of vantage—refuges from hostile man and the equally hostile heat of summer—leads us to the question involved in the title of this work,—How far such resources may be availed of, and what general advantages may be reaped from them?

The writer has consistently ever advocated the massing of British troops in healthy localities; and

* Gell.

though, doubtless, the space embraced by most of the positions noted may be very limited, still it is believed that these *pieds-de-terre* of the "Highlands of India" may well enter into our attentive consideration as possible stronghold refuges, or local centres of strength, for the dominant race in times of peril. Some of them, as above stated, have already been availed of as "sanitary" retreats from the heats of summer, chiefly for the convalescents of the Poona division of the army; others are, as stated, but slenderly garrisoned by our native soldiery, or even altogether abandoned. Should an imperial system of relief for our native troops be introduced, and natives not bound by hereditary ties to Mâhârâshtrâ ever occupy these quarters of the present Mahratta forces, we may anticipate that some of these elements of strength may be more fully utilised than has hitherto been done under the "Presidency" system, a *régime* which, in a military sense, seems so heavily to have curbed the development of the Indian Army, and pressed on its resources. I do not doubt but that in the future that system—which, however, in its time has worked well practically—is doomed to the common fate of effete systems. Thus much I venture to anticipate on a point so far bearing on my subject, "The Highlands of India," that its dissolution would no doubt facilitate the development suggested in this work.

NOTE.—The "Inyadri Hills," on the edge of Candeish in the Dekhan, present an extraordinary example of trap rock cropping up into fantastic shapes, often by successive terraces of level rock rising like steps on to a flat table-land-like summit, on which an isolated columnar mass often crowns the mountain.

SECTION XIV.

THE WATERSHED OF "CENTRAL INDIA;" THE PLATEAUX OF OMERKANTUK AND SEONI.

The Vindhya, Sathpoora, and Kymore Hills; Pachmari, and Basins of the Nerbudda, Tapti, and Godavery.

The Highlands of the Dekhan; Omerkantuk, and its Offsets: Vindhya, Sathpoora Hills, etc.

BEFORE passing on to the hills north of the Nerbudda, it seems expedient to dwell a little further on the Highlands of the Dekhan; especially to mention Omerkântuk, the most northern and the most elevated of the mountain tracts which encircle the table-land of Central India, and which may indeed almost be included within the area of Mâhârâshtrâ, as defined in the preceding section. This plateau constitutes the watershed of Central India, as on it originate the great rivers Nerbudda and Sône, which respectively pour their waters into the western Indian Ocean, and through the Gangetic Valley into the Bay of Bengal. The great river Mâhânuddy also rises on this plateau, which after draining a large mountain basin, empties itself direct into the Bay of Bengal.

The plateau of Omerkântuk—whose elevation at its highest points approaches 7000 feet above sea level—is the central axis-block whence radiate the chains that extend north-west across the Nerbudda, and west into the Dekhan. The table-land, however, rises considerably above them in altitude. Below Mundla, where the Nerbudda falls over its precipitous terrace, it sends out offsets westwards on both sides of the Nerbudda. These take the form of three distinct ridges:—(1) the most northern being the Vindhya Mountains, (2) the middle range the Sáthpoora, and (3) the Southern, which constitutes the northern dip of the table-land of the Dekhan, has been sometimes called the "Northern Ghauts,"—the Mâhâdeo Hills lying between the two branches of the Tapti. Between these three ranges lie the parallel valleys of the Nerbudda and Tapti.

The Northern Ghauts, Chandore & Mahadeo Hills.

2. The Northern Ghauts, thus defined, commence about 22° north latitude, and between 78° and 79° east longitude, with the "Highlands" on whose *eastern* declivity are found the upper branches of the "Wurdah," an affluent of the Godávery, and on whose western declivity the springs of the Tapti are found.

These mountain masses have an approximate elevation of 3000 feet, and send off a very distinct and well defined range some 2,500 feet elevation westwards between the two branches of the Tapti. This range is called the "Mâhâdeo," and attains its highest elevation near the fortress of "Gâwulgurh." Continuing westwards along the southern side of the Tapti, the Northern Ghauts extend to 74° east longitude, to Chandore and Soolgána, where they blend in with the Western Ghauts or Syhoodria Mountains. The range appears of considerable elevation, and rises very abrupt and steep from the valley of the Tapti, but its descent into the table-land of the Dekhan is moderate, not being more than 500 feet above it. The mountain passes are very difficult across this range. The best pass from the valley of the Tapti to Aurungabad leads close to the celebrated rock temples near Adjunteh.

River Godavery.

The Godávery—the largest of the Dekhan rivers—rises in the north-west corner of the table-land of the Northern Ghauts near Nassick in the Chandore range. The Wurdah, one of its chief northern tributaries, drains a considerable basin, extending along the southern declivity of the Northern Ghauts and the elevated table-land of Omerkântuk, between 76° and 80° east longitude: it receives the Wynegunga, on which Nagpore, the modern capitol of Berar, is built. Mountains rising to 2000 or 2,500 feet abruptly, lock in the Godávery at its junction with the Wurdah. The river is here a mile in width during the rainy season.

3. The Vindhya Mountains are of a very indetermined axis. Geologically viewed, some geographers have held them to commence in Behar and terminate near Cape Comorin; offset ridges ramify in various directions, and, locally, bear different names. The true Vindhyas—as so termed by the natives—commencing near the western coast, extend only as far as about *Jubbulpore.* Here they merge into the so called "Kymore" Hills, which extend down the valley of the Sône to near Patna, Rhótas, and Sasseram, sending branches off to Mirzapore, Banda, and even Gwâlior; where, however, they are of lesser elevation. To the north, where they extend along the Nerbudda, the true Vindhyas may be termed the broken wall or buttress of the plateau of Malwa; there they scarcely exceed 2000 feet elevation, and only in a few spots such as "Shaizghur—the highest peak in the Mandoo range—only attaining 2,610 feet elevation. The Vindhyas, and Kymore Hills

The drainage of the Kymore branch of the Vindhyas in Behar finds its issue chiefly into the River Sône, which falls into the Ganges near Patna. These are generally flat-topped hills; they attain their greatest elevation in the Peak of Omerkântuk, near 7000 feet elevation. Further south-east these hills are called the "Rajmahals" or "Goomehs." In Behar the flat shoulder of "Párasnaûth" attains an elevation of 4,230 feet; its highest peak being 4,500 feet. Some spurs, also, near "Beejaghur," a fortress famous in story and romance, near the head waters of the Sône, attain altitudes of 3,400 or 4000 feet, almost the only elevated points needing remark. The country can hardly be said to present ground for colonization; even as a temporary refuge for Europeans it is a doubtful locality; but the eastern watershed of these hills, into the Sône and its tributaries, is well known to be rich in auriferous deposits, and also contains coal measures; a fact which may affect its development in the future, when India shall have entered on another phase of social history.*

The Sathpoora Mountains.

4. The Sáthpoora Mountains are the block range between the Nerbudda and Tapti. They do not, at their highest peak, rise above 2000 feet. They possess the same geological structure as the Vindhyas, though the outlines differ in having bolder peaks of amygdaloid and greenstone. The River Tapti rises in the Nyardi Hills (a parent knot of the Sáthpoora Hills) 56 miles north-north-east from Ellichpoor. Gawulgurh† is in this district—15 miles north-west of Ellichpoor—near the sources of the Tapti and Poorna Rivers, which has its other source in the Sáthpoora range.

Pachmari.

The elevated plateau of *Páchmári* dominates these hills. It occupies a commanding and central position as towards Goondwâna; as also towards the Nerbudda valley; the plateau itself being about 3,600 feet elevation. The sandstone peak of "Dhûpgurh" = 4,380 feet, and Andeh-Kóh, a wild glen, = 2,500 feet elevation, are points in its close vicinity; Mopáni being the chief centre of the coal measures found in the basin of the Nerbudda. Páchmári appears first noticed about 1818, when Appa-Sahib, ex-Rajah of Nagpore, sought refuge amongst the wild tribes of the Mâhâdeo Hills, which brought on the temporary occupation of this plateau. It now holds a flourishing British sanitarium. The geological structure of this district consists of sandstone with trap overlaid, and coal is found towards Omerkântuk.

Goondwana Elevations.

5. Deoghur (above the Ghauts) a district of Goondwâna, may here be mentioned as an elevated tract looking down to the north on the valley of the

---

* See end of this section, para. 10.

† Wellesley took this place in 1803 after a siege of two days only. It was originally a "Goond" possession, and was captured by Ragajee Bhonsla in 1754.

LIV.

The Pachmari Escarpment. Section XIV.

LV.

The Mahadeo or Pachmari Hills from the south, showing the great escarpment. Section XIV.

Nerbudda. The most elevated of the ridges traversing it is in the vicinity of Bhútkágur, having at its other (west) extremity the mass of the Mâhâdeo mountains (2,500 feet), the highest of which is called "Damlâgahâri." The rivers Wurda and Wynegunga, to the south of this district constitute its outlet by water transit, and drain its basin.

The following are a few elevations;—

Ambawarra	-	2,500 feet elevation.	
Chindwarra	-	2,200	"
Tárághaut	-	2000	"
Kumapáni Ghaut		1,750	"

Sirgoojah, in the Goondwâna country, is the capitol of a large province of the same name. About three marches to the south-east is the mountain and table-land of Mynput—3000 feet elevation—enjoying a temperate climate as compared with the adjacent plains. Here the thermometer often falls as low as 28°, and the average heat does not exceed 72°—80°. It forms the watershed of a considerable region,—to the north into the River Sône, and to the south into the Mâhânuddy.

The Wurdah River rises in Goondwâna and flows into the Wynegunga at Sëoni. The Wynegunga is the largest of the Goondwâna rivers. It rises on the "Sëoni" plateau at 1,850 feet elevation, and finally enters the River Godávery near Chinoor, contributing an equal quantity of water. Floats of timber descend this river, whose water communication with the coast and the excellent little harbour of Coringa, at the mouth of the Godávery, is thus established.

Historical Notice of the Goondwana Chiefs.

The history of the Goond Rajahs is of considerable interest, though of somewhat obscure antiquity. They rose to some eminence and power under the Môghul emperors, of whom they became vassals; and in the person of Rajah "Bukt-Bullund," adopted the Mahomedan religion; but they were overthrown by the Bhonsla family, who usurped the country. As far back as the reign of Aurungzébe we find Goond chiefs as rulers of Mundla, Deoghur, and Chanda, the ancient capitols of the mountain kingdom of Goondwâna—Nagpore being the modern capitol. This tract may perhaps be mentioned amongst the "Highlands of India."

The Course of the Godavery, S. Points of Interest

6. Following the course of the Godávery, the "Anantagherry" Hills near Hyderabad Dekhan, may here perhaps be mentioned as a quasi-sanitary, but I believe they are assigned lands. Districts in the Berâr valley and Sáthpoora range within the basin of the Tapti, are perhaps favourable for enterprise and partial culture at such points as Chikuldah, Mokloh, Dhoolghât, etc., etc. They are inhabited by Goonds—a primitive race. The chief products are sugar-cane, turmeric, grain, &c. The scenery is very fine. Parts of Berar, which are bounded by the river Wurdah, a tributary of the Godávery, would have an outlet to the seaboard should "Sir A. Cotton's" scheme for the navigation of that river be carried out. A few blocks of land in Raichore district, over 3000 feet, may also be named as favourable for temporary if not for permanent residence for European capitalists.

Still pursuing the course of the Godávery, we should find on the northern bank, near the sea-coast, the "Marmédi" Hills, attaining an elevation of 4000 feet on the north of that river, and the "Thöamool" Hills (3,500 feet), which are still better adapted for settlement. These two blocks of mountain have been already described (Section II., paras. 5, 6) as enjoying a modified temperature, partly from elevation and partly from proximity to the sea. They are adjacent to the harbour of Coringa already alluded to.

Highlands.

7. The mountain tract north of the valley of the Mâhânuddy is a mountainous table-land elevated between 3000 and 4000 feet above the sea, but traversed by ridges running east and west of not less than 5000 or 6000 feet. North it blends in with the plateau of

Omerkântuk, and south a single ridge projects towards the Bay of Bengal, where it terminates west-south-west of Bálasore, and is here called "Nilagherri," ending in the bluff called the "Mylagiri" Hills.*

8. On the south-west of the table-land of Omerkântuk rise the Tapti and Poona Rivers, constituting the two branches of the Tapti. The mountain range between these two branches is called "Mâhâdeo," and rises to 2,500 feet. Its average width is about 20 miles, and it rises abrupt on both sides, which are covered with forest. After the junction, the Tapti flows through the Sáthpoora Mountains 280 miles to the sea. **Rivers.**

The course of the Nerbudda, from its source at Omerkântuk, and its precipitous fall over the table-land at Mundla to Husshangabad, along the base of the Vindhya Mountains on the north and the Sáthpoora Mountains on the south, has already been mentioned (para. 1). These two great rivers have been stated to drain the basin of the Dekhan westwards.

9. All the regions here described as constituting the Highlands of the Eastern Dekhan, contain dense forest tracts swarming with wild animals, the usual heavy game of the Indian jungles. Recent writers have described the wild and beautiful scenery of these regions often called "Central India." Although the writer has more than once passed across this country he has not had such full opportunities of examining the country as would justify an opinion as to its feasibleness for European settlement. On the whole, he must incline to the belief that it scarcely presents such encouragement as other districts already described. Lovely glades and vales bathed in perpetual spring, braced in by mountain tracts nearly above the zone of malaria, no doubt might be found, but in too restricted an area to attract colonists. A few plateaux, however, might be occupied, and the scheme of **General Remarks on the Highlands of Central India.**

* See end of this section, para. 10.

sanitary settlement such as has been tried at Páchmári in the Sáthpoora Mountains might succeed. Possibly a "Reserve Circle" might be established for Central India on some of the plateaux named for a military settlement *sub vexillo,* but its area of expansibility could be but restricted.

In the dry season, hot and arid are these intricate clusters of mountain, which, however, when the rain falls, are at once converted into fresh green pastures, and, it must be feared, malarious, though lovely forests in which, defying sickness, the British sportsman has loved to roam and hunt the tiger, sambur, and—southwards—the bison (or Urus) and elephant, with the other running game of an Indian forest. The lover of the picturesque also would find in these elevated forest tracts ample scope for his admiring eye to expatiate, or his pencil to limn the natural features. This is scarcely the place to dwell on such features, albeit in the settlement or colonization of new regions, assuredly such attractions in the vicinity are by no means an unimportant adjunct as attractive to the Anglo-Saxon race. Several recent writers have written pleasantly on this subject, and to them I would refer the reader for detailed information on the districts under notice. A few profiles, and elevations of the scarps of this district as an adjunct to the foregoing partial description will be given, as illustrative of the geological structure.

Parasnauth and the Rajmahal Hills

10. Párasnaûth (4,624) and the Rajmahal Hills being in Bengal are not strictly within cognizance of this section of the work, but as they may be regarded as offsets of the central plateau described in para. 3, may perhaps be here conveniently introduced.

The Mágasáni and Mylagiri Hills are also alluded to in para. 7 as found on the course of the Mâhânuddy, and will also be here noticed.

A short notice of Párasnaûth, the culminating summit of the Rajmahal Hills north of Bengal, seems

LVI.

Mount Parasnauth, Bengal. Elevation 4,624 feet. Section XIV.

LVII.

General View of Mount Parasnauth, Bengal. From east peak, looking west. Section XIV.

called for, as it forms a small sanitarium and residence for a few Calcutta people during the very hot weather, its temperature being some 10 or 12° cooler than that of the Bengal plains.

Mount Párasnaūth (Pârswanâth) is situated at the confines of Bengal and Behar, in territory belonging to the Rajah of Pálgunge. It is faintly visible from Hazári*bâgh*, another quasi-sanitary station for British troops in the Rajmahal Hills. It is one of the most sacred places of pilgrimages for devotees of the "Jain" sect, throughout India. The name of the mountain on which the temple, or series of temples (goompties), is situated is named *Sámet Sekher*, Párasnaūth being the deified or holy name of the shrine, and there are no less than 12 goompties (shrines)—corresponding to the 12 Jaina Tirthankars — crowning the summit. It is a singularly beautiful mountain, commanding a view of the whole surrounding country, and is the loftiest summit in the valley of the Ganges, being 4,483 feet in elevation. The chief ascent is from "Pálgunge," where the devotional duties of the pilgrims commence; another ascent is from Mahdëobund south-east from Mathopore, which is at the 147th milestone from Calcutta on the G.T. road. The sides of the mountain are clothed with magnificent "sukooa" trees and creepers. The flora on the sides of the hill is sub-Himalayan. Sál, toon, sisso, jarool, bamboo, and a tree peculiar to this district—the "sahr jain"—abound.

About 1000 feet below the summit, at an elevation of about 3,500 feet, there is a plateau which might be utilized for cultivation. Stone and timber are plentiful. The hill is of syenite (or gneiss), and the temperature 10° or 12° below that of the plains at the base of the hill, where there is a dâk bungalow. The highest summit, according to the Government Survey of 1861 = 4,624 feet. The watershed is on the north, where springs exist, owing to a dip in the strata northwards.

A ground plan and elevation will tend to show the characteristics of this really grand, though isolated, southern mountain.

The Hazari-baug Plateau. The Plateau of Hazári-bâgh*, an elevated region of the Rajmahal Hills, within sight of the fine mountain just described, is not less than 28 miles in length, but though elevated 1,800 feet above sea level it is not free from malaria, and is scarcely to be reckoned amongst the "Highlands of India." Its highest peaks, after Párasnaūth, are as follows:—

The Chendwár Peak	-	2,816 feet elevation
„ Jalinga „	-	3,057 „
„ Baragáti „	-	3,450 „

being 1,300 feet above the "Chutea-Nagpore" Plateau; and others approximating to 3000 feet. The watershed of the "Damoodar" River is not above 2000 feet. The forests of this region are not valuable, but the pasturage is good, and the soil is favourable to the growth of tea. The population are Sonthâls, Bishoos, etc. The geological formation is plutonic, with marine deposits superimposed. Coal is also found in the basin of the Damoodar.

"Khuttock Hills."

The Magasani Hills in Khuttock. 11. Some account of the "Magasáni" and "Mylagiri" Hills, in Khuttock, may perhaps conveniently here be given. The former (Magasáni) group, about 40 miles inland from Balasore, consists of a plateau 3,800 feet elevation, and, though scarcely sufficiently elevated above malaria, enjoys a temperature 12° or 14° lower than the adjacent plains. The route from Balasore is across a level plain of "kunker" and ferruginous gravel, and the summit peak, and ridges are reached by gradual slopes, and abound in stone suited for building pur-

---

* I am doubtful whether this word is referable to Bágh (gardens) or Bāug (tigers). From the "tigerish" character of the country, however, I incline to the rendering *Hazáré-bāug* (a thousand tigers).

poses, at elevations of from 2,500 to 3,500 feet. The soil is rich below the summit. Water is good and pure, and there are perennial springs near the summit. At about 3000 feet there is a fine grassy plateau of several miles in extent, well watered, and covered with large forest trees. The soil—a rich marl—is subtended by a rolling country 40 miles in length, by 10 or 12 miles in width, and is admirably adapted for coffee, wheat, potatoes, and vegetables; tea might also grow.

On the whole, these hills are better adapted for a colonist than for a sanitarium, for which their elevation is scarcely sufficiently raised above the malaria of the plains; the temperature being 13° cooler than Calcutta, and 13° hotter than the Nilgherries, is consequently exactly a medium temperature between those points. The trigonometrical station on the highest peak of the Hill of Magasáni is 3821-53 feet above sea level in latitude north 20° 38′, and longitude east 80° 24′, and is 38 miles from Balasore in a direct line, nearly due west.

12. The Mylagiri Hills in Palleyra, are even better **Mylagiri Hills.** and more interesting than the Magasáni, but their situation—120 miles as the crow flies, from the seaboard —reduces their value as a sanitary resort, otherwise they enjoy a finer site for building than the Magasáni plateau, as they possess a fine ridge running some 14 miles north-east at an elevation of about 3,500 feet. To the west of this ridge there is an extensive table-land at a slightly lower elevation, well watered, and containing many villages, one of which, "Jombarum Dehi," is beautifully situated in a lovely valley watered by a hill stream, which here falls over cliffs of "red jasper" 550 feet. "Kúmtar" is perhaps the chief trigonometrical station of this range of hill and valley, and is situated on the extensive ridge already mentioned.

The Mylagiri (trigonometrical) station, from which the whole range takes its name, is 3,880 feet high, with plenty of good water near the top, and easy access might be made from the southward. There is ample ground on the top for building, and even for gardening purposes.*

* Captain Saxton's Royal Trigonometrical Survey.

SECTION XV.

RAJASTHAN,

AND THE MOUNTAIN REGIONS NORTH OF THE NERBUDDA.

(1) The Vindhyas further described; (2) Malwa; (3) The "Uper-mal," comprising the Harrowtie and Chittore Hills; (4) Mount Aboo and Offsets of the "Aravelli" Mountains; with (5) a Notice of the "Kathiawar" Group of Highland Temples, etc., etc.

The Vindhya Mountains.

THE Vindhya Mountains begin on the west, between 73° and 74° east longitude, with the high hill of Powaghur near Champaneer—that blue mass one sees from Baróda to the east—and extend eastwards along the valley of the Nerbudda. The western portion, as far as Chikulda, has not the appearance of a continuous range, being broken up into isolated groups, and presenting many steep summits. Its width here is considerable, and to the north it blends in with the mountain tract which extends north-north-west along the river Mhye, and which unites the Vindhya Mountains with the Aravelli Range. East of Chikulda the Vindhya range approaches the Nerbudda, and continues along it like a steep wall, having a broad-backed surface without peaks; its general elevation being about 1,700 feet above the vale of the Nerbudda, and not more than 2,200 above sea level.

As the table-land extending to the north (where it is contiguous to this range) is itself 2000 feet above sea level, the mountainous character of the range disappears on that side; but towards the Nerbudda its declivity is exceedingly steep, and indented by short transverse cuts, which in places give the appearance of projecting bastions, on many of which fortresses have been built, now mostly in decay.

Such are the Vindhya Mountains as far east as the road which connects Bhopal—on the table-land of Malwa—with Hushungabad on the Nerbudda; and *it is to this portion of the range alone that the term "Vindhya" is applied by the natives.* East of this point the Vindhya range blends in with the table-land of Omerkântuk (see page 185), and merges into the "Kymore" range, which buttresses in the course of the River Sône towards Patna on the Ganges. It declines in height as it approaches Mirzapore to 1000 or 700 feet above sea level. The roads across the Vindhya and valley of the Nerbudda have been already mentioned. They mostly converge on the chief cities of Malwa or the Uper-mal district, such as Oojein, Mhow, Indore.

Passes across the Vindhyas and River Nerbudda.

(1) The Baug Road from Chikulda leads across the Tanda Ghaut to Oojein and Oodipore. (2) Next comes the Jaun Ghaut, which rises to 2,328 feet above sea level, to Mhow, and on to Indore and Oojein. (3) A third pass leads over the Vindhyas to Bhopal from Hushungabad, this road has already been mentioned and described (Section XIV.). (4) Near the table-land of Omerkântuk a road leads from Jubbulpore to Belhári. Other roads traverse the mountains of the Kymore range from Chúnár; and, more recently, the great Agra and Bombay mail road crosses the very heart of these mountains over the Seöni plateau; and the railway now (1874) has pierced these forest solitudes, and whirls the commerce and traffic of the Gangetic valley and north-west India to the western seaboard.

Malwa and the Uper-mal: their Topography.

2. A triangle, whose base would be the Vindhya Mountains (properly so-called) lying along the valley of the Nerbudda, and whose apex would be near Jaipore or Ajmere, would embrace a table-land of considerable extent, *viz.* that of Malwa, which occupies its southern regions, and is enclosed by mountain ranges, and also a large mountain region called *Uper-mal,* which extends on the north of the table-land. The Vindhya Mountains thus form the southern

LVIII.

On the River Nerbudda. Vindhya Mountains. Sections XIV. and XV.

LIX.

Powergurh Hill, Vindhyas, from the Valley of Sooki. Sections XIV. and XV.

LX.

The Thall Ghaut, Kandeish. Sections XIV. and XV.

boundary of the table-land of Malwa. On the north the Harrowtie (or Mokundra) range closes it in.

The Mokundra Pass, forming the great outlet of the country, has played a very conspicuous part in the destinies of Malwa. It is the scene of a British defeat, but it would be too long here to enter on the historical episodes of which it has been the arena. It leads to the Uper-mal or eastern section of the triangle supposed in the text. To the east the Mokundra Range stretches into the offsets of the Vindhyas near the sources of the river Sonar near Chandpoor (79° east longitude). It embraces an area stretching north-west as far as Neemuch, where it is connected with a mountain region south of Oodipore, and joining the *Aravelli* range near 24° north latitude, and 73° to 74° east longitude. This range is of insignificant elevation, and is broken up in places by the rivers and torrents which, originating in the Vindhya Mountains, traverse the table-land of Malwa, and forcing their way through the Harrowtie Hills, descend in numerous cataracts and rapids through the narrow valleys. The table-land of Malwa dips towards the north from about 2000 to 1,300 feet elevation. Indore, in the Vindhya Mountains, =2000 feet elevation; Oojein=1,650 feet; Baróda, near the Chumbul=1,520 feet; Rampore-Vaikree, under the Harrowtie Hills,=1,275 feet. These towns, which are built on the Chumbul river, indicate the dip of the table-land northward. On the table-land itself are several cities of importance, such as Bhopal, Indore, Dhar; and Oojein in the centre of Malwa is a very ancient town through which the first meridian of Hindu astronomers is drawn. It was formerly the residence and capitol of Scindia, now removed to Gwâlior. Bhanpore is important from its command of the Mokundra Pass, which leads over the Harrowtie Hills to Uper-mal. Pertábghur, situated on the road to Goojerat is noted for its works in gold. A line drawn from thence to Dohud marks the western boundary of the table-land of Malwa. The Kántel, west of this line, is a mountain tract about 50 miles from east to west, connecting the Vindhya Mountains with the Aravelli Range. This region is full of forest valuable for timber, which includes teak. This region is called Kántel, and is chiefly inhabited by "Bheels," who will be described further on (para. 9).

Mountain Ranges of the Uper-mal, or Highlands of Rajpootana.

3. On the north of the table-land of Malwa, separated from it only by the Harrowtie Hills, lies a mountainous region called by the natives *Uper-mal* = The Highlands. This region is intersected by several parallel ridges from the Aravellis, decreasing in altitude as they trend eastwards towards Rewâri.

The Chittore Hills are nearest to the Aravelli, and terminate in a kind of mountain knot, in which the Harrowtie Hills also terminate on the west. Neemuch is near the bluff of this range, which runs north-east towards Agra, terminating near Dhôlpore on the Chumbul. They do not rise beyond 2000 feet above sea level, and not more than 600 feet above the adjacent country at their base, but from their steep and broken character they oppose great impediments to the traversing the parallel valleys comprised in this region between the Chumbul and Bunnáss Rivers.

Forts or Towns of Rajpootana.

Chittore, Kôtah, Bhoondi, Jaipore, Indurghur, are towns of this mountain tract. Strange isolated rocks from 400 to 600 feet above the plain, are found in the northern parts of this region. The town of "Alwar" is even as much as 1,200 feet, perched on the highest of these strange rocky islands of the plain.

Oodipore is another celebrated city—the capitol of Mewar—whose chief claims precedence of all Rajpoot princes; and, still further north, are Ummerghur, Bhilwarra, and Bunaira. In the extreme north-east corner of this tract is Ajmere in the Aravelli chain which will be described further on. Gwâlior is a strange island rock west of this region.*

---

* Where this work was commenced.

LXIII.

Specimen of a Rajpoot Fort, "Bunair." Section XV.

NOTE. It is an essential feature of a Rajpoot Fort that the Town or Village is clustered round the base of the rock on which it stands. In predatory times the chief's followers and clansmen would naturally seek protection under the ægis of his stronghold. Further to the east, an example of this is presented in the great rock fortress of GWALIOR, which is one and a quarter miles in length, under each end of which a city containing ten or twelve thousand inhabitants is found built; that at the west end being originally the "Lushkur," or camp of the Mahratta Prince "Scindia," whose capitol it forms at the present day. The author, whilst in command of this interesting fortress, commenced the early chapters of this work.

I do not know that much more need be said of this region, which is cursorily noticed here as amongst the quasi-"Highlands of India," though it does not come within the area of healthy refuges, or even contain *pieds-de-terre* for sanitary circles such as have been suggested.

4. All the rivers which traverse the table-lands of Malwa and Uper-mal, just described, fall into the Jumna, the watershed of the country being north-east. Mostly originating in the west of the table-land of Malwa, with a slow current, they break through the Harrowtie chain in narrow valleys, where they form a series of rapids and cataracts. The largest — the Chumbul — rises on the northern declivity of the Vindhya Mountains in three branches, between which are built the towns of Dhar, Segore, and Indore. The other rivers of this region—the Sinde, Betwah, Cane, and Tonse, which all drain eastwards to the Jumna—are also full of cataracts, and none of them navigable beyond a very short distance from their respective mouths. **Rivers of Rajpootana.**

The most eastern of the rivers of the mountain region of Northern Hindostan, the Sône, rises on the eastern declivity of the table-land of Omerkântuk, near 23° north latitude, and 82° east longitude: it skirts the table-land north-north-west to 24° north latitude, when it suddenly turns to east-north-east, and flowing through the cliffs of the Kymore range, in a narrow valley to "Rótásghur," enters the Gangetic plain, and becomes navigable till its junction with the Ganges above Patna.

5. We have now fairly worked our way north as far as the Aravelli range, beyond which it is scarcely proposed to carry the reader at present.

To enter on historic study of these regions would involve too elaborate a retrospect, and take us back into the very dawn of history, when the early Aryan immigrations, fixing on these sheltered table-lands, **Historical Note.**

imported the great Rajpoot stock, and colonized the country of "Râjâsthân." Twenty-two principalities ruled over by scions of this great stock are still extant to attest the former grandeur of their race. Proud and patriotic, they resisted Mahomedan usurpation to the death; and the episodes of their struggles against the Moghul power are heroic, and full of most romantic interest. They extorted their "suzerain's" respect, and became "allies" rather than feudatories of the Moghul empire.

In the 18th century, and in the early years of the present century, successively overrun by the Mahrattas and Pindaries, they bent before the storm, but have recovered, and with our aid and support are, it is believed, contented, and loyal to the power which guarantees their integrity.*

A long period of enforced peace, and consequent idleness, has perhaps tarnished their former warlike character, and enervating habits may perhaps have impaired their original native energy; still they possess elements of warlike aspiration, and in our service have proved good soldiers. Even yet, it is believed that the Rajpoot principalities could bring into the field a united force of cavalry amounting to 150,000, which reduced to discipline, and organized, might give us perhaps 50,000 or 60,000 auxiliary light horsemen for the defence of British India. This feature may be called their *objective* power. Their *defensive* power resides in the natural character of their country rather than in its artificial strength; and it especially derives strength from the remarkable range of mountains now to be described.

The Aravelli Range.

6. The "Aravelli"† Range, extending along and covering the whole northern front of their country for

---

* The small Principality of Tonk alone remains a witness of the Pindarie irruptions and conquest. It is ruled by a descendant of the Mahomedan usurper "Ameer Khan."

† The literal rendering of Aravelli = *The Strength of Refuge.*

LXI.

View on the River Bunass, Rajpootana. Section XV.

LXII.

Distant View of the Aravelli Range from near Oodeypore, Rajpootana. Section XV.

300 miles or more, constitutes a grand defensive rampart for Northern Hindostan. The breadth of the Aravelli range is about 60 miles at Komulmari on the south, but decreases as it trends north to Ajmere, where it ends in the bluff of "Tara-Gurh," and breaks into ridges and offsets in several directions. The average height of the Aravellis does not much exceed 3000 feet, though a few summits may attain 4000 feet, and Mount Aboo, the highest peak, nearly 5000 feet.

The southern extremity of the Aravellis joins into the Vindhya range by a mountain tract extending from Edur to Lunâwarra and as far as Champaneer. The author has ridden along the greater part of this region, and to some extent explored and noted its physical characteristics, and is of opinion that he would be a shrewd leader who could make good his entry into the rich plains of India by the route of Rajpootana, covered as it is by the north deserts "Ḿároosthâli"—the "Plains of Death," as the natives call them—backed by the Aravelli range and its offsets.*

7. This range is composed of plutonic or primitive rock, superimposed on slates of a dark blue character, which occasionally extrude above the flooring of igneous rock. Quartz crops out here and there, and isolated rocks of gneiss or syenite jut forth into fantastic cones and pyramids, which appear in places like spires or columns athwart the deep blue sky. On the summit of Aboo many such may be noted. The author once dwelt under ono such quaint rock called the "Nun," which offered a marked resemblance to such a figure. At other points, especially near Ajmere, the "diverging ridges and the summits are quite **Geological.**

* During the Mutiny, however, in 1858, Tantia Topee, the Mahratta rebel, traversed several of these passes with considerable bodies of followers, and threaded the intricate country in its rear in various directions, followed by British columns. The remarks in the text therefore admit of exceptions for small bodies of troops.

"dazzling with enormous masses of vitreous rose-"coloured quartz." Not without an element of the picturesque are even these sterile, barren plutonic slopes.

Mount Aboo and its precincts.

8. *Mount Aboo*, the last of the *hill stations* to be considered, is situated on a spur of the Aravelli range, which here rise to the altitude of 4,500 feet; the highest peak, "Gooru-Sikra," being 5000 feet above sea level. It may be defined as an elevated block holding a small plateau surrounded by a ridge, of which it forms a basin, containing about a dozen villages. It may not inaptly be compared to the Nilgherrie plateau on a small scale, though situated as it is—so much more to the north—its flora is essentially different, and its geological structure differs, but the same undulating, though more broken, *terre-plein*, and the same exterior barrier-ridge or wall of peaks—corresponding to the Nilgherrie "koondahs"—are found: even the little semi-artificial lake, more rocky and islet-studded, however, completes the parallel similitude. It is situated in the territory of the "Sirohi" Rajah.

The Jain Temples of "Dilwára," on the plateau, contain some of the finest Hindoo carving I have anywhere seen. They constitute an interesting feature to the archæologist, and invest the mountain with a sacred character, which, however, is not without its drawbacks in a military point of view, or as a residence for Europeans. These temples were built on the site of other and more ancient temples dedicated to Siva and Vishnoo. The founder is stated to have been one "Bimul Sah," a Jain merchant of "Anhelwâra," who, about A.D. 1236 dedicated the chief temple to "Richabdeo," the second to "Nanni-nâuth," at a cost of eighteen millions sterling. The other temples are more recent, and are not more than 400 years old.

Altogether, Mount Aboo is a pretty little hill, enjoying a restorative climate. Situated on the main roads between Rajpootana and Guzerat, it thus possesses considerable strategic value, and dominates the whole northern face of the Aravellis, but being an isolated elevation raised above the adjacent spurs, it is not capable of much expansion. Its chief value in time of peace is that it forms a small sanitarium or refuge for the British residents of Rajpootana and Guzerat from that dire enemy the "heats of summer;" and in war time it might become a site of the utmost importance to the safety of the whole district; hence I would name it for a small *reserve military circle*, such as has been advocated in this work.

In the adjacent forests—towards Oodipore—are some very remarkable ancient cities and temples, now for several centuries overwhelmed by dense forest trees, especially "Chándräolis" or "Chándrawáttie," some 12 or 20 miles south-east of Aboo, and about equidistant from Sirohi, the capitol of the small Rajpoot state in whose territory Mount Aboo is situated. In 1860 the writer of this paper hunted them up with a line of 30 Bheels, and lived for three days in the principal temple of "Chándräolis." It was apparently a Jain temple, and surrounded by cloisters, in one of the cells of which we found a half-eaten "sambur" (deer), which had evidently been dragged here by a tiger or leopard, whose lair it constituted. I mention this to show the wildness of the place, and to note the existence of large game in this district; which contains, besides the tiger, leopards, bears, and the usual denizens of an Indian forest. **Adjacent Forests. Archæological Remains.**

9. As regards the inhabitants of these regions, besides the Rajpoot clans, we find the *Bheels* south of the "Mhair" country. The Bheels—"Vanâpootrâs," (children of the forest) as they style themselves—are a hardy, dogmatic little race of men, interesting to study. The Rajpoot clans, with whom they are on jealous terms, affect to despise, but in reality fear the little men, with whom the blow precedes the word; and who do not scruple to use their bows and arrows

freely on the smallest provocation. Like many oppressed populations, they are shy and distrustful, but faithful when once their confidence is secured.

North of "Kumulmair," in the mountain regions also, we find the *Mhairs*, a wild race, whom we have, however, enlisted into our service, and quarter in garrison at Ajmere, Beaur, and Erinpoora, as local corps; their country "marches" with that of the Bheels.

Ajmere and Tara-gurh.

10. With this slight sketch of Mount Aboo I must conclude the notice of the *Hill Stations of India*. There may be others left undescribed, as hill stations are increasing year by year, as the desirability of locating British troops in mountain air is becoming more and more recognized.

Besides hill *stations*, there are of course scattered over the country of "Râjâsthân," as elsewhere, isolated summits and hill forts at various points, too long to enumerate, such as are found in most Indian hill districts. These often form pleasant refuges for the sick soldiers or convalescents from the arid plains during the summer heats; instance, "Tara-Gurh," an old fort perched on the bluff overhanging Ajmere (the ancient capitol of Rajpootana), at an elevation of perhaps 3000 feet, a point whose military position is valuable as holding in check, and commanding, north-east Rajpootana. It is situated on the eastern extremity of the Aravelli range, as those mountains from this point throw off offsets north-east, east, and south-east (towards the Vindhyas), much lower in elevation than the main axis. Rose-coloured quartz may be seen hereabouts cropping out of the rocky ridges, which contain also copper, lead, tin, sulphur, salt, and iron. Ajmere (with Tara-Gurh) has appeared to me worthy of notice as a subsidiary—perhaps native—"military circle," and I have so marked it on my sketch map. An interesting lake from four to six miles in circumference is here seen. The environs of Ajmere are interesting, and the old fort of Tara-Gurh affords a retreat to the

LXIV.

Lake at Mount Aboo, Aravellis. Section XV.

LXV.

The "Nun," a syenite rock at Mount Aboo, showing also the interior gneiss slopes of the bounding ridge above the lake. Section XV.

British convalescents of the adjoining military station of Nusseerabad from the heats of summer; and if put into a proper state of defence, might form a position sufficiently strong to defy the surrounding country. I name this point as one of those valuable posts of vantage to be found throughout the land for "refuges" of a local character in war time, but should the concentration of British troops be more effectually carried out hereafter on to the tactical bases and strategic points of the land, in "Hill Stations" or "Reserve Circles" such as have been suggested, such small positions would be gradually abandoned, as tending to fritter away the (British) garrison of India; when probably their place might be taken with advantage by native or auxiliary troops, in pursuance of the policy to be found in the preceding chapters of this work of the *hills for the British, the plains for the native soldiery.*

Doubtless spurs of the Aravelli range, rising to near 4000 feet, might be found; isolated rocks also—those islands of the plain may be found in Râjâsthân as in other parts of India—as Posts of Vantage; but enough instances to illustrate the "Highlands of India" have probably been adduced.

Powarghur and Champaneer.

11. Going westwards from Mount Aboo we might perhaps find a few heights with a modified degree of heat, but as a rule, malaria prevails up to 4000 feet elevation, and renders them uninhabitable by European convalescents. Such is the old fort of "Powarghur," 28 miles east of Baróda, on an isolated hill—perhaps a bluff of the Vindhyas—rising to 2,800 feet, where the ruins of the city of Champaneer—that blue mass so enticingly visible from Baróda—lie at its base. It enjoys a temperature 12° to 20° lower than Baróda, and as a resort, *in the hot weather only*, can be availed of after January; during the rest of the year the malaria of the "Baria" jungles to the east renders it unhealthy. I may mention *en passant* that Champaneer was founded before the Christian era (about

Samvat I.) by Chumpa, a Bheel, whose descendants possessed it 13 centuries, till A.D. 1244, when it was subdued by a Chohan Rajpoot named "Pallumshi," in whose family it remained eleven generations more. It was finally conquered by "Sultan Mahomed Béghura," who left it a ruin. Other accounts state that Champaneer was taken A.D. 889, after a long siege, by Mahmood, 7th King of Guzerat; and was subsequently captured by the Emperor Humaioon in A.D. 1534. It is described by Abul Fuzl in A.D. 1582 as even then an extensive compass of ancient Hindoo and Mahomedan ruins. On the decline of the Moghul empire Champaneer fell into the hands of the Mahrattas, and it became an appanage of Scindia in A.D. 1803.

Kathiawar and the Highland Temples of Kepar Kot, Bhairava-Jap, etc.

12. As the last point to be mentioned here, the Hill Districts of "Kâthiawár" may be cursorily alluded to. The "Girnar" Hill, about four miles from Joonaghur, reaches 3,500 feet above sea level; and the stone of "Asoka," a monolith, is outside the citadel of "Kepâr-Kôt," which is built at an elevation of more than 4000 feet in the adjacent jungle. Here again the Jain temples are most remarkable; the largest, sacred to "Memi-nâuth," having cloisters measuring 190 by 130 feet, was repaired to its present form about A.D. 1278.*

In this district also is found the grand solitary rock called "Bhairáva-Jâp," whence the "leap of death" is taken by fanatic suicides, and "Amba-Mátá," the temple of Cybele, the universal mother. All these form a group which may perhaps find a place in this work; details are to be found in (Bombay) Government Reports. Thence also may be seen the Peaks of "Góra-Kanâtha," "Delatrya," and "Kálika," attaining elevations of 3,500 feet. From this spot a grand view is obtainable:—"The sea, 60 miles "distant, sparkles in the horizon at Veráwul. "Extended to the south lies the forest of Gir—*nutrix* "*leonum.* The hill of 'Sutrunjáya,' above Palitána

* From Bombay Government Reports.

"(itself a most wonderful agglomeration of Jain temples) "on the east; on the west, the hills of Alich and Barda." Jeipore has, I believe, been proposed as the central point of the railway system of Kâthiawár, in which case these interesting groups of highland temples will be rendered more accessible to the traveller. Any further topographical description of Kâthiawár need not be here entered on; suffice to say that the comparatively modern name is derivable from the "Kâthis," who some centuries ago came from the west through "Katch," and gave to the ancient Hindoo province of "Sômâshtrâ" its present name of "Kâthiawár." I mention this district also as a fine field for the sportsman; amongst other large game the (so-called) Babylonian or maneless lion is still to be found in considerable abundance in its wild forest tracts; and, as before stated, its archæological remains are highly interesting.

13. I have lingered perhaps over long on points scarcely to be considered as amongst the "Highlands of India,"—the theme is inviting. Now, however, I approach the end of my attempt to partially put before the reader the "Hill districts and stations of India," as sites for *reserve circles* or *refuges* for the dominant race, either as government settlements or for private enterprise. In the preamble of this work I have sufficiently dwelt on the argument in favour of colonization (especially military) for India; and now I believe I cannot end these papers better than by adopting (slightly modified) the words of an able writer,* who says—"The high plateaux of India have lovely hills "and dales bathed in perpetual spring; the long range "of the Himalayas offers Alpine homes to the Anglo-"Indian. The whole land asks but the application of "capital by English intellect to pour the treasures from "her teeming lap. Surely the blessings of permanent

General Remarks

* Money: in his work *How to Govern a Colony.*

"English settlement in India are worth trying for, "although their realization might convert the natives' "dearly loved laziness, with its consequent poverty, "into industry and riches."

Conclusion.

If the natives of India can by some such scheme of culture and colonization as is advanced in these papers on the "Highlands of India," be in any way associated with the dominant race in the honourable task of improving the soil and developing the grand resources of the great Indian peninsula, we may expect an empire to arise such as "it never hath entered the heart "of man to conceive;" with a revenue double its present figure; the military and strategic points occupied by an industrious and contented citizen soldiery to supplement the British marching garrison of India; we may see armies put into the field, such as India has hitherto had no experience of hosts,—fit to cope with all Asia, with Russia at its back; armed with all the weapons and latest improvements for scientific warfare; able and ready to engage the "world in arms."

SECTION XVI.

INDIA ALBA.

(1) THE KURRUM BASIN AND THE WATERSHEDS TRANS-INDUS; (2) THE SULIEMAN MOUNTAINS AND THE RANGES BETWEEN INDIA AND KANDAHAR; (3) SMALL HILL REFUGES ON SPURS OF THE SULIEMAN MOUNTAINS *(a) Shaikh Boodeen, (b) Dunna Towers, (c) Fort Munro, etc.*; (4) PISHIN AND THE BASIN OF THE LORA.

India Alba

THE original design of this work—written chiefly in 1874-5—had contemplated ending with the last paragraph of last section, but recent events have brought into such prominence the north-west frontiers of British India across the Indus—the country called by the ancients *India Alba*—that I will devote some small space to a few remarks on the *Highlands* of those regions:—1st, as far as they have come under my own observation; 2nd, as described by recent geographical surveys, and other authorities (mostly military), quoted further on (page 228). My own experience of these highlands not going much further than the Kurrum Valley and the Dérajhât, with the mountains immediately bordering the Peshawar, Yoosūphzaie, and Kohát Valleys, I must leave to others the description of the direct routes on Cábul and its surrounding mountains. I assume that these highlands can scarcely be regarded as fit habitations for European settlers, or as in any way affording sites for *colonies*, under present political circumstances.*

Cashmere, the true strategic defence of India, N.W.

I will at once remark that my own theory of a defence for north-west India has long been the subsidizing

* *Native* Military Colonies (of Goorkhas, Sikhs, or Dogras) perhaps excepted.

of Cashmere, as the country flanking the five Döabs of the Punjâb; thence, in case of invasion, to operate on the communications of an enemy advancing from the north;* but inasmuch as our armies have entered Affghanisthán, and taken up what has been assumed to be a "scientific frontier," I bow to circumstances, and *now* would deprecate retreat from valuable strategic points conquered by our arms, and justly our "heritage of war!" The flanking lines shown on the sketch map of this work will roughly indicate the strategic flanks contemplated as subsidiary to the main idea of *Cashmere the true strategic defence of India!* I emphasize this, as I have always wished to associate my military diagnosis of this problem therewith. My ideas on this point are briefly conveyed in para. 3, Section I. of this work on the "Highlands of India."

Small Sanitariums trans-Indus.

2. Setting apart therefore the possible settlement of the future in the highlands of Affghanisthán such as the valleys of the Cábul, Loghmán, Pághmán, Bamian, Tezeen, and the Dámun-i-Kôh, etc.; or even the ultimate absorption of wild tribes such as the "Siahpōsh Caffres," etc., etc., into civilization; let us not forget that Russia is a *colonizing* as well as a conquering power in Asia, which England is *not* at present. I will simply, in this first place, sketch such portions of the Dérajhât and mountains closely adjacent to our frontier as have fallen to my lot to view. These regions are perhaps some of them suitable for *native* colonization, but assuredly not for European. There are, indeed, spots of fertility and beauty which might attract us for a temporary location or cantonment, such for instance as are to be found in the upper parts of the Kurrum Valley and elsewhere; and a few mountain tops or plateaux might be found where the scorching heat

* *Vide* the preamble and Section I. Para. 3 of this work, *passim.* The Post of Kurrachee and the Indus Valley Railway may also be regarded as having the same value on the other flank, especially for the transport of munitions of war.

of the valley or the adjacent plain might be mitigated in summer. A few of these points were briefly alluded to in Section II., paras. 10 and 11. If possible, also a few sketches as explanatory of the girdle of mountains which embraces the Yoosuphzaie plain, and the Peshawar valley will be reproduced,—made by the author during his various rides, some on duties of inspection of frontier forts in this district.

Shaikh-Boodeen.

Cherât has been described at Section II., para. 9, but a few additional words as to Shaikh-Boodeen (4,500 feet)* may here be given. Assuming the valley of "Bunnoo" to be surrounded north by the Cábul Kheyl Hills (a continuation of the Suliemán range), south by the "Batánee" range, east by the Khuttock Hills, west by the Suliemáns. It appears that the latter throw off an offset south-east as far as Peyzoo, hence called the "Peyzoo Hill;" the prolongation of which ridge about six miles is called "Shaikh-Boodeen." This hill is of limestone and sandstone, and on the highest point is the sanitarium for this frontier. The rock here is stratified, and contains marine fossils, and perhaps the bones of miocene animals. I mention this in support of the theory stated in Section V., para. 1. In the Suliemán range lignite and pyrites are found in profusion. The Koorum River skirts the Cábul Kheyl Wuzzeerie Hills and enters Bunnoo, and unites with the "Gombelah;" the united stream joins the Indus at Esau Kheyl, having cut its way through the pass in the Khuttock Hills. It seems likely that originally the Bunnoo valley was a lake; and perhaps close examination might find fossils similar to those of the "Siwâliks" in the "Dehra Dûn," (Sect. V., para. 8).

The Kurrum Valley, Basin, etc. Topographical Features.

3. In lieu of a detailed description of the Kurrum Valley—which, with that of "Khóst," it is understood has been recently (1880) annexed to the Indian Empire—the author, having personally visited the country

---

* Dr. Costello's Report, 16th Feb., 1864, to Aux. Asiatic Society.

in a military expedition against the Cábul Kheyl Wuzzeerie tribes, may give a few profiles and sketches then made. His observation, however, scarcely extended so far as the upper waters of the Kurrum; which, descending in three streams from the Paiwár and Hazârdarakht ranges, unites with the Kármán River in the great range of the "Sufaid Kôh," and forms the highway of the valley to which it gives its name. Here some lovely spots are found, and towards the now celebrated Paiwár Pass the valley rises to 10,000 feet, affording a temperate climate, with a zone of forest and corresponding flora. The river Kurrum, besides its own basin, drains also the basin of the Khóst valley, of which the principal streams—the Shamil, the Matun, and Zumba—unite at Arun-Kheyl, ultimately joining the Kurrum at Hazár-Pír. The fluvial basin thus indicated is, of course, surrounded by lofty mountains, constituting the watershed from which its waters originate. To the north, one sees the great range of the Sufaid-Kôh, which may be called the main axis ridge of the Suliemáns. "Sikh-arám" (or Sitarâm) is the great dominant peak of this range (15,600 feet). Other peaks are "Bodin" (14,000 feet), "Matungurh" (12,800 feet), Lakerai (10,600 feet), the "Shútargurdan" (10,800 feet), Keraira (15,000 feet?). Several of these are shown in the sketch, but most lie more to the west. One large hill near "Thal," named "Kodimukh," = 4,900 feet. Other ranges, such as the "Paiwár," rise from 9,400 to 11,000 feet, and the great mountain "Matungeh," north over "Ali Khél," overlooks the best pass from the Ariāb Valley (the Lakerai Kôtal = 10,600 feet) across to Jagdalak and "Gundamuk." Here the scenery is described as "exquisite, "and quite Alpine in many parts." It is not proposed however, to enlarge on this theme. These regions, though undoubted "Highlands of India" (Alba), can scarcely claim our notice as "refuges" or sites for "Military Industrial Circles," such as have been considered in this work.

Mountain Peaks; Altitudes, etc.

LXVII.

Camp at Shewa. Valley of the Kurrum. The Pushtoo Mountains (Speen Wan, &c.) in the distance. Section XVI.

LXVI.

The Pushtoo Range from the Valley of the Kurrum, showing the Peak of Jooni, &c. Section XVI.

The great deodar forest of "Spinghar-Kôtal" may be mentioned: it clothes the upper reaches of the Ariāb valley for miles. Ilex, pines, deodar, juniper, with the birch, rhododendron, etc., are found; and on the slopes the gooseberry, currant, honeysuckle, walnut, daphne, cotoneaster, berberis, coleaster, roses, jasmine, a few ferns, and grasses. Lower in the valley, the plane (P.Or.)—especially near Sháluzân, a lovely spot —walnut, mulberry, apricot, plum, apple, pear, grapes, peaches, quince, pomegranate, almonds (olives on the lower hills), are found; and willows and poplars fringe the streams. The flora of a temperate zone is here found. The people are agricultural.

Aspects of the Highlands of the Kurrum.

4. Across the Kurrum one *did* enter on Cábul territory, and when we crossed the range in 1859-60, I noticed the top of the plateau, paved as it were with sheet rock, cracked into fissures by the frost, as though the whole had been broken up by a giant pavior for slabs. The mounted portion of the expedition could not of course proceed very far in such a country, but we viewed the infantry driving the enemy—the Cábul Kheyl Wuzzeeries—into the slopes of the Suliemán range. Other "Highlands of India" may be termed the *Land of Snow*, the *Land of Forest*, or the *Land of Grass;* so assuredly I would apply to these highland regions the epithet of the *Land of Stone.*

The Sulieman Mountains.

5. The "Sufaid-Kôh" already alluded to runs north east to south-west, and is visible from the stations all along tho Indus west of the Cábul River, where it is called the *Suliemán Mountains.* This range ramifies in two branches, an inner or main western range forming the water-parting of the Indus basin and the inland Affghan valleys; and an outer or eastern range rising from the plains of India. On this last is found the peak of the "Takht-i-Solimán," which gives to this range its name. The inner (or western) of these two branches of the Suliemán Mountains extends to the Bolán Pass, south of which it is called the "Halla"

Range. It extends further, 350 miles or more—as far as Cape Munza, the westernmost point of British territory on the Arabian Sea. To attempt to describe in detail the features of this intricate country, or to enumerate its tribes, would be a work in itself. The reader may be referred to the valuable papers on the geography of Affghanisthán in the numbers of the Journal of the Royal Geographical Society for January, February, and March, 1879, by C. R. Markham, C.B., the able secretary R.G.S.

Ethnological. (See para. 18)

The author has had the advantage of reading a native work—the Tarikh-i-Affghan—on the tribes of Affghanisthán, of which only two copies are extant. The one consulted was borrowed by a Candaharie friend from a town beyond the "Tartara" mountain (6,800 feet), and copious notes were taken. Not only were the Pathân, or Affghan tribes alleged to be descendants of the Israelites, and a most graphic history of their progress eastwards given, but the origin of each particular tribe, or branch of a tribe, was given. It may be stated generally that this *historical romance* (as it was pronounced to be by Löwenthál) stated that at the period of the return from the captivity, two Jewish chiefs, with a following of about 2000, declined to return to Judea, marched eastwards, and entered the service of the Amir of Balkh; thence they extended their arms to Ghuzni, and either in support of, or themselves as dominant, proclaimed a chief; became possessed of that seat of dominion, and thence extended themselves over Affghanisthán. In this work the origin, or rather the point of ramification from the parent stem, is given for each tribe or section of a tribe of the Pushtoo-Affghans; in fact, it constitutes a most elaborate geneological chronicle, in the main features of which I myself am inclined to believe, *viz.* that the Affghans are veritable descendants of Jews; but I am bound to admit that this view was not supported by the great Pushtoo scholar Löwenthál, to whom I submitted them, who gave several learned reasons why the whole thing was a romance vamped up to flatter the pride of the Affghan race. I of course submitted to such an authority, but was, nevertheless, not convinced.

6. Proceeding south-west along the Dérajhât—although I have incidentally visited most of the military frontier stations—I am not aware of the existence of any sanitary refuge* until we come to "Sinde:" there—about 50 miles from Dadar—we find the small station called "Dunna Towers" (4,500 feet). This small place is by route far distant from the localities mentioned, though, "as the crow flies," across the great western desert, not so far from Mount Aboo. It forms a cool retreat and a sanitary refuge for Shikarpore, Jacobabad, etc. The station is built on a ridge of the great Halla range about 50 miles south-west of Mahur. It overlooks the north-east portion of the Sinde valley, and the position is itself overlooked by the vast range of the "Khara-Luckha" (6000 feet), the barrier between Sinde and Beloochistân. The rocks and soil are chiefly sandstone, limestone, and marly detritus, quartz, pyrites, and carbonate of lime. Rugged watercourses and cliff terraces bear evidence of powerful water action; denudation of the higher ranges also attest it, and as characteristics of this region, boulders of many tons in weight are found in the flanks of the watercourses. (Compare para. 2.)

The Derajhat: "Dunna Towers," etc., in Sinde.

"Herár" is a pretty valley three miles south-west of the "Towers," and contains an abundant supply of water. Here a fort was built by the Amir of Sinde, but was soon abandoned. The soil is a yellow rich marl. The rivulet or stream from Herár possesses some curious peculiarities, being lost amidst vast boulders and

* *Fort Munro*, however, a small sanitarium for the civil residents of Dera-Ghazie-Khan—south-west—at an elevation of 6,158 feet may be here mentioned. The summit of the range reaches 7,400 feet hereabouts.

rocks for the distance of half-a-mile, through petrified vegetable matter and *débris*. European vegetables grow, but can scarcely be said to flourish here. It is a wild, barren spot, with much of the characteristics as to soil and climate of Shaikh-Boodeen in the Déra-jhât, already described (para. 2). Its desolate aspect, however, is relieved by flocks of sheep and goats, who here find herbage amongst the stunted shrubs and trees. In June and July the temperature is considerably above 80°—rising to 90° and even 100°—but *endemic disease is absolutely unknown*, and the nights are generally cool, and the climate very healthy. To sum up its advantages, "an elastic and buoyant atmos-"phere, trying to escape from the enormous superin-"cumbent pressure, constitutes its most pleasant "feature, in providing a refreshing relief from the "lassitude of the plains during the summer heats."

The Passes across the Sulieman Mountains, east.

7. Five Passes will be observed indicated in the sketch map:—(1) The *Khaibur;* (2) the *Kurrum* or *Paiwár;* (3) the *Gômul;* (4) the *Sanghár;* (5) the *Bolán.* Most of the invaders of India traversed one or more of these passes. Alexander the Great, Baber, Nadir Shah, and Mahomed of Ghazni, came by the *Khaibur;* Baber by the *Khaibur* and *Gômul;* Prince Mohommud-i-Dara Shukoh—a son of Shah Jehan—passed by the *Sanghár*, to and from Candahar; Nadir Shah and Ahmed Shah Abdalli by the *Khaibur* and *Bolán.*

Geological.

As regards the geological structure of the Suliemán range, which these passes traverse, it seems to require further examination; but is presumably of freestone, sandstone, and other *stratified* rock, containing marine fossils. Water action is obvious, and its structure supports the theory ventured on in Section V., para. 1, of this work. Gneiss, and, I believe, *trap* also are seen on the spurs of the inner or west Suliemáns, but no granite is found on either of the ranges.

The Sufaid-Kôh has been mentioned as culminating

in the Peak of Sitarâm (15,622 feet)—its general elevation may be estimated at 12,500 feet. Its northern geography is beyond the sphere of this sketch. The southern and eastern offsets of the Sufaid-Kôh stretch to the Indus, and divide the Peshawar and Kohât valleys by the *Zaimukht* and *Khuttock* hills, on which the sanitarium of Cherát, already described (Section II., para. 9) stands; and which is the watershed ridge between them.

The South-east Offsets of the Sufaid-Koh towards the Indus embrace the Khuttoch and Zaimukht Hills.

The Samana Range contains Table-land 6000 8000 ft. elevation.

The parallel spurs of the Sufaid-Kôh also enclose the Samána range (6,600 to 9000 feet) abutting on the Miranzai and Hangu valleys, up which the expedition of 1859-60, already alluded to, passed on its way to the Kurrum Valley to attack the Cábul Kheyl Wuzzeerie tribe. In this range are several table-lands of sandstone and limestone, at elevations of from 6000 to 8000 feet. Afreedies are the chief tribe of this region, and he would be a bold colonist who would care to locate himself near their habitation! Many, however, have enlisted in our service in the Guides and frontier regiments; and although their traditional character is that of atrocious robbers for centuries past, they have proved hardy, brave soldiers, and "faithful to their salt."

The Kurrum Valley and Pushtoo Hills.

8. The Kurrum Valley has been partly described. It is about 60 miles long and from three to ten wide. The valley is not without beauty, with smiling green fields and pleasant orchards. The river is full of Mahaseer fish, and in 1859-60, when seen by the author, was very clear. The river basin is bounded by the Sufaid-Kôh on the north, and by the parallel Suliemáns on the west and east. The range called the *Pushtoo Hills* are seen to the west, and contain the peaks of *Speen Wán* and *Jooni* shown in the sketches. This inferior range is considered by the natives to be the dividing ridge between India (Alba) and Cábul, and beyond which it is not proposed to carry the reader.

Valley of Khost. The valley of *Khóst* is south of the Kurrum valley, about 40 miles long, and shares its general features. Timber and pasturage are found on the surrounding mountains, and flocks of sheep, with some cattle, abound.*

Valley of Dawar. *Dawar* is another valley 40 miles in length, of a similar character.

These three districts are, it is understood, now incorporated within our possessions;—the new "scientific frontier" as defined by the treaty of Gundamuk. To sum up, the "fluvial basin" includes the valleys of Kurrum, Hariab, Kerman, Furmul, Khóst, and Dawar. Jagis, Turis, and Mangals, inhabit it; and it is essentially the country of the *Wuzzeeries.*

The Kurrum Pass. Historical Note. 9. The Kurrum Pass has always been regarded as one of the chief passes across the Suliemán Mountains. In the days of Mahomed Ghori (1193-1205) Kurrum was the seat of government of his lieutenant Ilduz, and thence the latter advanced over the Shutargurdan to the conquest of Ghazni.† It was down the Kurrum pass that Genghis Khan hunted the Prince of Khúrism in September, 1221. In 1398 Timour's grandson, Pir Mahomed, advanced from Kandahar, and laid siege to Mooltan. Timour himself shortly followed, and both in going and returning adopted this route; halting at Kâfr-Kôte, one of the remarkable mountain summits shown in sketch (4,500 feet).

The Emperor Baber, who traversed most of the passes across the Suliemán range, mentions four, *viz.* (1) the Bangash or Paiwar; (2) the Nāgr-Kôte or Kâfr-Kôte; (3) the Furmul, by Tochi valley; and another, as all good—especially the Furmul, leading to

---

* On Christmas eve, 1859, no less than 5000 head of captured sheep and cattle were driven into our camp at Thal.

† Many particulars of the following four paragraphs are derived from the masterly papers by C. R. Markham, C.B., the able Secretary of the Royal Geographical Society. *Vide* Proceedings for January, February, and March, 1879.

Kandahar. It leads from the Kurrum fort across the western Suliemáns into Zurmat, but has not been explored in recent times; it is probably, however, a far easier pass than the Shutargurdan.

It is not proposed here to touch on the inner watershed of the *western* Suliemáns, being beyond the borders of India Alba as defined in this paper.

Eastern Sulieman Altitudes. Along the Dérajhât the range of the *eastern* Suliemáns is clearly seen rising like a wall above the lower spurs. The highest peak is the celebrated "Takht-i-Solimán." Its summit is described as a narrow plateau five miles long—north to south—with culminating points at each extremity; the north peak being 11,300 feet, and the south peak 11,110 feet above sea level. To the north are other lofty peaks, *viz.* Mount Pirghál (11,580 feet), and Shah Haidur (9000 feet).

Duns. Enclosed within the parallel ridges of the east and west Suliemáns are certain long valleys which have been called "Dûns," though scarcely like the Dûns of the Himalayas, being bare, arid, and uncultivated. On the hither side of the outer Suliemáns they have been called the "Batáni" Dûns, from the Pathán tribe which inhabits them. There are no less than 32 passes from the Dérajhât into these hills; the best being the "Tank" pass practicable for artillery, and the "Khusára, a pass further north.

The Wuzzeeree Clans. The Wuzzeeries are the chief tribes of these regions. They are divided into five great clans, *viz.* (1) Utmanzaies, (2) Ahmudzaies, (3) Mahsoods, (4) Gurbaz, (5) Lali. The Cábul Kheyls, who have played so turbulent a part in border warfare since our occupation of the Dérajhât, being a section of the Utmanzaies. These tribes united could bring 44,000 fighting men into the field. A remarkable feature of the Mahsood Wuzzeerie country is the elevated scarped plain of "Ruzmuk," seven miles by two, at 6,800 feet above sea-level.

The Gomul Pass. 10. South of the Wuzzeerie country is the Gômul Pass, indicated roughly in the sketch map. It proceeds up the course of the Gômul River—as indeed all the Cábul passes do up a river—in a continuous ascent of 145 miles, to the "Kôtal-i-Sarwand," 7,500 feet above the sea. Beyond, is the plain where the Gômul river is joined by the Zhôb from the west Suliemáns, up which river is a pass, but quite unknown. The pass of Gômul or Sarwand-i-Kôtal is that traversed for centuries by the "Povindahs" or Cábul merchants, as they are called in India; sellers of fruit, horses, etc. They date back as far as the time of Mahmûd of Ghazni, and have carried on the trade in military fashion for centuries; fighting their way through the rough tribes *en route.* In 1505 Baber found them, attacked their camp, whose chief he killed; and then proceeding by a pass south of the Takht-i-Soliman, which joins the Gômul, passed the "Abistada" Lake to Ghazni.*

The "Sanghar" and other Passes south of the Gomul.

11. The Sanghar Pass is the intermediate pass between the Gômul and the Bolán. It leads from near Dera Ghazie Khan, and was formerly—if it be not still —the one most used route from Mooltan to Kandahar. Prince Dara, son of the Emperor Shah Jehan, marched with an army of 104,000 men and 40 cannon to besiege Kandahar by this route. The heavy cannon were however sent by the Bolán pass. Prince Dara returned by this pass—the Sanghar—with an escort of 1000 cavalry after an unsuccessful siege, in October, 1653.* The country adjacent is occupied by Belooch tribes (Khosah and Lagháris). The Sekhi-Sawar Pass is a branch of the Sanghar occupied by the Lágharis, and forms an important alternative route from the plains to Kandahar.

There are many other passes across these mountains, south of the Takht-i-Soliman, occasionally used, such as (1) the "Shaikh-Haidari," up the Zhôb Valley to Kandahar, (2) the Darwazi Pass leading into the Draband Pass to the south; this joins the Dahina Pass,

* Ap Raverty.

and so on to Kandahar. Next come the Guioba, Walia, Chaodwar, Tarzoi, and Chabwi, local passes. The Dahina and Wahwa Passes to Kandahar are more important; the latter is held by the Kihtránis, who are the last Affghan tribe along the outer Suliemán range, their next neighbours south-west being the Kasráni tribe of Beloochis.

Passes into the Beloochisthan highlands.

South of Dera-Ghazie-Khan again are many small passes—as many as 18—into the Bōgdar and Laghári country, which need scarcely be enumerated. Viewed from the Indus (which the author once descended as far as Ooch from D.G.K) they appear like nicks in the wall of the Suliemáns, which are visible from the plains as far as Mooltan. Well does the author remember his first view of them afforded by the setting in of the cold season, which dispelled the lurid veil of dust and heat which enshrouded our camp before Mooltan at the close of the year 1848, after an unsuccessful siege, and whilst wearily waiting for reinforcements from Bombay to recommence the attack of that fortress, which in fact surrendered to our arms on the 21st January, 1849.

All these minor passes need not be even named; the Cachár, however, is of slightly more importance in the southern Dérajhât. Till rendered dangerous by the depredations of the lawless Beloochis, it was a frequent thoroughfare for caravans coming from the Zhôb (Zawa) and Sanghar routes. To the south of this, however, we come to a remarkable plateau called the "Phylaunsham Plain," 1,500 feet above the sea amidst the *sham* or watershed of the Cachár and Kaha Rivers. Several passes—such as the Baghari, Jahagzi, Thok, Chuk, Muyhal, and Taháni—lead on to it. It is 30 by 25 miles, with area basin of 900 square miles. Could a colonizing native population maintain themselves against the lawless Mári and Būghti tribes adjacent, this plain might form a favourable site for settlement; it is well watered, and has good soil. At present wild asses, hog, deer, and horses roam it in freedom.

Watershed of the Suliemans, W.

South-east of this plain of Sham, an isolated ridge called "Mount Gandhari" forms the angle where the outer or east range of the Suliemáns turns westwards towards Dadar, and the mouth of the Bolán pass. The inner or western Suliemán range continues to form the watershed, and terminates at the "Tukáta" Peak, 12,000 feet. This (Tukáta) ridge, north of the Bolán pass, forms the dominant axis of this range. The general elevation is not less than 7000 feet; and towards the north-west are several lofty peaks, such as Toba, Kánd, and Tukáta. From the former (Toba) a plateau range, also called Toba, ramifies, of which one portion is called "Khojeh-Amran," over which passes the now celebrated Kohjak pass, on the main road from Quetta to Kandahar. On the Toba range was the sanitarium* where Ahmed Shah Abdalli, the founder of the Affghan kingdom, died in 1773. It seems to be the watershed between the basins of the Argandâb and Lóra.

The Bolan Pass.

12. The *Bolán* Pass is the last great pass leading up to the Highlands of *India Alba,* which is noted on the sketch map of this work. It is too well known to need much remark. Its crest is about 5,800 feet above sea level, and its total length from Dadar = 60 miles. The road hence leads to Quetta and the *Highlands* of Beloochistan; Quetta being 5,537 feet above sea level.

From the Tukáta peak the great Halla range extends 280 miles to the seaboard. On this range or its spurs is placed the sanitarium of "Dunna Towers" (para. 6).

The *Bolán* pass is—like all the other approaches to the Highlands of Affghanisthán—simply the bed of a river—the Bolán river—which rising at Sir-i-Bolan (4,400 feet), flows with diversified current down the pass, at one place being lost amidst boulders and pebbles for 14 miles. This pass was (as has been stated)

* Perhaps the rock fortress *Siazgai* (para. 16).

LXVIII.

The Spurs of the Kirtar Hills near Sehwan, impinging on the Indus. Section XVI.

LXIX.

Quetta and the surrounding Mountains. Section XVI.

LXX.

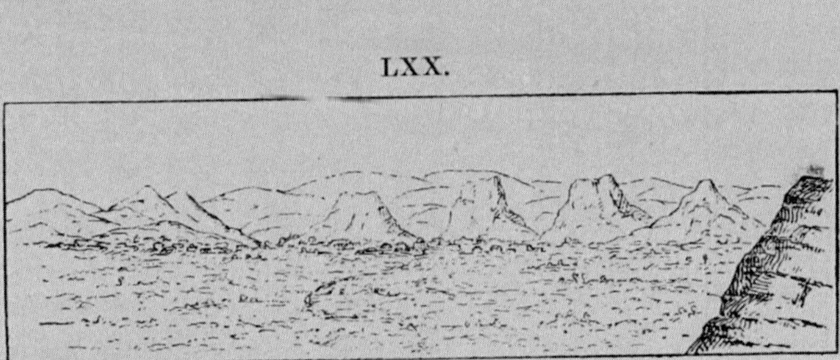

Distant View of Candahar. Section XVI.

used by Prince Dara for the passage of his heavy artillery for the siege of Kandahar. Ahmed Shah Abdáli descended it when he invaded India. In 1839 the army of the Indus marched to Kandahar by the Bolán, and more recently the left column of the army of Affghanisthán traversed it with heavy guns. It is well known, and needs no further description here.

There is still another pass that may be mentioned as leading across the Halla range to Kelât and the Belooch Highlands, *viz.* the Múla Pass; and there are as many as ten other paths in the 60 miles south from the Bolán. The top of this pass = 5,250 feet; it is 100 miles in length, and then turns north through the Nal valley to Khelât, the capital of Beloochistan. From this point the Halla ranges extend 200 miles to the coast at Cape Munza, but they are called the Kirthar Hills as far as "Sehwan," where their spurs impinge on the River Indus; south-west of this they are called the "*Pubh*" Hills.

The Kirthar summits reach 7000 or 8000 feet, and the table-land of Beloochistan, which is buttressed by the Halla range = 6,800 feet, at Kelât. The range ends in a bluff at Cape Munza, in two peaks, one = 1,200 feet, and Jebel Pubh = 2,500 feet, on the sea coast.

The Plateau of Beloochisthan. Quetta, the Pishin Valley, etc., to the Khojeh Amran

13. On emerging from the Bolán on to the plateau of Beloochisthan the plain called "Dasht-i-Bedaulat" (6,225 feet) leads to Quetta, at which point the line of march on the objective, Kandahar, commences. Soon after passing the Shalkôt plain and the Sogarbund defile, the extensive plains of Pishín are entered, and here I would refer the reader to the able lectures by Major-General Sir M. A. Biddulph, R.A.,* who has had

* *Pishin, and the Routes between India and Kandahar,* by Major-General Sir M. A. Biddulph, K.C.B., read at an evening meeting of the Royal Geographical Society, 9th February, 1880. *The March from the Indus to the Helmund and back, 1878-9,* by the same officer, read before the R.U.S. Institution on 16th of June, 1880.

exceptional opportunities of studying these districts, especially Pishín, and the basins of the Lóra and Argandâb—rivers of *Arachosia*, the *India Alba* of the ancients.

It may here be briefly stated that the watershed ridge between the east and west Suliemáns is found at or near Quetta, of which range the peaks of Kánd, Surghwand, Muzwah, Murdár, and above all, Tukáta (already mentioned at para. 12) are dominant elevations, and which are not less than 8000 to 12,000 feet.

In view of such references as have been mentioned, it would seem unnecessary here to enter upon a detailed description of the regions referred to. It may be stated generally that Pishín may be considered as the basin of the Lóra, which originates in several branches from the Zhôb valley, the Tukáta, Múla, and Barai Hills, also from the Khūrg-Bárak pass south of the Bolán and Quetta. It joins the Argandâb below Kandahar, skirting the "Khojeh-Amran," over which the *Gwaja* pass (6,988 feet), and the Khojak pass (7,380 feet), lead to Kandahar. These elevated plains have only been partially explored, and the boundary is indeterminate.

Limits of Pishin Basin. From Tukáta and Chiltân (12,000), on the south-east, to the mountains bounding the Toba plateau on the north-west; and from the Zhôb valley on the north-east, to the Khojeh-Amran spurs on the extreme edge of the desert south-west, appear to be the diameters of the basin of Pishín,* which moreover embraces subsidiary valleys and minor ranges with local names, presenting a wild and extraordinary sweep of country at a general elevation of 5000 or 6000 feet, rising to even 7000 or 8000 feet, amidst which several points suitable for military stations, and even sanitaria, have been noted by the authorities quoted. Especially on the west and north-west the skirt of the mountains

* The diameters are not less than 80 and 60 miles respectively.

rises rapidly, and leads by the Karatu pass by a steep gradient, and so to the edge of the Toba plateau (8000 feet), which appears an important strategic point, as covering the roads both to Ghazni and Kandahar. This extensive plateau extends to the Khojeh-Amran. "Here are the summer camping grounds of Kakars "and Achakzais, and the elevation of 7,500 feet would "appear to present a suitable sanitarium for our "troops." The height of the Khojak peak = 8,017 feet. The Khojeh-Amran itself forms a regular rampart between Pishín and the country beyond, which is 2000 feet lower than the plain of Pishín. From the summit of this range General Biddulph describes the view as one of the most surprising he ever saw. "The "plains of Kadanai, leading on to other plains, are laid "out like a map, and seen in the marvellous clearness "of the frosty air of December, the effect is most "extraordinary. Beyond the plain the ranges of "strangely isolated masses of hills run in parallel "lines north-east and south-west, and jut out towards "the desert, which lies to the south like a sandy shore. "There are rocky hills far away in the midst of the "desert appearing like veritable islands, and islets "occur in the Kadanai plain."

The Toba Plateau

These hills are of gneiss and trap; no granite has been found. They form the natural rampart of the Quetta-Pishín position, and are the only obstacle to be encountered between the Bolán pass and Kandahar.

The Sarlat range runs down as far as the 30th parallel, or the left bank of the River Lóra.

The Tang Hills are the prolongation of the Khojeh-Amran southwards where they are lost in the desert, itself probably the ancient bed of a shallow ocean.

Passes over the Khojeh Amran.

There are other passes over the Khojeh-Amran. The Roghání (5,112 feet); the great Kafila road to Kandahar lies intermediate between the Khojak Pass (7,380), and Gwája Pass (6,880 feet), but is only fit for horses and foot. The Spinatija-Kôtal = 6,888 feet, 10 miles west.

Sketches and profiles of this country, could they be introduced, would alone show the varied outlines of this stony and inhospitable region—mazes of mountain and ravine, and long spurs impinging on to the sandy tracts of valley, dotted, however, here and there with strips of verdure along the river banks; but as a recent writer

General View of Affghanisthan.

on this country—"Holdich"—says: "It is from the "mountain tops alone that one becomes aware how "narrow are these bright green ribbons of fertile beauty "winding and spreading here and there into broader "plains amid the desolation of the hills and the weary "wilderness of sand and rock.* So much of Affghan-"istan consists of land that must be unproductive "through all time, that whatever the revenues of the "country may at present be, it is only too abundantly "certain that they can be increased no further by the "spread of agriculture; nor do I believe that the culti-"vators have much to learn in the science of making "of their narrow slips of cultivable land. The art of "irrigation in particular—both by open cuttings and "the underground system called 'karez'—has been "brought to great perfection. It may in truth be said "that the Affghans use up their whole water supply. "It is a fact that both the Cábul River and the Har-i-"Rud which waters the plains of Herât, are absolutely "dry at certain seasons of the year. So far, indeed, "the resources of Affghanistan have been fully devel-"oped. But though their total area is limited, these "narrow bands of cultivation stretch far, winding into "nearly every valley, and occasionally broadening out "on to the open plateaux between the mountain ridges.

"Scattered among the fields are well defended and "thickly populated villages, which are connected by "fairly good roads, so that a traveller might well pass "through Affghanistan from one end to the other, and "describe it as a very Italy in Asia. Here and there,

* *Geographical Results of the Affghan Campaign*, by Captain T. H. Holdich, R.E. Lecture before the R.G. Society, 13th December, 1880.

"indeed, it is distinctly Italian in character. Anyone "who has strolled from Florence towards Fiesole or "Vallombrosa, passing first through the narrow high-"walled lanes which conduct him past the suburbs, "and thence, from the gradual ascent to Fiesole, has "turned to look at the matchless scene below him, will "probably ever remember some of its chief character-"istics. Terraced vineyards sloping step by step down "the lower spurs of the hills, with villages climbing "and clustering into the water-worn ravines, towers "showing brightly in the evening sun, amid the olives "and the orchards of the low-lying lands that border "the Arno, the glint of the river, and the glitter of the "snow-capped peaks of the purple mountains beyond "—even the same soft light to mellow the whole "picture into harmony—all this may be seen with just "a few of those slight changes with which nature al-"ways varies her pictures, among the skirts of the "mountains—the Koh-i-Daman—about a long day's "march north of the city of Cábul."

The Highlands of Beloochisthan.

14. We have now arrived within hail of our objective, "Kandahar." Our hitherto guide, philosopher, and friend, General Biddulph, had the opportunity of proccoding further, as far as Girisk and the Helmund, which are conjectured to be near the limit of "India Alba" of the ancients; but it falls not within the scope of this work to more than mention them. They can in no wise be called "Highlands." Such points as *Pishín*,* *Toba*, and *Bálazaie*, do indeed show a plateau rising into something like altitudes where friendly coolness is sometimes found. The Toba plateau has been already mentioned as containing possible sites for sanitary resort should it be eventually decided to hold Kandahar and the supporting plains of Pishín.

---

*A Toorkie tribe called Bálish or Válish emigrated from the vicinity of Ghazni in the 9th or 10th century, whence they settled south-west in Pishín, or Afshineh—an equivalent.—*Sir H. Rawlinson.*

Question of occupation of Kandahar considered.

The arguments for and against such, appear to me so nearly balanced, that I shrink from expressing an opinion. My own former ideas *were* to advocate a strictly *defensive* action, readily convertible into an *offensive;* but, under the altered circumstances of the present, I confess I incline to think that having gained a forward strategic point—our objective, Kandahar—we ought to maintain it. I should have preferred a "feudatory" to conduct the civil government, but I would deprecate a *receding wave.* If we *do* abandon this fine objective let us see that it is held in our interest by a strong ally, bound to us as his suzerain; otherwise we may have to fight our battles over again. Under all the circumstances I would, if possible, adopt the old maxim, *divide et impera!**

Routes to the Indus.

Our communications with India would of course have to be improved. Railways would connect these objective points with our bases on the Indus, to which, I suppose, the "line of least resistance" may be the Gômul pass, leading through the valleys of Togai (?) (8,277 feet) and Zhôb, and skirting that of Pishín already mentioned. The route by the Barai Valley, which adjoins that of Zhôb, seems an alternative route towards the plains of India from the head of the Pishín basin. The valley stretches 100 miles, with a width of five to ten east and north-east; also to the south the Barai river escapes through the Anumbar gap towards the plains. The passes between these two great valleys—Zhôb and Barai—appear easy, and afford lateral support for parallel columns advancing towards the objective, Pishín or Kandahar—a valuable military feature; and, if I infer correctly from General Biddulph's description, an elevated table-land called "Sahara" exists to the east, which I should suppose

---

* These remarks were of course written whilst this question (now set at rest) was still pending. *At present* the result seems in a measure to justify the policy of withdrawal.—D.J.F.N.
8th Dec., 1881.

well placed on the highland watershed as a point for a Depôt or Sanitary Support. The rivers of Zhôb, Barai, and Rakin rise thereon. "It is visible from Fort "Munro looming in the distance as a dome-like mass, "with the Rakin plain stretching towards it."

Of this route we scarcely know anything; it has not been explored since Baber traversed it, and he left but scanty records. Its length from Kandahar to Dera Ishmail Khan = 320 miles, so that it is at anyrate the *shortest* route. A rough sketch is given in the text, and the elevations of a few points of the regions closely adjacent to this route as given by Biddulph, will be found at para. 16.

15. Before finally ending this notice of *India Alba*, I may perhaps add a few words as to (Is) Kandahar, the city of Alexander the Great, as no doubt it may be considered.* Situated at the corner of the desert it must, from the earliest times, have formed the pivot of the routes diverging on the one way to Herât and Persia, and Turkisthân, and on the other to north Affghanisthán and India by the Indus. From the days when the Aryan tribes emerged from their native seats in north-west Thibet and the Pâmir, this must have been a dominant point for occupation. After the able histories placed before us by Elphinstone, Malleson, and others, to enter on its history and natural resources would be a work of supererogation, so I will leave the subject, referring the reader to those pages. **Kandahar and its supports.**

I believe I cannot better conclude this imperfect sketch of new regions claiming to be called *Highlands*

* Modern Kandahar was founded by Ahmed Shah (Abdali) in 1754, but the seat of government was removed to Cábul by Timour Shah in 1774. *Olán Robát*, in the valley of Tarnak—near Kandahár and Ghazni—seems to have been the ancient capitol of Arachosia or *India Alba:* it was a flourishing city in the time of Alexander the Great. *Bost* or *Bist*, whose ruins are near Girisk, was another great city of the ancient Arachosia. These cities were probably destroyed by Timour the Tatar (Tamerlane) about 1380-5.

of India (Alba) than by quoting the following opinions of the latest, and perhaps best, authority on the subject —Sir M. A. Biddulph, K.C.B.—

Military opinions cited.

"With Kandahar and Pishín in possession, our mili-"tary position in South Affghanisthán would be perfect; "and if connected with India by rail, so many objects "would be secured that we might afford to resign other "more intricate advanced posts in North Affghanisthán. "However, whether we cede or hold Kandahar it is our "duty to push on the railway, and Khorassan must be "made central, that it may not become the scene of "military activity. Should Kandahar be resigned, the "importance of our position in Pishín is much en-"hanced. In this case it will be incumbent on us to "hold the Khojeh-Amran from some well defined point "on the north edge of the Toba plateau, down to where "the range terminates in the desert. And to command "the range effectually we must possess the glacis-like "plain as far as the left bank of the Kadani stream. "Posts of observation would command in the Kadani "plain all the routes leading into South Affghanisthán, "including the road from Kelât to Kandahar through "Sherawak. This frontier would also secure the "country to the valley leading towards Kelât *viâ* "Ghilzai and Ghuzni, and control the hill country "regions to the north of Pishín. All the territory east "of the Kadani, *i.e.*, Pishín and Sherawak would form "part of the empire.

"The strength of the Pishín position lies in the great "breadth of the plain, in the peaceable character of "the inhabitants, and in the security given by its left "flank resting on the desert. No military position is "perfect, and the defect in that of Pishín is caused by "the continuous mountain mass to the north. The "belt of mountains to the east is not so much an im-"perfection; it is narrow, and opens into valleys so "arranged that there is no difficulty in moving about "them in any desired direction. As the Quetta position "required the addition of Pishín, so the latter also re-"quires something to make it secure, and if it is shown "that the improvement can be carried out without "incurring embarrassment, it is our plain duty to make "the addition."

Such are the arguments by an able advocate for the retention of Kandahar and Pishín, and there can be but little doubt that in a strictly *military* point of view they are unanswerable; in a political, and especially financial, they may be open to doubt. Should they, however, finally prevail, and the retention of Kandahar or Pishín be decided on, the routes connecting them with the base on the Indus, will naturally rise to great importance. The Bolán, the Sherawak, and Gômul Passes will be thoroughly secured, and military posts placed on the strategic points commanding the country, if possible at elevations affording a temperate climate. Several such have been pointed out in the able article so much quoted from. The *Toba* plateau has been mentioned. The *Tal Chótiâli Valley* might be occupied;—to my eye, it seems a point of much importance. *Balazai*, on the north-east corner of the *Pishín* valley, is noted as an important point. It commands the roads descending to Quetta and Pishín, as also the passes leading to Zhôb, Barai, and Tal; whilst at Gwal—13 miles south—lies the exit to Sibi and Tal, by which the trace of the projected railway has, I believe, been laid out. This important project has been dwelt upon in an able paper by Sir R. Temple,* to which the reader may be referred. The projected trace is, I believe, up the Barai valley, by Sibi, on to the plain of Pishín at Gwal. The Kohmughzai pass = 6,327 feet, is found on this line.

Steps to be taken in the eventuality of its retention.

16. Elevations given by Biddulph are as follows, *viz.*, Balazai = 6,392 feet; Matazai Kôtal = 7,139 feet; the Mosai = 7,078 feet; the Togai stream = 6,954 feet; its peak rising to 8,277 feet. At Yussuf-Kach = 7,180

Elevations. Topographical points in the Highlands of Beloochisthan.

* R.G.S. Vol. II., No. 9, for September, 1880.

"feet, 15 miles from Mohturia Serai is the watershed; "the Suiklah flowing to Pishín, and the drainage of "Nara plains to the Indus by Sibi; here we find the "pass of Momandzai (8,457 feet), which also is the "watershed of the Barai valley."

We must not leave these *Highlands* without remarking on the highly picturesque character of the country, particularly between the two passes. "Mazwah and "Spinskar rise abruptly into grand rugged forms, having their lower slopes gracefully disposed and varied "with a growth of cypress and other trees and shrubs. "In our travels we have not seen anywhere so luxuriant "a growth. Momandzai, is the division between "Khorassan and India, and also between the Panizai "and Damar sections of the Kakar tribe."

It is believed that the Barai valley—100 miles in length—and Zhôb, must contain similar points of strength.

The Siazgai Rock

Three miles east of Chinjai stands the singularly formed table-mountain of Siazgai which rising well out of the plain is a natural fortress. This point seems to be of strategic value. It was formerly held by the Moghuls as a military post, and might again serve for such in the future. "It stands out in noble "proportions in this strange yet grand landscape. On "the top of the hill remains of tanks, cultivation, and "ruined walls still exist. Near here also the outlets "of the *Barai, Sonalan,* and *Tal-Chótiâli* valleys find "their exit. Thus are found three great valleys having "their origin in the Highlands east of Pishín, so disposed as to offer choice of routes towards the Punjâb."

Sketches of these interesting points, could permission be obtained to reproduce them, would give better ideas of this country than any description. One isometric view or section of the route from the Indus to the plains of Pishín and the Khojeh-Amran will at any rate be given. The altitudes embraced evidently entitle the intermediate country to be reckoned amongst the *Highlands of India* (Alba).

LXXI.

The Ruined Moghul Fortress of Siazgai. Section XVI.

LXXII.

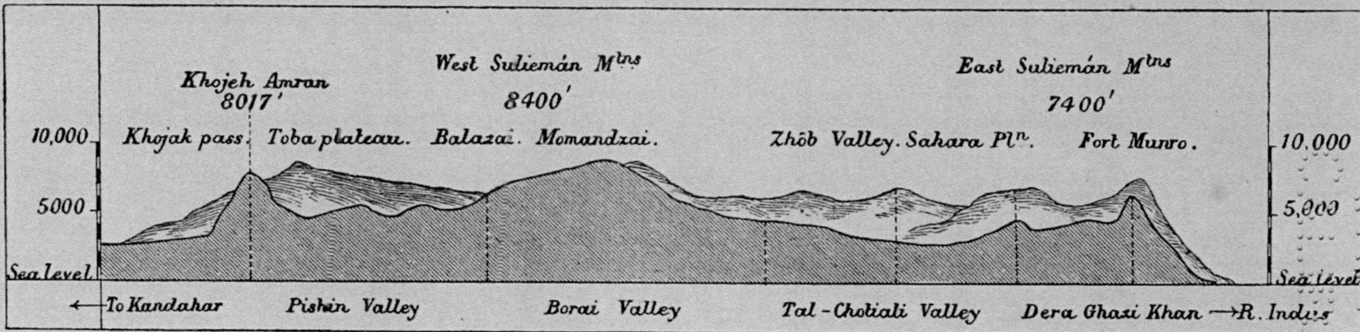

SECTION OF THE HIGHLANDS OF INDIA ALBA FROM THE INDUS TO CANDAHAR. Section XVI.

17. We have now considered, in however sketchy a manner, the three features of this section as proposed in the preamble, *viz.*—(1) The Basin of the Kurrum, (2) the Basin of the Lóra, (3) the Passes across the East Suliemán range leading to them. This country, with the connecting valleys such as Zhôb (scarcely yet explored) with the Barai and Tal-Chótiâli valleys, comprises the chief part of the new territory to be incorporated by the treaty of Gundamuk, and subsequent arrangements, within our empire. No doubt the day may come when the glacis of the British Empire will extend beyond the Hindoo Khoosh, as far even as the Oxus—India's "furthest,"—perhaps to be fought for in a great battle of the future; unless, indeed, we shrink from our responsibilities, and allow our receding wave of conquest to give place to an advancing wave of conquest of our great northern neighbour; in which case the final struggle for the great Dependency of England will *possibly* have to be fought *within* our own frontier. Every military consideration, however, now points to Herât as the probable point of contact in the future, and that should now be considered our *objective.* Perhaps diplomacy will step in to solve this question as between ourselves and Russia; and at least one eventuality leading to a pacific solution occurs to me; but *la haute politique* is not our present cue, and such speculations need not be entered on here. **Concluding Remarks. Summary.**

18. A very few words on the inhabitants of the regions described, and this sketch—already too long extended—must be brought to an end. **Ethnological.**

The generally accepted history of Affghanisthán is not very ancient, and cannot be traced to remote antiquity. Originating in central Asia or west Thibet, the dynasties which have ruled Affghanisthán—such as the Toorki, the Ghori, the Moghul, the Ghilzai, and the Abdáli, are all within the last 800 years. Of true Affghans the principal tribes may be enumerated as (1) Abdális or *Doorá nis,* (2) *Ghilzaies,* (3) *Kákars,* (4) *Wardúks,* (5) *Povindahs,* (6) *Bérdmánis.*

(1) The *Dooránis*—formerly Abdális—are paramount in the south-east. Of the three great subdivisions of this tribe who have given kings or khans to Cábul are (a) the Populzaies, (b) Sadoozaies, (c) Bárukzaies; and the internecine struggles of these rival branches have at times convulsed the country; and, indeed, formed the chief cause of the constant anarchy which has prevailed since the end of the last century. The Bárukzaies have finally predominated, and in the person of that strong old ruler, Dost Mahommed, established the present dynasty—Sher Ali being his grandson. In 1747 Ahmed Shah *Abdáli* was crowned at Kandahar, and in 1773 was succeeded by his son Timour Shah. Zemaun Shah, his son, reigned till 1800, when he was dethroned by his brother Mahmood, between whom, however, and his brother Shujah constant vicissitudes of power took place, till they eventually both became fugitives in 1826. At length Runjeet Sing of Lahore stepped upon the stage of Affghan politics, conquered Peshawar and Cashmere, and extended his protectorate to the third brother, Zemaun Shah, who had been blinded by the successful Bárukzaies, in which section of the Doocáni clan the chief power has since resided.

(2) The *Ghilzaies* formerly conquered Persia, and established there a powerful, but short lived, dynasty. They are still, however, a powerful tribe.

(3) The *Kakárs* are a lawless tribe who mostly hold the south-east passes to India, and inhabit the adjacent Suliemán hills. They play in those regions the part of Affreedies in the north, and exact black mail, robbing friend and foe with impartiality.

(4) The *Wardúks,* on the west of the Ghilzaies, are an agricultural, peaceful people. They are beyond the confines of India Alba.

(5) The *Povindahs* are soldier-merchants, and were alluded to in para. 10 of this section.

(6) The *Tor-Tarins* hold Pishín. They also are an

agricultural people of peaceful habits, and would probably prove good subjects should their country—as has been recommended—be annexed to the British empire.

(7) The *Kussilbashis* are of Persian origin, and are an exceptionally intelligent class. Employed as soldiers of the artillery, and guards of the sirdars, etc.

Other tribes on the north and west, such as the *Usbegs, Hazaras, Aimaks*, etc., need scarcely be mentioned; they live beyond India Alba. They are mostly Tatars or Moghuls by descent, and inhabit the lofty regions from north of Cábul to Herât. The *Tájiks* and *Hindikies* are the shopkeepers of the country. The *Amazais, Othmanzaies*, and *Jadoons*, dwell in the skirts of the Mahábun and Black Mountain, along the river Indus. The author has had opportunities of studying these tribes as high up the Indus as Torbela and Derbund, and will endeavour to present a panoramic sketch of the River Indus, embracing the whole of this territory, made during the campaign against the Sitána fanatics in 1863-4.

Yoosoophzaies, Bonairs, Móhmunds, and *Affreedies* carry on the tribal chain to near Cábul northwards. Hereabout we find the nidus or seat of the ancient kingdom of Sewâdgére, so often alluded to in native MSS.; and in the high mountains due north are found the *Siahpōsh* (black-capped) *Kaffirs;* that mysterious people of whom so little is actually known. They are however, probably the indigenes of these mountains, driven to this corner by conquering races. They have lately been identified with the ancient Gándháridæ by Bellew.

The *Wuzzeeries* have been mentioned in para. 9 as occupying the Kurrum Valley and adjacent hills.

The *Shiránis* and *Ashtaránis* occupy the Suliemán range about the Takht-i-Solieman and adjacent ridges as far as the Khúri pass, which point is the southern limit of the Pathán (Affghan) people. South of this, the *Balooch* tribes occupy the Suliemán range.

We have now briefly enumerated the chief Affghan tribes; to enter on details or subdivisional clans would be a work in itself. The Affghans are of course the inhabitants of Affghanisthán, but it is a fact that they themselves do not use that term—which is of Persian origin—for the soil of their country, the meaning of which seems to be the land of "weeping" or "lamentation;" but whether in allusion to its melancholy desert character or to the "grief-giving" character of the people themselves, seems doubtful. They call themselves *Patháns* (the people of the *flag* or *boat*), and assert that they descend from Prince Afghána, son of Irmiah or Bárukáiah, a son of Táloot or Saul, King of Israel (see para. 5), and the author is inclined to believe —notwithstanding all discredit thrown by scholars on the idea—that they *are* descended from Jews.*

HISTORICAL NOTE.

Historical Note. Affghanisthan.

19. The early Mahomedan chronicles mention the rulers of Cábul as guebres or infidels, and the remnant of these are now probably represented by the Kaffirs on the north-east of Cábul, who dwell amidst the lofty peaks of the Hindoo Khoosh, an interesting people whom, however, it is not here intended to more than mention. The Abdális embraced Mahommedanism in the 9th century, and the rest of the Affghans followed suit, but the first authentic notice of the Affghans commences about A.D. 997, when *Sebuktagin*—son of Alptegin, an officer of the Sámáni Khan (Mansúr) who had rebelled in 976—succeeded his father, and soon after defeated *Jaipal*, King of Lahore, at a great battle at Loghmán near Cábul, and spread his arms over

* Sir W. Jones alone, of philologists, fancied he detected traces of the Scriptural Chaldäic in the *Pushtoo*—the language of the Affghans —else so far removed from all known ancient languages. The author himself holds a pedigree or geneological descent of Abdur Rahman and Abdoola, sons of Khaled, whom the Affghans claim as their immediate ancestor, and whose pedigree—38 generations—is traced to Saul (or Táloot) King of Israel.

LXXIII.

PANORAMIC VIEW OF THE INDUS FOR A DISTANCE OF 25 MILES.

Taken from the Mountain above Derbund in Upper Hazara. Section XVI., page 237.

Affghanisthán, making Ghazni his capitol. His son, *Mahmood*, who succeeded about 1001, greatly extended the empire. He defeated *Anand Pal*, son of Jaipal, at the great battle of Hazro near Attock (see sketch map and page 43) A.D. 1002, and consolidated his kingdom. From Attock he pushed on to Nagr-Kôt—the modern Kangra (Section III., para. 11)—where he sacked the great temple and treasury of the Kuttoch kings, obtaining an immense booty. On his return to Ghazni (1010) he utterly defeated the Ghilzaies, who had waylaid his army, He undertook as many as 10 or 12 expeditions to India. In 1012 he invaded the Punjâb and sacked Thanésur. Between 1013 and 1015 he conquered Cashmere, but in the latter year he lost an army in that country through stress of weather and loss of his road amidst the mountains. In 1016 he invaded and overran Khórism (Khiva). In 1017 he again invaded India, penetrated as far as the Ganges, attacked Muttra and Kánouj, where he again obtained immense plunder. In 1021 he again invaded India to chastise the Rajah of Kálingar in Bundelkund, who had killed his ally, the Rajah of Kánouj: the enemy fled without fighting; the mere terror of his name leading to victory. In 1022 he turned his arms against Kafiristhán, Swât, and Bajaor. He sacked Lahore also this year, and set up there a Mahomedan government. In 1023 he again attacked Kálingar and Gwâlior, who propitiated him by a speedy surrender. His final and last invasion of India was to the south. He descended on Mooltan; thence marching across the desert to Ajmere. There he organised an attack on Somnauth in Kâthiawár. After a desperate resistance the place fell, and Mahmood was rewarded with treasure stated to have amounted to ten millions sterling.

I have thus enumerated Mahmood's invasions of India because the passes through which he descended have been alluded to in the previous paragraphs of this section. With Mahmood the Ghiznivede Empire culminated· It lasted till 1159, when it was overturned by the Seljook Tartars and Ghazni burnt; but Bahman its representative maintained the throne, invading India also according to the fashion of the century.

The house of Ghor in the person of Mohomed then (1160) became dominant, and extended the empire from the Tigris to the Ganges; but whilst conquering abroad, their own territory became the prey of the stranger; and whilst Affghans ruled in India, Genghis Khan and his descendants gained a foothold in Affghanisthán.

In the early years of the 15th century Tamerlane invaded India, and on his death in 1405 Affghanisthán appears to have enjoyed independence till about 1506, when the Emperor Baber—a descendant of Tamerlane —seized upon Cábul and Ghazni prior to his invasion of India in 1506. Affghanisthán was then divided between India and Persia, the Affghans preserving local independence. The history of the country, however, during this period can hardly claim separate notice; it is nearly that of the Moghul Empire, of which the chief part of Affghanisthán formed a province or integral part. (1) Baber, (2) Humaioon (who fled to Cábul from the temporary usurper Sher Shah Affghan), (3) the great Akbar, (4) Jehángire, (5) Shah Jehán, (6) Aurungzébe, successively occupied the throne of the *Great Moghul.* On the death of Aurungzébe in 1707 the Ghilzaies grew strong, conquered Persia, and in 1720 took Ispahan, and established a vast but transitory empire; but in 1737 their own country was completely subjugated by Nadir Shah of Persia, who annexed Affghanisthán to the Persian Empire. In 1747, however, when Nadir Shah died, Ahmed Shah (Abdáli)—an officer of Affghans serving in Nadir's army—fought his way back to his own country, and having overthrown the Moghul Emperor of Delhi (whom, however, he reinstated) returned to Kandahar and was there, in 1747, crowned ruler of the *Duráni* Empire: the term Duráni being a term invented by himself, and meaning "Pearl of the Age." From that period till the death of his son, Timour Shah, in 1793, the empire maintained its splendour. The sons of Timour Shah—Zemaun, Mahmood, and Shūjah—after vicissitudes of power, were finally all fugitives about 1820, when Runjeet Sing, the Sikh Chief of Lahore, stepped on the arena. Throwing the balance of his power into the scale, a final blow was given to the Suddoozaie family of Affghans and the Bárukzaie—represented by Dost Mahomed—gained the ascendancy, which they have since maintained, and in the person of *Sher Ali* or (1881) in that of *Rahmán Khan*, his cousin, still rule in Affghanisthán.

20. The rest of India Alba is occupied by the tribes of *Beloochisthán*, whose capitol (Khelât) has been alluded to as attained from the plains of India near Dadar by the Múla pass. Khelât appears to be the crown of a mountain region whose general altitude is not less than 7000 or 8000 feet above the sea. It embraces several plateaux—such as Sohrâb 35 by 15 miles, Khôzdar 20 by 15 miles, and Wudd 20 by 10 miles—in the way of terraced plains, decreasing in elevation as they recede from the central mass, and enjoying a healthy and quasi-temperate climate. The great Halla range, running due north and south, intersects these, and forms the axis range. In the north of this highland country are found Mustong and Shâl—Quetta already mentioned—and here the table-land approaches nearest to the Indus, and has been described. **Beloochisthan.**

Another mountain system of this province culminates in the Sirhud Mountains, north, towards the desert, between 29° and 30° north latitude. Their spurs are covered with trees—even teak, tamarind, sissoo, etc.—and abound in mineral wealth, but are almost unknown to Europeans, and are beyond the scope of this sketch.

The uplands about Khelât and Quetta abound in

European fruits, such as apples, apricots, peaches, pears, plums, currants, pomegranates, cherries, melons, mulberries, almonds, etc.; and excellent vegetables such as are found in England, and most Indian and other grains are grown.

Historical Notice. The people inhabiting this country are chiefly Beloochis* and Brahuis; of the former three chief tribes are named—(1) Kharaes, (2) Rhinds, (3) Mághzais. The last named giving the representative reigning Khans, and the former his minister and feudatories—in short, an elaborately constructed limited monarchy is attained, not without an element of wisdom in it. Originally—250 years ago—a Hindoo Rajah called Sewah, ruled the country; perhaps a Jut, which tribe is still found scattered over the pastoral parts of the country, who being bullied by robbers and others, applied for aid to one Koombae, a neighbouring Brahui chief, who, enacting the part of most powerful allies, ended in himself seizing the government and usurping the country as Khan. He was succeeded in regular succession by his son (2) Sumbar, (3) Mahomed Khan, (4) Abdoola Khan, (5) *Nassir Khan I.*,

* I will here add a note from some "Remarks on the Warlike Races of India," formerly (1872) noted for the U.S. Institute for India. "The Sikhs and Beloochies are the only two races who *rally* well, or evince persistent aggressive courage in returning to the charge after a repulse. Pathans, Rohillas, Rajpoots, perhaps Mahrattas, are good at a rush or 'hulla,' but don't rally well. Note a custom common to several tribes of Beloochisthan, that of passing a rope round the waist of each man and so charging. It becomes an interesting question how far a moral bond of union—shoulder to shoulder—would thus be established, and remain after the rope is withdrawn. The Beloochis do, in a degree, exhibit this trait of charging *in line* shoulder to shoulder. Of course the moral motive lies deeper in the higher nations of earth than can be supplied by a rope bond. The idea, however, leads up to the questions (19 and 20) as regards 'the lesson taught by recent warfare in India,' as against undisciplined enemies, I would sum them up that the *moral is to the physical, not merely in the Napoleonic ratio of two to one, but as twenty to one*, and that a happy, well considered, and persistent audacity is the great lesson taught by recent campaigns in India."—D.J.F.N.

an ally of Nadir Shah of Persia, who bestowed on him Mustong and Shâl (Quetta). This wise chief seems to have consolidated a considerable principality, which, after a reign of forty years, he transmitted to his son, *Mahmood Khan*, in 1795; who, however, after a stormy reign of sixteen years, was assassinated by his younger brother, Mustapha, who, however, was himself killed in 1812 by the forces of the late khan. A state of anarchy, and consequent weakness, ensued; and in 1830 Runjeet Sing of Lahore stepped upon the plateau of Beloochisthán, and tore from it several provinces, which he annexed to the Punjáb.

In 1838 the British Government invaded Affghanisthán, and the Kandahar column, passing by the Bolán pass and Quetta, was assailed by the tribes under the instigation of the then Khan of Khelât—*Mehráb Khan*—or of his minister; and in November, 1839, a force was sent to depose him. Khelât was taken by storm, and the khan died, sword in hand, in the breach. After some difficulties, Mir Nasir II., his son, was elected khan, and confirmed as such by the British Government on the 6th October, 1841, who, on our second advance into Affghanisthán in 1842, did his best to fulfil his engagements.

In 1843, the province of Sinde being conquered by the British, Khelât was thereby brought into closer relations with the British Government; but raids and intrigues prevailing, an administration was created on the Sinde frontier in 1847—with Major John Jacob as its head—with a view to their repression; and this object was, by that officer's vigorous measures, obtained. By a new treaty, Nasir II. of Khelât bound himself to strict alliance, but was in 1857 made away with by the party hostile to the English. His younger brother, Khódadád Khan succeeded, but being weak, and influenced by evil advisers, his country has, till very lately, become the scene of intrigue, rebellion, and hostility to the British, on whom, as successors of

Runjeet Sing, the suzerainty of 200 miles of frontier "marching" with Beloochisthán had devolved. Márees, Bhûgtis, and other quasi-independent Belooch tribes were pushed into hostility, and vexed at times the frontier till 1874-5, when the British Government determined to put an end to such a state of things, and deputed Major—now Sir R.—Sandeman to the Mári and Brahui chiefs; and ultimately he was welcomed by the khan and his sidars as the arbiter of their disputes. In 1876 this officer was invested with powers as envoy, and supported by a military force, which was located at Quetta; and this measure has proved the salvation of Khelât, and been of inestimable value to our advance since 1878 into Affghanisthán.

SECTION XVII.

CEYLON,

CANDY, NEWERA ELLIA, ETC.

IN the Index to the Frontispiece Map of this work reference has been made to *Newéra Ellia* in Ceylon (6,210 feet), and so a few words on this beautiful island may perhaps not be out of place before closing these papers on the "Highlands of India." **Ceylon.**

Although Ceylon is so far independent of India in that it possesses a separate government, directly ruled by the British Crown, still it may, I think, be regarded as an *Indian* island. It is in fact almost the *only* island of importance adjacent to the sea-board of India; unless, indeed, we regard Bombay as such.

Its former connection with the mainland of India doubtful.

Ceylon has often been regarded as a fragment of the Indian Continent; but though perhaps *ethnologically* it may be chiefly Indian, grave *geological* doubts exist as to its ever having been joined to the mainland. The supposed ancient connecting causeway called "Adam's Bridge," seems attributable to marine deposit rather than to disrupted connection with the mainland; and the madripore and coral formation of its northern coast further strengthens this doubt. The island probably owes its origin to *upheaval* rather than to the *subsidence* attributed in native annals to the ancient Lanka. (On this subject see further on, page 247).

Geological formation.

Although much of the rock is primitive, gneiss also abounds, and from its detritus and that of quartz, the soil of the island is principally formed. Granite, quartz, hornblende, and dolomite, are found. Basalt is seen in places on the east, and laterite in the west. No tertiary rock is found, though limestone appears in localities; and the whole island is surrounded by a zone of sandstone rock. There are no volcanoes, nor any vestiges that suggest their former existence; indeed, scarcely any evidence of plutonic actiŏn appears anywhere, except, perhaps, near Petiagalla Harbour on the east, where masses of broken rock are superimposed on each other in huge blocks. Basalt also is seen in Galle and Trincomalie Harbour—a grand basin—and the existence of hot springs in the vicinity seems to indicate the proximity of subterranean fire. The Ceylon mountains, however, are of stratified crystaline rock—chiefly gneiss with some quartz and granite intruded—the strata being much contorted, and tilted at all angles to the horizon.

On the whole, I suppose the geological structure of Ceylon to be *metamorphic*, and closely assimilating to that of the Nilgherrie plateau and Travancore mountains.

Few metallic ores are found, iron and manganese being chief; but most of the metals are represented in extremely small quantities, except iron, which is good. Gold has been said to exist, but its presence is doubtful. On the other hand, most of the crystals of quartz abound, and are exhibited in rose-quartz, amethyst, topaz, garnet, sapphire, imperfect diamonds, catseye, chryso-beryl, etc., but above all the *ruby* of Ceylon is celebrated.* Chalcedony is used by the natives for gun flints. Most of these gems are found in the alluvium of the gneiss and granite rock, where they appear to have been originally crystalized.

Geographical. 2. The extent of the modern island of Ceylon is about 270 by 136 miles, and the mountains contain about 4,212 square miles. Hindoo astronomers draw the first meridian of Lanka south-east of the present island, and assert that it formerly included a large

---

* A list of 37 gems—chiefly found in the alluvium of the hill districts—is given by the Swiss Doctor Gygax.

continent extending to the south-east;* but for this opinion there seems little ground beyond the fact that the island of *Giridipo,* on the east coast, is stated to have been submerged about 306 B.C., in the time of King Devenipiatissa. The Basses Rocks on that coast are apparently relics of that island.

The original submersion of "Lanka," however, is stated by the Rajavali† to have occurred in 2,387 B.C., and may perhaps be referable to the Mosaic deluge. The second immersion is ascribed to the age of Pandurvása, 504 B.C., and the third—as above stated—to that of Devenipiatissa, 306 B.C. Thus traditions of no less than three cataclysms exist; but on the whole—if there be any foundation for this tradition—the area of the ancient island would seem to have fallen rather to the *west* than east; geological indications rather pointing to the Maldives and Chagos archipelago as a more probable site of a submerged continent. *Sri-Lankapoora* is fabled to have been the antique capitol of this kingdom—now submerged in the waters of the Indian ocean,—and the ancient Indian province of *Sugriva* (Section XII., para. 9) was in the estimation of Hindoos closely adjacent thereto.

3. From earliest ages when men first "went down to the sea in ships," Ceylon must have become known to the nations of earth: situated on the highway between Western and Eastern Asia; and "cursed with the fatal gift of beauty," this lovely island must have soon attracted conquest: we shall accordingly find it, in its subsequent history, becoming in all ages the prey of the stranger, from remote antiquity. **Historical.**

Passing by the fables of the "Râmâyânâ," with the invasion and defeat of Râwan—by the mythic hero Râma, Prince of Adjudia (Oude)—we are informed

* Perhaps some obscure idea of *Sumatra* may account for this fable.

† The "Máhábansa" is the chief chronicle of Ceylon; and as in the case of the Raja Taringini—the ancient Cashmere chronicle—is still current.

that the island was for long ages inhabited by a race of savages—Yakkas and Nâgas—who seem, however, to have had some sort of organised government when invaded by Wijayo from Bengal in 543 B.C.

Greek & Roman. The Greeks and Romans knew Ceylon as Taprobane. Onesicritus and Nearchus, who commanded Alexander's fleet from the Indus to the Persian Gulf—325 B.C.—make mention of it; and the reports of Megasthenes, the ambassador from Seleucus Nicator to Palibothra (Patna) on the Ganges 323 B.C., appear to have thrown further light on the state of Taprobane or Singhála at that period. In fact, the island had then only recently been conquered by Wijayo from the Gangetic valley.

Pliny quotes Eratosthenes and other Greek geographers on the subject.

Arabs, 1000 to 1200 A.D. Ceylon was known to the *Arabs* as *Serindip*, and in the 11th and 12th centuries they appear to have entirely usurped possession of the island and its products; and from early times Malabars, Siamese—and even Chinese—vexed its shores, and at times usurped the government.

Portuguese, 1505 A.D. The *Portuguese*, under Almeida, in the early years of the 16th century found Ceylon harrassed by Arabs and others, and persuaded the king—then residing at Columbo—to pay a tribute of cinnamon in return for his alliance to expel them.

Dutch, 1603. In the first years of the 17th century the Dutch arrived, and soon after (1632) allied themselves to the King of Candy against the Portuguese; whom, after a long and sanguinary struggle, they finally expelled in 1656, but the usual effects of unequal alliances soon developed themselves, and wars between the Dutch and Candians shortly ensued, in which the latter, trusting to their hills and fastnesses, escaped utter subjugation, though the Dutch held the sea-board and maritime provinces, and monopolized the entire trade.

British, 1796 A.D. In the closing years of the 18th century the British appeared on the scene as opposed to the Dutch, and between the years 1803 and 1815 completely subjugated the island, but in 1817 a rebellion broke out, which lasted till 1819, when peace was made; and the island has been since ruled by a succession of able governors —appointed direct by the Crown of England—who have brought it to a high state of prosperity.

Population.

4. The inhabitants of Ceylon are Cingalese, Candians, Malabars, etc. Many are Mahomedans and Boodhists; though one half the population—which in 1864 barely exceeded one million—profess Christianity. The aborigines—a wild race called "Veddahs"—are found in the forests on the south of the island, and will be alluded to further on.

Climate, etc.

5. The climate of this island is temperate and salubrious; the temperature not averaging above 70° at Newéra Ellia, and 80° on the sea coast. Ceylon is therefore cool as compared with the mainland of India, though so much nearer the equator. Frequent thunder storms clear and cool the air; and when selection is made so as to avoid certain malarious sites, the seaboard is equally salubrious with the uplands. The rainfall may average from 80 to 100 inches, being rather more in the hill districts than on the coast.

The Highlands of Ceylon.

6. The Highland country of Ceylon—which comprises an area of about 4,212 square miles—lies mostly between 7° and 9° north latitude; the central mass being in the territory of Candy, whence the axis runs due north, the loftiest plateau—that of Newéra Ellia —being south, in about 7° north latitude, but offsets south-south-east, and south-west approach the coast, forming subsidiary watersheds between the valleys, which are drained by rivers originating in the central mass. Adam's Peak (Samanella, 7,420 feet) was long considered the loftiest summit of Ceylon, but is exceeded in elevation by several others.

Well does the author of this paper—whilst coasting along the shores of this lovely island—recall its appearance hanging in the clouds of the approaching monsoon. The "spicy gales of Araby the blest" have been held to be mythical, but the author can attest that the appellation of "Isle of Spices" is no misnomer as applied to Ceylon! Clearly did we on board ship, several miles out at sea—whilst wafted by the land breeze—perceive the spice laden gales of this lovely Eastern isle.

From the central mass of the Candy mountains a watershed ridge runs due north as far as 9° north latitude, forming the western boundary of the basin of the Mahavelli Gunga, the chief river of Ceylon. This ridge is, in fact, the waterparting of the island, as rivers originating on its west side flow into the Gulf of Manaar on the west.

The Mahavelli River has a course of 134 miles, and drains a basin of 4000 square miles. Originating in the mountains of Newéra Ellia, it encircles Candy, and falls into the sea on the east coast near Trincomalie.

Candy. 7. The Town of Candy may be considered the capitol of Ceylon,* though Columbo enjoys far greater importance as a commercial mart. It stands low (1,467 feet) as compared with the circumjacent hills, which rise 6000, 7000, and even 8000 feet above sea level. The town is almost encircled by the Mahavelli Gunga River, which in former times constituted its chief defence; aided also by thick bamboo hedges in form of lines of circumvallation. In 1803 a British detachment gained easy possession of Candy, but owing to sickness was, the same year, so enfeebled as to be reduced to the necessity of capitulating to a large native force which surrounded it, and by whose treachery it was afterwards cut off in the intricate country beyond Candy, and all but annihilated.

But the veritable Highlands of Ceylon must now be described.

---

* Prakrāma Bahu III. founded the city of Candy about 1266, and made it the capitol of Ceylon.

LXXIV.

The Upper Lake of Candy, Ceylon. Section XVII.

LXXV.

Rock Fortress of Si(n)giri, Ceylon.
Section XVII.

8. Newéra Ellia (6,210 feet) has been noted on the index of the panoramic map, attached to this work, as amongst them. This plateau may justly be included amongst the points suitable for European settlement in the East, and has in fact been largely availed of in that point of view—coffee planting being especially developed. The plateau itself is about 15 or 20 miles in circumference, at a general elevation of from 5000 to 6000 feet above sea level, rising to 6,210 feet at the town of Newéra Ellia. **Newera Ellia, (6210 feet).**

The following are a few elevations of the Highlands of Ceylon:—

Pedrotallagalla -	8,280	feet above sea level
Kirrigal-petta -	7,810	"
Totapetta - -	7,720	"
Samanella (Adam's Peak)	7,420	"
Nammoone Koola -	6,740	"
Newéra Ellia -	6,210	"
The Knuckles -	6,180	"
Diatallowa - -	5,085	"
Wilmanie Plateau -	6,990	"
Ooragulla - -	4,390	"
The Kaddooganava Pass,	1,730	"
The Upper Lake at Candy,	1,678	"
Town of Candy -	1,467	"
Badulla Plateau -	2,107	"
Maturetta Plain -	5,500	"

The Newéra Ellia country lies about 33 miles direct south of Candy, and its average elevation may be estimated at 5,300 feet above sea level. It is surrounded by ridges corresponding to the "koondahs" of the Nilgherrie plateau. As is well known the coffee planting interest has attained conspicuous development in the Highlands of Ceylon; but at present (1882) seems slightly on the decline, and inclined to give way to cinchona and perhaps tea. **Topographical Description.**

The road from Candy to Newéra Ellia—about 50 miles—leads by a sharp gradient to a much higher level, and at the distance of about 47 miles south-west of Candy the Town of Newéra Ellia is reached. The road winds through a bold mountain country, with many streams and picturesque valleys. The road crosses the Mahavelli Gunga by the bridge of Peradenia, where the river often rises 60 feet in the rains. Hence one road leads by the Rambodde Pass, and the other *viâ* Kewahatti and the Maturata Valley and the lofty mountains, which tower above the whole island. The pass of Attabaggé, and the station of Pusilava (3000 feet) is found on the former of these roads. Hence one passes the Kotmalé and numerous streams, which, rushing down the sides of the neighbouring mountains, form a grand basin, in the centre of which they unite in a deep, rapid stream, which ultimately empties itself into the Mahavelli Gunga.

The Pass of Rambodde rises abrupt 3000 or 4000 feet, near which are some remarkable cascades. The sides of some of the precipitous rocks are level, and their summits crowned with gigantic forest trees. The pass is 13 miles in length, with a gradient of one in ten. The sides of the hills are terraced, and rice is cultivated. Here we come on numerous fine coffee estates and farms; amongst which may be enumerated "Rathoongodde" (3,910 feet), which enjoys an equable temperature of about 66°, not varying above 6° for the *whole day and year!* "Patula" is another estate. "Ambogammoa," "Doombera," "Pusiláwa," and "Badulla," are also important coffee centres, and are covered with plantations. Park-like scenery, with frequent waterfalls, characterizes this region.

Newéra Ellia was accidentally discovered by a shooting party in 1828, during the government of Sir Edward Barnes, whose appreciative mind at once recognized its value. It was at that time uninhabited, or visited only by occasional hunters. The plateau is surrounded by lofty hills, of which the highest—Pedrotallagalla—rises to 8,280 feet, Adam's Peak on the south-west angle being 7,420 feet. It is a place of pilgrimage, and on its summit is seen a strange indentation, two feet in length, fabled to have been the mark of Adam's parting footstep on leaving Eden—this of course being a Mahomedan legend. The Boodhists ascribe it to that of Boodha, on ascension to heaven or absorption into final beatitude (Nirvána).

The plateau of Newéra Ellia is divided by a low ridge into two parts, through which runs a river which has been excavated and dammed into a lake. The soil is well suited for European vegetables, and peat is found in places as on the Nilgherries. On this plateau the temperature varies more than at lower elevations: the nights are cold, but the thermometer does not rise over 70° in the day time, and free exposure to the sun is usually at all times harmless. Subtending the table land lie the Ouda Pusilava Hills, and the (so called) Elephant Plains, where elephants, elks, and wild men (Veddahs) roam the forests. Newéra Ellia is above the zone of leeches, so troublesome in the lower country.

Botanical Products and Flora of Ceylon.

9. The vegetable products of Ceylon have already been briefly alluded to: coffee, tea, and cinchona, have been named as products of the hills, and cinnamon of the plains. The whole soil of the island is of disintegrated gneiss, mixed with vegetable mould and silicious quartz, and in this it would seem the cinnamon finds its home. It grows chiefly on the sea coast, and has its chief centre at Columbo, where the gardens are a fine sight, occupying an area of white sand, detritus of quartz or gneiss. This product was formerly a government monopoly, and constituted the chief item of revenue of Ceylon, but is now collected on the export. The plant grows best in silicious sand, which in places is of a dazzling whiteness. At Columbo it may be seen to perfection; but this cannot now be indicated as a promising industry for Europeans. Many *palms* are found,—the *cocoa*, *palmyra*, and *areca* amongst

them. The cocoa nut especially is an appreciable item of revenue. *Tobacco* of fine quality is grown. Fine woods are exported. The *grain* grown on the island is still collected in kind, as in so many ancient provinces of India—especially Cashmere.* *Indigo* used to be celebrated, but is now neglected. The ruined irrigation works of antiquity attest decay in low ground culture. The lakes and tanks of Kandelay and Minery, north-west of Trincomalie may be cited as instances. The giant tank near the ancient capitol, Anoorajapoora—now a dry lake—contained in the year 1791 no less than 24 villages in its basin, and has an area as large as the lake of Geneva. The lake of Kokalai is 20 miles in circumference; the tank of Padivil perhaps 40. All the above may be cited as examples of the vast irrigation works for which ancient Ceylon was so celebrated.

The foliage of Ceylon is perennial. Lemon grass clothes the slopes as on the Annamallay and Palnay mountains. Bamboos abound.† The *tea plant* thrives. *Apples,* when established, display unexpected characteristics, as they become "evergreens," and replant themselves like the banian tree of India. The *nilloo (strobilantes)* are richly represented, there being as many as 14 species in Ceylon. They form the chief undergrowth of the upland forests, where the jungle fowl feed on the fruit. Tree ferns and rhododendrons flourish. A flora similar to that of the Khásia hills and Southern Himalayas (Sikhim) is thus presented. Adam's Peak is clothed with rhododendrons to near its summit. The *coral, asoka,* and *seemul*—cotton tree—are found as lofty trees. The sacred bo-tree —*ficus religiosa*—is found near all temples, ruins, etc.

---

* See Section I., page 23.

† The natives of Ceylon have a practice—noted also, I believe, in the Malayan peninsula—of perforating this tree with holes "through which the wind is permitted to sigh." The effect is described as charming, producing an æolian symphony!

The specimen at Anoorajapoora is said to be over 2000 years old, having been planted by King Devenipiatissa in 288 B.C. The *Indiarubber* (snake tree), though exotic, is largely diffused in Ceylon. The *cow tree* affords a milk-like exudation, whence its name derives. The *talipat* palm is often met with 100 feet in height, and with leaves 12 or 20 feet in length. Ironwood, teak, ebony, tamarind, and many palms, may be added to the timber flora; and of aquatic plants, the lotus—red, white, and blue. The *baobab* tree is represented; that of Putlam—now destroyed—was 70 feet high and 46 feet in girth.

The fauna of Ceylon is peculiarly rich, but cannot here be entered on. The elephant, as is well known, is celebrated, and his capture and reduction to servitude of man was formerly a state affair, and his value as a military animal appreciated. It appears to be of the *Sumatra* (or *muckna*) variety. **Fauna of Ceylon.**

For further details on the natural history, and other cognate subjects, the reader may be referred to the valuable and exhaustive work on Ceylon, by Sir J. Emerson Tennent, K.C.B., LL.D., etc., whose work—fourth edition, 1864—I have had the advantage of consulting in drawing up this paper.

10. Besides the great tanks for irrigation mentioned in para. 8, the ruined cities of the north are numerous. Many of them are associated with *Mohindro* the Boodhist, and King Devenipiatissa his *eléve*. **Archæological.**

Anoorajapoora was the ancient capitol, and some idea of its extent may be conveyed by the fact that one street alone (Moon Street) is related to have contained 11,000 houses: and the brazen palace of Dutugaimūnū was supported on 1,600 pillars of rock.

The Abhayagiri dagoba was built 87 B.C. by Walagam Bahu to commemorate the defeat and expulsion of the Malabars from Ceylon. It was originally 405 feet in height. Other dagobas, containing enormous masses of masonry, are found at Ruanwellé, Abhayagiri, Thúpárána, etc. The "Lanka-Ramaya," 276 A.D. Further north the "Jayta-wâna-râma," built by Maha Sen, A.D. 330, is still 249 feet high, and clothed to its summit with forest trees. It has been computed to contain no less than twenty million cubic feet of masonry.

The rock fortress of *Sigiri* was the stronghold of Prince Kasyapa, a parricide, who, murdered his father, King Dhatu-Sen, about 477 A.D., and fortified this singular rock to escape the vengeance of the second brother, Mogallana, who had escaped to India, where, however, he raised an army, and returning to Ceylon, slew his brother Kasyapa in battle—515 A.D.—thus avenging his father's death. The general tameness of Cingalese annals is chequered by the above story, which is authenticated.

The invasions of Malabars from the continent of India which prevailed from before the Christian era, especially from the Pandya kingdom, should doubtless afford interesting episodes, but few are recorded of any interest.

Hiöwen Thsang, the Chinese traveller who visited India 629-45 A.D., corroborates the native accounts of these invasions, and the anarchy and weakness to which Ceylon had been reduced; and in fact between 520-640, and even up to 1000 A.D., the island was almost depopulated by the Malabars, who usurped the whole country. In 1023 the King of Ceylon was carried away captive to India, where he died in exile, and Ceylon became the prey of strangers.

Strategical aspects.

11. I will now venture on a few remarks as to the strategic value of Ceylon, as bearing on the general question—the "defence of India"—to which this work is partly subsidiary.

The geographical position of Ceylon being on the path of commerce, and the very pivot of the highway to the East, must in all ages have conferred on it the highest importance. I should consider it a valuable site for a *naval* depôt. It guards one of the chief arteries of our naval, commercial, and colonial systems, and might at any time rise to the utmost value as a depôt of coal and naval stores for our war ironclads and ocean cruisers, and in this point of view I believe its harbours—the harbour of Trincomalie especially—to be almost indispensable to the stability of our naval empire. On this subject I would refer the reader to that most valuable and comprehensive essay, "Great "Britain's Maritime Power, How Best Developed:" by Captain Philip H. Colomb, R.N,—the prize essay for 1878 of the Royal United Service Institution—which touches on this particular development; as also to the paper on "The Naval and Military Resources of the "Colonies, March, 1879, by Captain J. C. R. Colomb, R.M.A.;" two essays of the most searching and comprehensive character, and which may well commend themselves to the attention of every thoughtful Englishman, whether a naval or military "soldier!" In this point of view the island of Ceylon—a fragment as it has sometimes been called of the continent of India—seems to deserve a passing notice in a work treating of the military development of India.

It is presumed that the important harbours named—chiefly on its east coast—when defended as they would, could, or should be, by harbour block-ships—and perhaps torpedoes, as also by forts*, with ocean cruisers ready for immediate service—would be self-defending, and require but slender military garrisons in peace time. In war time, three regiments of infantry, and as many batteries of artillery—beside local levies—would probably more than suffice to aid the harbour defences named. The British troops would be located in cool elevations, perhaps at Newéra Ellia—the *Royal Plains* of ancient Ceylon—ready at hand to occupy the defensive points when required.

* Trincomalie harbour when visited by the author some years ago seemed poorly provided with harbour defences. The harbour forts, I recollect considering paltry, and utterly inadequate for the purpose.

The "Highlands of Ceylon" may therefore justly claim our attention in a *military*, as well as *sanitary* and *industrial* point of view, in furtherance of some of the suggestions contained in the argument of this work; though, as a point for the creation of a "reserve" for India, the area is too restricted, and almost beyond the scope of the Indian imperial defensive system advocated. Nevertheless, India has ere now been glad to find a "reserve" close at hand, and I need scarcely remind the military reader of the year 1857, when the troops destined for China were diverted from their original destination, and arrived at Calcutta in the very nick of time to support the Government of India, when under such stress to find troops to oppose the great mutiny of 1857.

Sanitary. 12. An author (Mouat) whom, chiefly in a *sanitary* point of view, I have consulted in drawing up the present paper, associates and compares the climate of Ceylon with that of the *Mascarenhas* group (Bourbon, Mauritius, etc). Of all three he pronounces the climate to "possess many advantages over our hill "sanitaria," and especially praises that of Bourbon, as "superior even to the interior of Ceylon." He declares it to be "probably one of the finest and most healthy "climates in the whole world for Europeans, though "extremely prejudicial to the negro race. Containing "also grand and beautiful scenery, and mineral waters "of rare virtue and excellence."

The "Mascarenhas" group is beyond the cordon of "Indian" resort of the present day, still as I have found these *pieds de terre* in the Indian Ocean associated with Ceylon in a work treating of the "Sanitaria for India," I have thought it scarcely out of place to just mention them in a work on the Refuges of India, with which they were doubtless in olden times more closely connected than at present. Being on the path of the long sea route round the Cape—that natural highway of the English to India—they may perhaps hereafter recover some of their former importance as depôts for naval stores, coal, etc.* As regards the mutual support derivable from India and other British colonies in imperial interests, I have always thought that an interchangeable relief of troops—especially including native troops—and extending even as far as the Australasian continent, could have been advantageously introduced into our army system.

To sum up, Ceylon viewed as a support not only for India, but for our entire colonial empire—a central point of vantage—must be pronounced strategically valuable, and may perhaps in the future rise still further in the scale of colonies, and play a future part in history even more important than its past. As one means to this end a scheme to attract foreign settlers —perhaps including Chinese—has been suggested, and no doubt the "rice" cultivation alone would support many times the present population of Ceylon which—as evidenced by ruined cities and villages, aqueducts, and terraced mountains—must in ancient times have been vastly in excess of its present figure.

---

* I believe the "Mascarenhas" group to be of volcanic structure; warm mineral springs exist on the island of Bourbon (or Reunion). As regards Mauritius, I have been informed that marine shells have been found *in situ* on the "Pieter Botte," and on the very summit of the "Pouce" mountain on that island. I do not know how far—or if at all—this fact strengthens in any way the suggestions offered in Section V., as also in para. 6, Section X . of this work.

The author must needs take some interest in *Mauritius* especially; his father having, in his youth, been a prisoner of war there to the French early in the century (1810), having been captured after a severe naval action by a detachment of the fleet of the French Admiral Lenoir. The good old gentleman, who afterwards himself rose to be Commander and Commodore H.E.I.C.S., would narrate many strange old world stories of the island in those early years of the century. Having a cousin of the same name (David Newall) on the staff of Sir David Baird—the commander of the expedition from India which recaptured the island in 1810—he stepped from the misery of a prison hulk in Port Louis harbour to all the luxury of a guest at Government House. The author may perhaps be pardoned introducing this anecdote, as it bears in a way on the point raised in the text—mutual support between India and the outlying colonies and islands.

HISTORICAL NOTICE.

Historical.

13. We now come to an historical consideration of this fair island. The Rámáyáná, containing the fabled wars of the Titans on this arena, has been already mentioned. Here we rely on that ancient chronicle, the *Mahawanso*—or "Genealogy of the Great"—which extends from 543 B.C. to 1758 A.D., and offers a striking analogy to the Raja Taringini of Cashmere. Both are written in "slokes" (verse); both were collected about the same period (13th century) at an age subsequent to their original inditement; and both seem to be in a way still current; men of learning being appointed from time to time to carry on the cotemporary annals of the country.

The "Mahawanso" seems to have been *originally* written in part by Mahanamo, uncle of King Dhatu Sen (459-77 A.D). There are other chronicles which relate to Ceylon, such as the Rajavâli, and the Raja Taringini also mentions that King Meegwahan of Cashmere visited Ceylon about 24 A.D., and ascended Adam's Peak. There is no want of material from which to form a history of this beautiful isle, but it was reserved for Turnour to give anything approaching an epitome of its annals, which he did from its invasion by Wijayo 543 B.C., to its conquest by the British in 1798—a period of 2341 years.

The annals of Ceylon are rather bald, and void of interest; but a few salient events may be fixed on as turning points in its history. A chronological list of the native sovereigns of Ceylon is given at page 320 of Sir J. Emerson Tennent's work, already quoted; but it is not here proposed to enter on so elaborate a record.

The annals of the "Great" dynasty—from Wijayo to Maha Sen, and of the "Lesser" dynasty, from the latter to Sulu-wâna—were compiled by order of King Prakrāma Bahu 1266 A.D., and the history carried on by other hands to 1758, the latest chapters being compiled by order of King Kirti-Sri, much of which was recovered from Siam; many original records having been carried away by Raja Singha I. about 1590, whilst the Portuguese were dominant. This king was an apostate, who exterminated the Boodhist priests, and transferred the care of the shrine on Adam's Peak to the Hindoos.

Unlike the testimony of the Raja Taringini, corroborative evidence is not wanting to that of the Mahawanso. The evidence of Megasthenes, who was ambassador from Seleucus Nicator to Sandracottus (Chândragûpta) 323 B.C., mentions the conquest of Ceylon by Wijayo; and allusions to Alexander and his successors are not wanting in the Mahawanso — a striking omission from the chronicles of the Raja Taringini—and its general tone tends to elevate *Boodhist* above *Hindoo* annals.

Gautama Buddha—Prince of Magadha—as is well known, was founder of Boodhism; and *Mahindro,* who finally established it in Ceylon, was great grandson of the King Chândragûpta already mentioned.

The sacred Boodha is stated to have visited Ceylon three times; and the sacred indentation on Adam's Peak is considered by Boodhists as the print of his farewell footstep previous to ascension to the heaven of Nirvâna, or absorption into the divine essence.

The following brief note on prominent events in the history of Ceylon may here be added.

543 B.C. *Wijayo,* the conqueror of Ceylon, is supposed to have sailed from Bengal, or possibly from the Godavery, about 543 B.C. He founded a dynasty which lasted eight centuries. Previous to his advent, the ancient inhabitants of Ceylon are called Nâgas and Yakkas, and the island called *Nâgadipo,* whose capitol was Lankapoor. These aborigines are probably represented at the present day by the *Veddahs*—wild men of the woods—who are chiefly found in the deep forests in the south of the island. Some resistance to the invasion was offered, and at first many viharas and

543 B.C.

dagobas built by the intrusive Boodhists, were destroyed by Yakkas and Nâgas.

307 B.C. The preaching of Mahindro, and planting of the sacred bo-tree, with the establishment of Boodhism in Ceylon may be assigned to about 307 B.C.

250. 250 B.C. The edicts of Asoka extended to Ceylon.

205. Usurpation of Elala: his wars and subsequent defeat by Datugaimānū, 205 B.C.

543 B.C. to 300 A.D. The "Maháwane" or "Great" dynasty.

301 to 1153 A.D. The "Suluwan," or "Inferior" *(61 kings).*

400 to 600. Embassies and intercourse with China established.

515 to 1008. Incursions by Malabars and other foreigners.

1100. Ceylon rescued by Wijayo Bahu (1071) and his successor, Prakrāma* Bahu (1153), who having expelled the intruders from the mainland, united the kingdom under one head, and restored the island to prosperity. He was proclaimed sole king of Lanka in 1155.

1197 to 1211. The Malabars again invade Ceylon in the reign of Queen Leelawáti, and establish themselves at Jaffna.†

1266. Prakrāma Bahu III. endeavoured to expel the foreigners—Malabars and others. Although partly successful, he found it expedient to fix his seat of government in the mountains, and after many migrations for security, founded the city of Candy, 1266 A.D.

---

* This king's name is the most celebrated in Singhalese annals, though Devenipiatissa as a religionist, and Dutugaimānū as a warrior, are also famous. He seems to have been animated with a religious spirit, as he is stated to have built 3 temples, 101 dagobas, 476 statues of Boodha—which religion he re-established—300 image rooms (and repaired 6,100), 230 lodgings for priests, 50 halls for preaching, 9 for walking, 144 gates, 192 rooms for offering flowers, 12 courts, and 230 halls for strangers, 31 rock temples and tanks, baths, and gardens for priests.

† The grand city of Pollanarua (Toparé) was probably ruined about this period. It was fifteen miles in circumference—built like Mexico on the margin of a lake—with one street four miles in length, and a shady causeway along the lake of two miles. For a glowing description of its probable aspect in its palmy days, see Sir S. Baker's *Eight Years in Ceylon.*

The King of Ceylon carried captive to China, and 1410.
Ceylon rendered tributary 1410 A.D. During this century a religious *rapprochment* between China and Ceylon is manifested.

1505 A.D. The Portuguese arrive. The Singhalese 1505.
embrace Christianity 50 years later.

Almeida arrives at Galle, 1515. The Portuguese 1515.
occupy and fortify Columbo about 1520. They retain possession of the maritime districts for 150 years, during which period, however, the Kings of Candy made frequent endeavours to oust the foreigners.

Raja Singha besieges Columbo, 1563, and is crowned 1581.
at Candy, 1581.

Raja Singha II. besieges Columbo, 1586. This king 1586.
seems to have endeavoured to play the Portuguese and Dutch against each other. He died in 1607.

1602 A.D. The Dutch arrive, and after a severe 1602.
struggle—which lasted from 1632 to 1656—they conquer the island from the Portuguese. Then commenced wars between the Dutch and their allies, the Candians. The Dutch took Candy in 1761, but had to retire owing to the sickness of their troops.

In 1782 the English took Trincomalie during the 1782.
war with the French, by whom however it was soon after retaken, and it remained in possession of the Dutch till 1796, when it was wrested from them by the English, to whom it was formally ceded at the peace of Amiens. Between 1803-15 the entire island 1803.
was taken possession of by the latter.

In 1817 a rebellion broke out which lasted nearly 1817.
two years, but eventuated in the complete supremacy of the English, who have since remained masters of this important island.

14. The whole of the Highland district of Ceylon Topographical.
is composed of a series of ledges, descending from the central mass of Pedrotallagalla at the "Newéra Ellia" plains, and of Totapella and Kirigallapotta at the "Horton" plains.

The highest plateau is that called the "Horton" plain, 7000 feet. Below this for twenty miles, as far as Newéra Ellia, the next plateau called the Totapella plain, forms a terrace averaging 6,200 feet or more. Six miles west of Newéra Ellia the district of Dimboola, at about 5,400 feet elevation, extends to the west: here the forest has been cleared, and given place to coffee plantations. Nine miles north of Newéra Ellia, at the same elevation of 5,400 feet, the so called "Elephant Plains" are found, a tract of grass land. These, with Dimboola, form the third ledge. Finally, nine miles east of Newéra Ellia, we arrive at the *Ouva* district (2,900 feet), forming the fourth descending ledge of these Highlands. It is suddenly viewed on emerging from the forest covered mountains of Newéra Ellia; described as a "splendid panorama stretched like a "waving sea beneath our feet. The road on which "we stand is scarped out of the mountain side. The "forest has ceased, dying off gradually into isolated "patches, and long ribbon-like strips on the sides of "the mountain, upon which rich grass is growing in "vivid contrast to the rank and coarse herbage of New-"éra Ellia, distant only five miles. Hence descending, "one reaches the district of *Ouva*—comprising about "600 square miles of undulating grass land—which "forms the fourth and last ledge of the Highlands of "Ceylon. Passes from the mountains which form the "wall-like boundaries of this table land descend to the "low country in various directions." *(Baker.)*

Pastoral avocations are thus suggested. Here is evidently the site for sheep farming, a probable remunerative industry of this region of Ceylon, of which the fertility—even of the cleared forest land—except for shrubs such as tea, coffee, cinchona, etc. is not great, the soil being poor and not adapted for the higher order of culture; the "patina," or black soil, also being disappointing for crops, and—according to Baker—not even as good as the forest land when cleared.

My impression of the general fertility and agricultural resources of Ceylon has been much modified by the perusal of Sir Samuel Baker's *Eight Years in Ceylon;* a most graphic and at the same time practical and suggestive work, which I had not met with when the preceeding paragraphs of this paper were drawn up. Nevertheless, the "flora" of Ceylon in general is undoubtedly rich and varied.

Sir S. Baker states that "gold" *does* exist in Ceylon in considerable quantities; and quicksilver and plumbago are well known to be plentiful; whilst the export of excellent iron is only limited by means of transport to the coast. Indications of "diggings," exist—chiefly for *gems*—especially on the east end of the plateau of Newéra Ellia (*anglice* "the *Royal plains*"), called the "Vale of Rubies" to this day. Pits, varying in depth from three to seventeen feet, are found all over the *Newéra Ellia* plateau, the *Moonstone* plain, the *Koondapillé* plain, the *Elk* hills, the *Totapella* plain, the *Horton* plain, etc., embracing a range of thirty miles. This, added to the ruins of grand old cities, aqueducts from the hills—even as high as Newéra itself—and mountains terraced to their summits, attest the decay in population before alluded to.

The former existence of a grand system of water supply—probably supervised by the ancient kings of Ceylon—is thus evidenced; and Sir S. Baker suggests that much of the power of the kings of Candy was based on this power of granting or withholding water from his subjects inhabiting the lowlands subtending these mountain plateaux. He attributes the depopulation of the island, and even that of the noble city of "Pallanarua" (alluded to in page 262) to famine caused by the water supply being cut off by the kings holding the watershed; and possibly this cause, added to sickness and the constant incursions mentioned in History, may have contributed to the remarkable decay in population of this formerly flourishing Eastern isle.

General remarks. 15. The reader has now been conducted through such regions of the "Highlands of India" as seem best adapted for the location of "Reserve Circles."

It will be observed that no attempt has been made at graphic description; for although the author has been all his life an ardent searcher after the "picturesque," and has taken great delight in viewing such localities, he has, nevertheless, rigidly excluded all "word painting" from the present work, in which he has simply aspired to place before his readers such materials—topographical and historical—as he has been able to collect during a long service in the East. The theme is so enticing, however, that he may perhaps be encouraged hereafter to present to his readers, in another volume, some sketches of the "Highlands of India" from a "Picturesque" point of view as supplementary to the foregoing rather crude and bald exposition of their Military, Industrial, and Sanitary aspects; when probably some pictures, as well as plans and profiles of country mentioned in the preceding pages, may conveniently be reproduced.

The "Highlands of India" comprise elements of the "sublime and beautiful" not to be surpassed on earth —and which may compare with any portion of the surface of the globe—and it has always been a matter of surprise that painters and artists of repute have not more frequently made them the arena of their explorations and studies. If the author could only impart to his readers a portion of the delight he has himself experienced in viewing these glorious mountains and lovely vales, he would not in vain have penned these notes on the "Highlands of India."

CONCLUSION.

"*Quod hodie esset imperium, nisi salubris providentia Victos permiscuisset victoribus.*"—SENECA.

BEFORE finally concluding this work, it seems appropriate to offer a few remarks on the general aspect of India as holding out inducements to the Military or Civilian Colonist. The reader has been conducted to such sites as seem fitted for occupation, as well as others calculated to afford refuge from the heat of the plains subtending them.

As industrial products tea, coffee, cinchona, wool, gold, copper, lead, borax, timber, coal, and many others, have been indicated as existing in the various districts treated of succinctly in the sections of this work. There is no lack of raw material on which the industry and capital of the British settler may be profitably employed.*

The occupation of the watersheds forming the true "Highlands of India" by Englishmen, and the establishment thereupon of settlements, would probably confer on our race the dominion of India in perpetuity. Is such an eventuality opposed to our fixed policy? Is the generous policy of the old East India Company

* On this subject I would refer the reader to that most valuable Lecture by Hyde Clarke, Esq., V.P. Statistical Society, delivered 21st June, 1881, at which I had the privilege and honour to be present as an invited guest, and derived therefrom much further enlightenment as to the statistics and resources of the districts I had already treated of. Besides the articles mentioned above I find iron, limestone, lac, caoutchouc, wax, honey, betel, oranges, cassia, ginger, catechu, hemp, gunny, glue, hides, gold dust, tea, live stock, musk, and many others. I could have wished whilst drawing up the sections of this work to have had the great advantage of earlier access to this source of information.

—and perhaps that of its successors—*India for the Indians*—ever likely to be realized, and the natives of India rendered fit to hold the reins of government *pari passu* with the dominant race?

The attempt to forecast the future of the great Indian peninsula is beset by so many elements of difficulty, and is so much dependent on developments of policy in Europe, that I believe no safe guess can at present be hazarded on the point.*

Judging from issues, it may be almost affirmed that no certain policy, foreshadowing a definite future for India, has ever been adopted as an invariable state maxim. The vessel of the state drifts on; or at times sail is clapped on or shortened according to the party in power; still it may be acknowleged that many a watchful Palinurus has presided at the helm, and the good old argosy—taken in tow and lightened of much of her cargo—has weathered many a storm.

It is perhaps inexpedient to speculate too closely on this matter: bye and bye no doubt, as the world goes on, the hawser may be loosed, and the old craft left to fight her own guns, alone, or possibly as an *ally* rather than a *convoy* of England; and one may be permitted perhaps to wonder how long the hawser will hold; and if severed, whether worn out by time or suddenly snapped by a political tempest.

The question already asked in the preamble of this work, "India for the English?" or "India for the Indians?" brings the matter to a crucial test. This question has already been partially answered.† May we not hope that a happy fusion of races—if not *social* at least *political*—may eventuate to decide it. India is surely wide enough for both, and we may confidently

* Here, and in other places, I have borrowed my former words as set forth in a little pamphlet—*Three Chapters on the Future of India*, for private circulation, "1875."

† Page 7 para. 9 of Lecture.

anticipate that a European population in the mountains would rather tend to consolidate our Indian Empire than the reverse. In such case—and when the hawser is finally cast loose—the cry will be "*Beati possidentes*" as regards those whose prudence and forethought has impelled them to take time by the forelock and acquire freehold estates in the mountains of India, bequeathing to their descendants the position of landed proprietors in a "Colony" of England.

In the day when England and Russia shall confront each other on the slopes of the Hindoo Khoosh or Indian Caucasus—the glacis of India—the time will perforce have arrived for a new departure involving "The future of India." In that day let us hope that a pacific solution will occur to the two nations principally concerned. The time has scarcely arrived when one can with propriety suggest a solution of this problem in imperial interests.

Let me now introduce the opinions of one who, in his day, had much to do with "Principalities, Dominions, Dukedoms, Powers;" in short, just such an agglomeration of states as we found—indeed still find—in India. It is interesting to note his maxims in so far as they bear on the same political complication we have passed—are still passing—through; but he had a more difficult task than lies before us *if we are wise; his* mission was to raise a small state to power, *ours* to render a great one more secure.

"When a prince acquires the sovereignty of a country differing from his own both in language, manners, and intelligence, great difficulties arise, and in order to maintain the possession of it, good fortune must unite with superior talent! One of the easiest and most effective methods which a new prince can employ is to go thither and inhabit the country himself, which cannot fail to render his possession more durable and secure. Another excellent method is to send colonists to those places which are considered as the key of the province. This measure must either be adopted or a military force maintained. If instead of forming colonies, armed forces are sent thither, the expense will be infinitely greater, and the whole revenue of the country consumed in the single purpose of maintaining peaceful possession, so that the prince loses rather than gains by his conquest.

"The Romans, in the provinces which they conquered, carefully practised this system. They planted colonies, they protected the lesser neighbouring powers without increasing their strength.* They humbled the overgrown power of others, and never permitted any foreigner whom they had reason to fear to obtain the smallest influence in them. The Romans on this occasion did what ought to be done by every wise prince, whose duty it is not only to provide a remedy for present evils, but at the same time to anticipate such as are likely to happen; by foreseeing them at a distance they are easily remedied; but if we wait till they have surrounded us, the time is past, and the malady has become incurable."

I have thus freely quoted from this author† because

---

* The reader will be reminded of the policy—
"*Parcere subjectis et debellare superbos.*"

† I refer to *Machiavelli*, that much misunderstood writer, and clearest headed politican of the 15th-16th centuries. A great man so misrepresented! but whose character has been greatly rehabilitated by Macaulay, as doubtless it would be in the estimation of all such as took the trouble really to study his works, wherein—apart from a few *lâches* in ethics, wherewith his age rather than himself should be credited—are to be found sentiments of *public* honour and social morality worthy of any author; but he takes a low estimate of the virtue and wisdom of mankind—especially of the age in which he lived—and assumes the wickedness of the nations for whose subjugation by his prince he lays down the sagest maxims. If a writer is to be judged by his works, in all fairness let the good be set off against the evil he may have penned. An impartial reader of this great Italian will find for every questionable maxim—and that some are *very bad* and open to condemnation I admit—at least a dozen that would do no discredit to the most virtuous of modern humanitarians. His wisdom is all his own, and his wickedness chiefly that of his age and cotemporaries. In short, with exceptions noted, well might Indian politicians study and note the real wisdom, polity, and forethought of this master mind, and astutest intellect of the 15th-16th centuries, where they do not shock the ethics of the 19th century. Thus much as a good word for old Machiavelli: should my English readers be scandalized at my citing such an authority, I can only bid them remember the old adage, "*Fas est et ab hoste doceri.*"

his remarks seem so apposite and applicable to ourselves and our present position in India.

At the outset, however, we are met with the dilemma of a class of Eurasians and "poor whites," whose haro cry of justice against ourselves has at times been heard in the land; and a growing class of loafers—European and native—nibbling at the crumbs which fall from the rich official table, demands attention. This class might perhaps be utilized in the formation of a reserve *sub vexillo*—under strict martial law—such as the Lecture forming the preamble of these papers takes cognizance of.

The time will probably arrive—has in fact already arrived in part—when the discovery of gold or other attractive magnet* may draw to the mountains of India the energetic classes of this earth, and so establish a population in these sparsely inhabited regions. Current history presents to our view many such parallel cases in barren regions of the world's surface.

Although perhaps in an æsthetic point of view, the historical student might wish to save any portion of the vigorous Anglo-Saxon race from retrogression into a semi-Asiatic amalgamated nationality, such as might result from any attempt at mixed colonization like the Spanish *encomienda* system in South America, still this sentimental view of the question would apply in a modified form to nearly *all* emigration from England, removed from whose soil no doubt her sons decline in *physique*, and perhaps *morale*.

Much of the land rights of India are of our own

---

* *Copper* abounds in the Himalayas, in Kumäon, Gurhwal, Nepal, and Sikhim. *Lead* is found in Kooloo, Gurhwal, and Sirmoor; and *silver* is associated with that metal in Kooloo and Lahoul. Alum is found in the Himalayan shales. Borax in Thibet. In Kumäon and Sikhim *graphite* or black-lead is found. The iron of Kumäon is famous. The *gold* of India has been alluded to in Section XII., para. 8, but has scarcely been dwelt upon so strongly as its probable value for development merits.

creation, and the natives as tenants of the soil have, in some instances, been endowed by us with rights prohibitory of its colonization by Europeans; nevertheless, vast areas of crown land are still available, and it only needs a non-obstructive policy on the part of government *and its employés* to render others equally so.

On the whole, colonization of at least the mountain ranges by Europeans, and of other regions by native colonists, seems expedient; and when we recall* that *Clive, Warren Hastings, Wellington, Munro, Bentinck, Metcalfe, Ellenborough, Dalhousie, Malcolm, Canning,* and the *Lawrences,* amongst others, favoured the idea of the occupation of the hills, we may well pause to consider whether our recent policy has not been retrogressive in this matter.

As I have already quoted the words—wise no doubt in their general application—of a politican of an age of hard dynastic ambitions and unscrupulous expediency, so let me now quote those of an enlightened and humane statistician, already mentioned.†

"In connection with the hills there comes naturally the consideration of our relations with the aboriginal populations. While we are stigmatised by some writers as recent invaders of India, the oldest populations bear evidence how epoch after epoch they have been subjected to grinding oppressions, from which our dominion comes to relieve them. The Mussulmans of various races were not our only predecessors as conquerors. The Hindoos have destroyed the religion and languages no less than the liberties of vast nations. It is not the millions of the Tamil speaking races alone which seek relief from Hindoo domination, but also the many millions of Kolarians, and particularly the tribes degraded to the position of pariahs.

"Whatever jealousy and hostility of feeling we provoke among those who have in later times preceded us as conquerors of India, to the Dracidians and the Kolarians we offer the prospect of deliverance from a bitter oppression. Unfortunately as yet we have not fully appreciated the duties of such

---

* See foot note page 3 of Lecture.

† Page 267.

a task, but have in some instances abetted or upheld the domination of the Hindoos.

"The hill aborigines include many hardy tribes, and they have a much greater disposition than the other races to cast in their lot with ourselves. Under judicious administration our relations with the hill aborigines would become the means of our acquiring the sympathies of other aboriginal populations of more importance, and affording to us valuable allies.

"Indeed the influence of civilisation consequent on our occupation of the hills is of paramount consideration. Whatever may be said in depreciation of our rule in India, the main fact remains that we have procured for the people peace and a participation in the advanced civilisation of the west. That is our great task, for which we need no apology, and the means of best advancing it are well deserving of our serious care.

"Much as has been effected by our sojourners in the plains, the result is small in comparison with the needs of that great portion of the human race committed to our rule. Although at first sight the specks in the hills may appear insignificant in comparison to the labour to be undertaken, yet it can be shown that more will be obtained from the exertions of the statesmen sent from England if placed under healthy surroundings, and still more if aided by the co-operation of a local English population.

"Thus with small means, and from small beginnings, we may constitute a new empire of civilisation in India, as we have constituted an empire of conquest with small resources, and almost by individual effort. In fact there is no subject connected with India so great in its associated capabilities as this one of the hill regions. It is not only the development of a field of enterprise for our people, but the best safeguard of the populations committed to our care, as well from foreign aggression as from the horrors and devastations of internal dissension. Indeed, it offers to us the achievement of our noblest destiny in the world, the promotion of good and of happiness among mankind."

The party cry of "India for the Indians," would seem at first view to militate against the suggestion of *European* colonization; but it will be seen that *native* colonization is also advocated in the preceding pages, as tending to the creation of a *Reserve* for India. When Indians become sufficiently enlightened to share the burden of government, and rule themselves, they will, by the mere force of public opinion, assume that part, and become associated with the dominant race in political power. Is it our fixed policy to reserve India for that far-off day, when the two races shall—if ever—become equally fit to rule? Has Providence ordained us to hold India as a *colony*, or after years of occupation to hand it over to a regenerated Indian nation for themselves alone?

In the march of nations, the least religious mind, if observant, cannot fail to recognise the element of design or destiny as governing this world's development. Let us then hope, that whatever our policy, it may be in consonance therewith; and that the action of our country in this particular direction may lead us "Heaven's Light our Guide," into the best and wisest course, not only for ourselves but for the millions committed to our charge to educate and raise to their proper place in the comity of nations. Thus, in the "India of the Future," we may hope, and confidently anticipate, an empire to arise, civilized and strong enough to hold its own like our other colonies, and fit to assume its natural place amongst the "great powers" of the world under the auspices and ægis of its foster-mother—that great British Empire—of whom it may well be said in the words of the Latin poet,

> "*Hæc est in gremium victos quæ sola recessit,*
> *Humanumque genus communi nomine fovit,*
> *Matris, non Dominæ; ritu civesque vocavit*
> *Quos domuit, vexuque pio longinqua revinxit.*"

D.J.F.N.

Printed by A. Brannon and Son, Holyrood Street, Newport, Isle of Wight.

APPENDIX TO "INDIA ALBA."

Views in the Highlands of Beloochisthán reproduced by permission of Major-Genl. Sir M. Biddulph, R.A., K.C.B., from blocks lent by the Council of Royal Geographical Society. (Section XVI.)

LXXVI.

MOUNT TAKATU.

LXXVII.

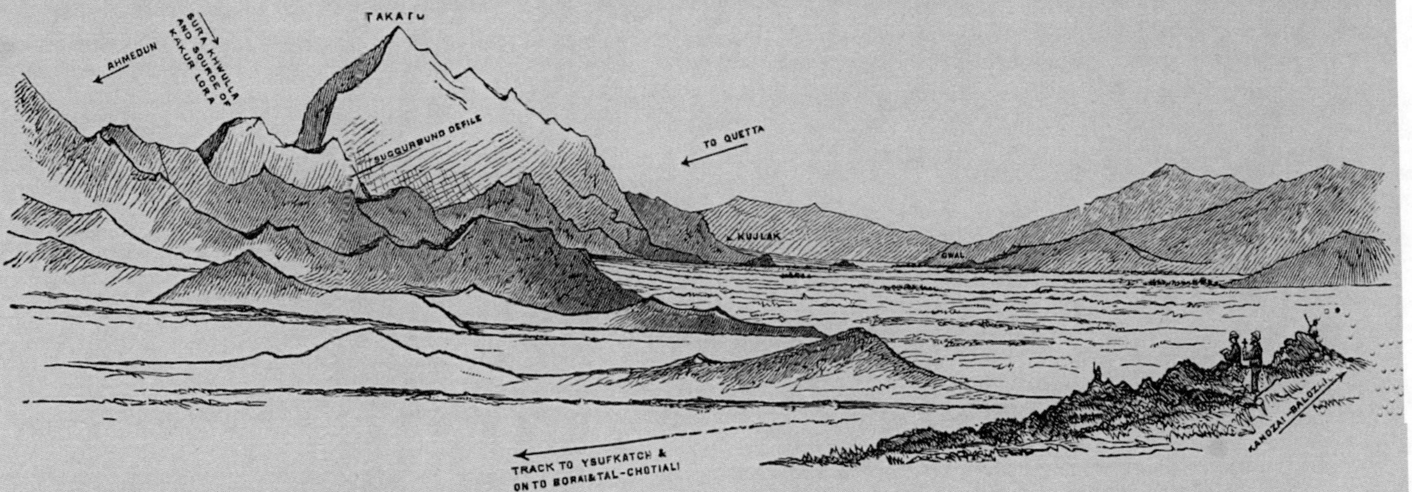

LOOKING DOWN THE VALE TOWARDS KUJLAK; SHOWING THE LENGTH OF THE PLAINS ALONG THE KAKAR BORDER.

LXXVIII.

VIEW FROM THE VICINITY OF AHMEDUN.

LXXIX.

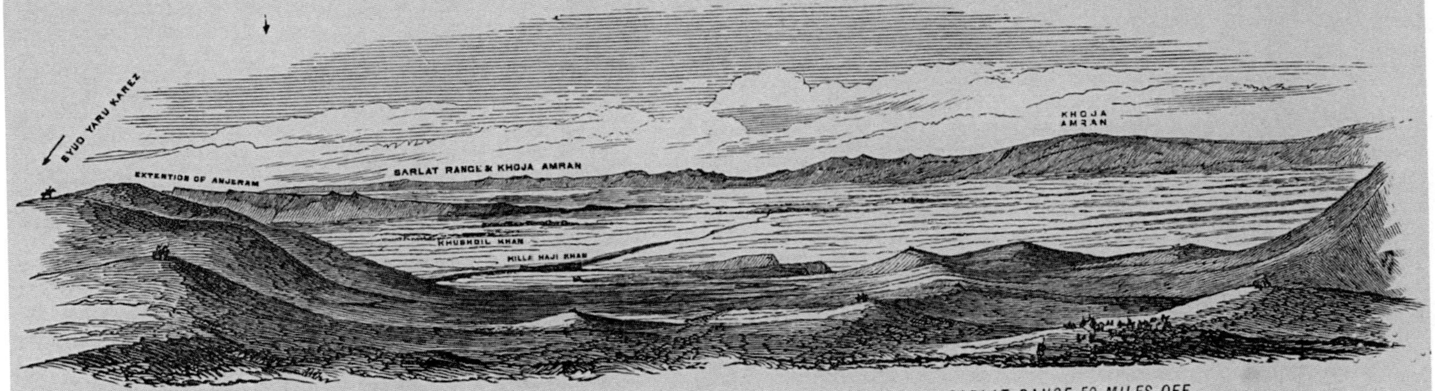

THE PLAINS OF PISHIN, LOOKING SOUTH-WEST. SHARAWAK IN THE FAR DISTANCE. SARLAT RANGE 50 MILES OFF.

LXXX.

View looking east by north down the Zhob Valley, from the Waterparting of Pishin and Zhob.

LXXXI.

View westward on march to Derajat. Watershed of the Pinakai in the distance.